Eve's Song

WITHIN ONE WOMAN'S STORY...
LIES EVERY WOMAN'S JOURNEY

Eve's Song
AN ALLEGORY

Maria,
from your
heart to
mine to
yours—
again—

Enjoy!

R O B I N   W E I D N E R

Personal Study Guide and Book Group Guide Included

Robin Weidner

Author of *Eve's Song* and *Secure in Heart*

rwcopywriting@comcast.net

ISBN 978-1-939086-23-5

Cover features original artwork by Jeffrey A. Little. Layout by Shari Poirier and Tara Price.

Printed in the United States of America.

ILLUMINATION **iP**
PUBLISHERS

6010 Pinecreek Ridge Court, Spring, Texas 77379-2513 • www.ipibooks.com

To Dave, my Adam,
from your ezer

ALLEGORY

A poem, play, picture, etc., in which the apparent
meaning of the characters and events is used to
symbolize a deeper moral or spiritual meaning.

A story that has a deeper or more general
meaning, in addition to its surface meaning.

SOURCE: DICTIONARY.COM

Table of Contents

Foreword IX

PART ONE: DARKNESS OVER THE DEEP I
Chapter One: The Cloak 3

PART TWO: RE-CREATION 17
Chapter Two: The Song 19
Chapter Three: The Springs 39
Chapter Four: The Shepherd 59
Chapter Five: The Sacrifice 81
Chapter Six: The Skins 103
Chapter Seven: The Shelter 123
Chapter Eight: The Storm 145

PART THREE: REST 169
Chapter Nine: The Return 171
Chapter Ten: The Redemption 193
Chapter Eleven: Eve's Song 215

Epilogue 239
Questions for Discussion 248
Afterword 260
Book Group 266

Foreword

WELCOME TO A STORY THAT WILL CHANGE the way you see yourself. Yes, an allegory told in the voice of Eve, but unlike any other book, story or conjecture you've heard before. I predict that as soon as you finish your first reading of *Eve's Song*, you'll find it calling you back for deeper study. Speaking to you in difficult moments. Bringing you fresh insights that thrill your soul. And if you are at all like me, there are times it will bring you to tears—not tears of despair but rather tears of recognition, cleansing and hope.

I first heard about *Eve's Song* when Robin and I were attending a ministry workshop in the Pacific Northwest. I was making my way through the hotel lobby early in the morning, a little bleary-eyed in search of a much needed coffee. Glancing toward the hotel restaurant, in a dimly lit secluded area (that later in the day would be the bar) I saw Robin, her Bible and laptop open, her head bowed, praying and writing. After I acquired my coffee, Robin caught my eye, smiled warmly and motioned for me to join her. As I sat down beside her, there was a noticeable radiance about her. It turned out she was immersed in Eve's life—as if she were living it herself, emotionally experiencing the story. As the visions grew in vibrancy within her mind, soul, heart, there was an urgency to get them onto the page—an urgency that drew her out of the bed early in the morning, to sit with God and see where he would take this story next.

You see, Robin prays while she writes—not the pause and bow your head kind of prayer (although that, too) but the constant communion kind of prayer where she sits in the presence of God while she writes. You will understand this once you start reading *Eve's Song*. Like me, you'll find your heart drawn to Robin as you make your way page by page through this story. Reading this book is much like being around her—every conversation and interaction oozes insight. So when Robin asked me if I would like to be one of the first to read *Eve's Song* (despite sorely needing more time for my own writing), I was eager to get started.

What did I find in this richly imagined allegory? As I read, I felt drawn into the very heart and soul of Eve in the aftermath of Adam and Eve's expulsion from the Garden. The story starts a year after Cain killed Abel. As Eve goes into seclusion to seek healing for her wounded heart, God joins her and guides her through seven memories. Chapter after chapter, I felt as if God himself was unveiling his constant presence, his nurturing love, his invisible blessings and his longing and power to redeem. By the end of the story, I had made a heart connection with Eve as a mother, a wife and a person. I felt the draw of temptation and the devastation of falling for the evil one's lies. I mourned with Eve in the way our own losses are sometimes magnified in our children's battles. I related to the angst that loss brings to a marriage and the difficulty of bridging it. Through the twists and turns of my own story, I felt Eve's fear that reconciliation with the Father, who once walked intimately beside her, might not be possible after such devastation and loss. And then I thrilled with Eve as she stared down the darkest parts of her experience and her own soul, to find a bright path to healing through a God of redemption. More than once, after reading (and loving) a chapter, I would muse...*this story can't go any higher. It's just not possible.* Page after page the story lifted, unfolding in meticulous detail higher and higher until the powerful climax.

The best way to read this book is to come with an expectation of meeting God in these pages. As you read, I would suggest marking passages that you want to go back through. I'm guessing you'll want to burn through these pages on the first reading, and then go back and re-read the passages you've marked, as well as the scriptures (appearing at the bottom of the page) making up the rich framework for the book. You'll also want to go through the study guide questions at the end of the book. This story also lends itself to being read with others in a book group format, where you can forge deep bonds by exploring the deep places of human sin, pain, and loss together. However you approach *Eve's Song*, I believe you'll find a personal journey within its pages.

Every person who has ever experienced grief, regret, confusion, or fear that God may be unable or unwilling to forgive will find exultant hope and relief in this poetic portrayal of Eve's journey with God. I predict *Eve's Song* will become a classic.

Linda Brumley, Seattle, Washington
Author, *My Beggar's Purse*

To tell is to mourn,
To mourn is to accept.
But redemption comes
From God alone.

Born of Adam's rib
and the breath of God,
Daughter of creation,
Helpmate of man.

My song rises and falls.
As much as it gives,
It takes away,
To rise once again.

But I wonder…
Is it my song or yours?
Or so one, we cannot
Tell the difference?

This I do know,
Adam proclaimed me,
Woman out of man,
Mother of life.

Yet I became to him
And all to come…
Bearer of sin,
Firstborn of death.

Now there remains
A song of Jehovah,
Only I can sing,
Only he can witness.

Then I wonder,
Is it my song or yours?
Or so one, we cannot
Tell the difference.

Darkness is over the deep.
Chaos laughs, mocks.
Then the spirit commands
A new Creation.

I cannot mistake
The love in his voice,
Echoing through my soul.
Embracing all after me.

So I must obey
As Jehovah whispers…
Sing your song, Eve.
Sing without shame!

Then I realize,
It is my song and yours.
Now so one, we cannot
Tell the difference.

PART ONE

Darkness over the Deep

Now the earth was formless and empty,
darkness was over the surface of the deep,
and the Spirit of God was hovering over the waters.
And God said, "Let there be light,"
and there was light.[1]

THE LIVING WORD THAT IS JEHOVAH[2]

[1] GENESIS 1:2
[2] *See* JOHN 1:1

I'll never forget the trouble, the utter lostness, the taste of ashes,
the poison I've swallowed. I remember…
the feeling of hitting the bottom.
But there's one thing I remember, and remembering,
I keep a grip on hope… He's all I've got left.[3]

THE LAMENTER OF JEHOVAH

[3] *from* LAMENTATIONS 3:19–23 (MSG)

CHAPTER ONE

The Cloak

I AM WALKING THROUGH THE FOREST ALONE. The trees burst with the early morning glow of the first sunshine filtering through the branches. Birds swoop overhead, darting from limb to limb. The undergrowth crunches beneath my feet as I make my way. I'm at peace with God and the world. Suddenly, I stop, panicked. I have a son. An infant. My mind starts reeling...When did I feed him last? I realize it's been days, maybe even weeks, since I've touched him. Desperation descends. How could I have forgotten that I have a son? I start running through the woods, frantic to get back to him. Is he still alive? I am stricken with guilt. *Why did Jehovah give me, a woman capable of forgetting, a child? What if something terrible happened to him? What will Adam think?* Then I realize that I'm not even sure where I laid him last. I go from place to place, frozen with terror. Until finally I find him. Miraculously, he seems alive. I quickly take down my tunic. Do I still have milk for him? I shake him gently. *Wake up, please, wake up. Oh, please, please! I'll never leave you again. I'm here now. Drink little one. Drink!* Has he forgotten how to eat? I touch his small bottom. Why isn't he soiled? "Please Jehovah," I beg. "Please, just let him wake up! Let it be like this never happened." I feel the milk surge into my breasts in anticipation. Thankfully, his little mouth opens and he latches on. He begins to suckle, first slowly and then more earnestly. I begin to weep as I nurse him, weep and rock, relieved at finding him, sorrowful at neglecting him. Then, I hear something behind me. When I glance over my shoulder, there is another woman motioning that she wants me to nurse the child in her arms. Soon, women are coming from every direction, all bearing infants.

I WAKE UP TO MY HEAD POUNDING AND MY HEART aching. It has been twelve turns of the month since the murder of my youngest son. I am wrapped in a deep brown wool cloak, dyed with black walnut shells, but it offers little solace. I long for the nights when I slept peacefully—when there were no nightmares of a lost child or of other women coming to me for help. I pine for the days when I took pleasure in creating new colors of cloth, experimenting with nuts, fruits and plants to discover new dyes, when I took satisfaction in making something useful, something beautiful. Where is the pride I felt in making garments for my sons, my husband and myself? I spent many months crafting this cloak for Abel that I now clutch tightly around me.

I remember surprising him with it during the time of year when the ground cools. I can still picture his sweet response—how he brushed my cheek with his lips, still soft but surrounded by the mounting stubble of manhood. How he made sure that I saw him wearing it as he left to tend his flocks. How he tossed a boyish grin my way while he hurried through the door.

That night he returned with the smell of goats and lambs on his new cloak. The scent of a boy turning into a man.

A boy who loved nothing more than to see a sheep give birth to a lamb.

A man who led his flock to better pasture.

A boy gentle enough to adopt a little lamb as a pet.

A man brave enough to fight off a wolf who threatened his flock.

Abel plopped down on a bench, ready for food and rest, yet knowing I would have questions. When he was impatient, he would finger the stubborn curl of hair that tickled his right ear. He couldn't help this hurry in his heart...this longing for his own story.

Later that night, long after our talk ended, as much as Abel could bear yet far too few words for me, I checked on him. Abel had wound that dark brown cloak tightly around himself, as if it offered security. Now that same garment, the cloak I wear as a protection against a world of thorns, offers only a semblance of security to me. It's all I have left.

I remember the first time I saw the deep spiritual desire in Abel. Our family was sitting by the fire. With legs crossed, Abel sat with his elbows on his knees and his head cupped in his hands. Adam was weaving tales, mostly truth, but embellished with the perspective of time. The stories had gone on for hours. Cain wandered back and forth, unable to sit still, yet Abel hardly flinched.

As Adam talked, his eyes danced and his hands moved in unison with the flames. When Adam started sharing adventures from his time with Jehovah at the dawn of creation, Abel's eyes were wide with wonder.

Cain, noticing my gaze on Abel, plopped beside his brother and whispered, "What are you doing, God boy?"

Abel pretended not to notice, not wanting me to be angry with his brother. Although Cain didn't let us see it, I knew he enjoyed the stories as well. I frowned for a moment, but then my frustration with Cain lifted, like smoke spinning upward into the dark sky. *Perhaps a little teasing is good for a little brother, a God boy who needs one day to become a God man. A boy so different from his older brother.*

Unlike Abel, Cain had never shown much patience to sit. He was a child who loved to run. After a day of digging in the ground, he came home covered with dirt. His fingernails were always filled with mud. No matter how much he scrubbed with the vegetable soap I made, the dirt just found new hiding places—in the crook of his arms, in between his toes and behind his ears. I finally had to give up on him ever being completely clean. It was clear that Cain was destined to be a man of the soil.[4] Cain's patience was of a different sort. Although he couldn't sit still for more than a few minutes, he could plant a seed and nurture it into a leafy masterpiece bursting with good fruit. Each day, he stood over his garden watching for small changes, tenderly picking away the persistent weeds, delighting in the buds that hinted fruit wasn't far behind.

I remember Cain's pride at giving God his first offering, a small yellow squash, curved and ridged, a marvel to run your hands over. As Cain declared, "yellow as the sun." I could see why Cain was drawn to the squash. Although Jehovah had breathed creativity into him, Cain was hard on the outside, more likely to shrug off a hurt or bury his anger, letting it

[4] *"Later she gave birth to his brother Abel. Now Abel kept the flocks, and Cain worked the soil."* GENESIS 4:2

simmer until he couldn't hold it in any longer. Some days he could be as calm as the river at dawn and on other days as energetic as a young buck. To me, he was pure sunshine.

Abel was more soulful. He couldn't keep pain from coming in or emotions from spilling out. It seemed that his heart had no protection from anything that life brought. He was moved to tears when he sensed injustice. Like one day when a baby bird fell from a tree. Abel found it hopping around on one leg with one wing folded at an odd angle. He ran home with it gently cradled in a few poplar leaves.

"Mother, we must do something," he choked out. "We can't let the little bird die. We must help it find its song."

Moved, I reached up and brushed a tear from his cheek, musing, "Perhaps your good heart will be enough to bring him back."

Late that evening, after the bird's small body grew cold, after Abel and I buried it underneath the fig tree by our home, I checked on Abel to find him cocooned in blankets to insulate himself from the pain. When I knelt down to kiss him good night, he started to cry. "How could this happen? Why did Jehovah let this bird die? It's just not right!" Now I'm pretty sure I understand how he felt.

Nothing can express the darkness of the last year—so dark it seemed that the night was the only light about me.[5] There are days on end when I do well to rise from my mat. On the difficult days, my sorrow flows like the Tigris at flood stage, sweeping away anything near its banks, including me.[6] Never satisfied, the grief holds me under the water and drags me along the bottom until I somehow find my footing again and heave myself out of the currents.[7] I have little desire for

[5] See PSALM 139:11-12
[6] "The hearts of the people cry out to the LORD. You walls of Daughter Zion, let your tears flow like a river day and night..." LAMENTATIONS 2:18
[7] "You hurled me into the deep, into the very heart of the seas, and the currents swirled about me; all your waves and breakers swept over me." JONAH 2:3

anything, anyone. The world seems the color of the soil, from which I came and where my beloved son Abel now lies buried.

My dream of wandering through the woods searching for my lost son is now my constant companion. The terror of losing him and the sorrow of finding him unnourished. The relief of putting him to my breast to find I still have milk, and the shame of women coming to me with their babes as if I have anything at all to offer them. And now, a second dream has moved in to accompany it...

I'm wandering in a beautiful field bursting with wildflowers. It's a glorious day. The sunshine is dazzling. Even the weeds hold drops of pure light. A warm breeze catches my hair and whips it around my face. I tuck a few strands behind my ear and resume picking wildflowers to take home for a special meal I'll prepare for my boys. Without warning, a shadow descends. The sun has gone under a cloud. I turn away, still picking, intent on finding more purple coneflowers. Then a chill runs up my back—the temperature is dropping. I glance over my shoulder and see dark grey clouds approaching rapidly, churning on the underside, unlike anything I've experienced. The daylight is quickly fading. I hear a voice in my head say, "Run, Eve, quickly. You are needed at home." I feel something fall on my head, and drops of water are falling from the sky. Is God weeping? A moment passes as I stand and contemplate fleeing. But it's like I'm stuck in the mud—I barely feel like I'm moving at all. My chest is heavy with an unknown dread. After struggling for untold moments, I finally break free and surge forward, only to find that I'm at the top of a high cliff. I try in vain to stop myself. I fall down and slide over the slippery edge, stricken with fear, unable to scream for help. I fall into the branches of a tree clinging to the side of the cliff. Now I'm entangled in the branches. My hands are scratched and bleeding, yet I grip for dear life, sure that if I let go I'll plunge to my death. How will Adam and the boys find me? I look up and see that I'm some 30 handspans down the side of the cliff. There is only one tree on this cliff, and I have fallen into its arms. *I'm not sure how long I can hold on.* Then I hear a whisper, "Eve. I'm here. Let go. I'm holding you. I won't let you fall." I look up. It might be possible to climb up since the tree clings all the way up the side of the cliff, but one faulty branch and I'll go sliding to my death. So I hang on even tighter.

ON THE REALLY DIFFICULT NIGHTS, THE NIGHTS when I have both of the dreams, I wake up longing for a comforting touch. Rolling over, I drape an arm around Adam, grasping for just a little security.

"The dreams again, my ezer?"[8] Adam says sleepily.

He rolls over and holds me for a moment as he lets me cry. I am grateful for this small mercy, because there are other times when he just sighs a little and falls back to sleep. In those moments, I wonder if Jehovah might take me to be with Abel and create a new woman from another of Adam's ribs—a woman without the smell of death about her. I sigh. Jehovah seems to have no such inclination.

Now Adam's dread of the dreams has settled over him like a deep fog. One morning, I wake up in tears, unable to move for hours on end. At the end of the day, Adam decides

---

[8] *Hebrew for helper* (GENESIS 2:18).

to assert his position given by Jehovah (as he occasionally reminds me) as firstborn of creation.

"Eve, don't you see that it's time to let go? The dreams come because you cling to your grief. The darkness hungers for you, but you must refuse it."

Adam looks away from me as he speaks. I wonder if he realizes that he has just alluded to my shame...all that happened with the serpent. He tries again, this time giving me his eyes, "I...I just want you to be happy."

"Happy? And what is your vision of this happiness, you who sees only straight ahead?" I immediately regret the sharpness in my voice, knowing I'm now casting thorns.

"Don't you see that you're clothing us in sadness?" Glaring at me in anger, Adam gets up and walks out.

I put my head in my hands and weep, never having felt so alone or ashamed. I desperately want Adam's comfort, yet I know he can't begin to touch my sorrow.

When Adam comes in later, he wraps his arms around my waist and buries his head in my hair—his way to make peace. I tell myself...*Keep quiet Eve. He doesn't need to know that the dreams are getting worse.* The truth be known, Adam desperately wants me to pick myself up, to start moving on. If he catches me in a wisp of a smile, he'll mistake that for hope.

"Eve, my ezer, why don't you put on a fresh tunic? Make yourself feel pretty?"

But Adam doesn't understand that if I take off this cloak, I'll lose the precious little that's left of Abel.

At times, I'm angry with Adam. His first words to God after we fell hard in the Garden still sting, "The woman *you* put here with me. She gave me some fruit from the tree, and

I ate it."⁹ *And you didn't stop me,* I think to myself, knowing my excuse is feeble, oh so feeble.

Underneath my accusation against Adam lies a bigger complaint. Although it roots into my soul and sends out bitter shoots, I dare not say it aloud.¹⁰ Yet in the difficult moments, after a night tossed by nightmares or a difficult talk with Adam, my bitterness is there ready to throw its seeds into the wind, a charge against the Almighty...

Jehovah, why didn't you warn me how far the rivalry between my boys would go?

Why did you have to make Cain a restless wanderer?¹¹ Wasn't losing one son enough?

Don't you understand that Cain's punishment is more than he can bear? More than I can bear?

After all, aren't you Jehovah God who made everything out of nothing?

Buried beneath my anger towards Jehovah is my hurt over Cain. I'm tempted to cut Cain out of my heart, yet I constantly fret for his safety. I'm devastated that he's gone, yet not sure what I'll do when, or if, I see him again. Heartbroken that Cain stole Abel from me, yet angry that Cain took himself away from me as well. I rehearse what I long for in my mind once more, the secret desire that I use for comfort on the difficult days...

I see Cain in the distance walking home. His head is hung low. I sense he wants to run, yet he will not. I see him brush away tears...he is weeping. And so I run toward my son. Before I can sweep him into my arms, he holds out his arms in protest and falls on his face before me. Adam runs up as well. We both watch as our son declares his sorrow over his

⁹ GENESIS 3:12
¹⁰ *"See to it that no one falls short of the grace of God and that no bitter root grows up to cause trouble and defile many."* HEBREWS 12:15
¹¹ *"Cain said to the Lord, 'My punishment is more than I can bear. Today you are driving me from the land, and I will be hidden from your presence; I will be a restless wanderer on the earth, and whoever finds me will kill me.'"* GENESIS 4:13-14

sin, with anguish that cannot be interpreted as less than a broken heart over his own actions. Cain says, "I cannot ask you to take me back after I murdered Abel. But I want you to know from this day forward I devote my life to Jehovah. Could you help me choose a sacrifice before I leave? I dare not choose myself." Adam kneels down and lifts Cain up. "You are our son, our firstborn…and today is a day of rejoicing. Come, we will offer a sacrifice together."

This vision of Cain, born of desperation, doesn't address my fear that I caused all this pain. And so my thoughts wash back in waves of regret over my banished son…

Was it because I worked so hard helping Adam provide?

Did I favor Abel's sensitivity over Cain's boldness?

Did I make Cain grow up too fast when Abel was born?

Or, was it because of that regrettable moment in Eden when, thirsting for a knowledge of my own, for something that I alone could give Adam, I stumbled and fell into a deep abyss, taking Adam with me?

I bit into a lie. I listened to a snake. Then I hid in the bushes, ashamed, afraid and appalled at my vulnerability.

How could I have fallen so far from the early days? The days when there was never a care. The days when I rejoiced in the knowledge of Jehovah, like the dew-drenched morning when I woke up to God singing over me. I long for the freedom I had in the Garden of Eden. The nakedness. The innocence. I long for the days when there was never any question whether our future held good things. I long for this not just for me or even for Adam. I want it for our boys.

How would Cain and Abel's lives have turned out if they had grown up in Eden? If Adam wasn't fighting thorny fields?

If I wasn't distracted by being alone so much of the time?

Surely, our path is barricaded with stones.[12]

Adam used to tell me when I would venture out in the late afternoon by myself, "When you see the sky darkening, turn for home." What he cannot see now is that the shadows in our marriage deepen by the day. I'm desperate to share my grief, but his attempts to comfort only make me sadder.

In his frustration, Adam finally lodges his own complaint, "Perhaps it would be better for us if I took Abel's cloak and burned it!"

"You are angry, Adam," I say, squaring my shoulders and lifting my chin. "This isn't just about me. It has to do with you and Jehovah as well. Now you seek to blame me, just as you did in the Garden!"

"And you're trying to tell me how I feel!" His face flushes red with emotion. "Do you live inside of me now? Does having my flesh and bone give you knowledge of my thoughts? I'm not angry!"[13]

Even as the words fly out of his mouth, they bite, latching on and burrowing themselves under my skin.

Adam sighs deeply and then continues, "I'm saddened by the way you've hidden yourself away under that cloak. Don't you see how painfully I toil, even as the ground cries out against me? Isn't that proof enough of my love?"

I see the chill in his eyes, as he motions toward the cloak... "Do you really think this honors Abel's memory?"

His words pierce me to the bone, sending a sharp pain along my rib...or perhaps his. I stand there for a moment daring Adam with my eyes to understand how much his words cut. Instead, he turns and walks out. I go to the place

13

[12] *"Even when I call out or cry for help, he shuts out my prayer. He has barred my way with blocks of stone; he has made my paths crooked."* LAMENTATIONS 3:8-9

[13] *The Hebrew word for rib,* tsela, *suggests both flesh and bone.* GENESIS 2:21 *is footnoted in the* NIV, *"Or took part of the man's side."*

where we sleep, pull the curtain shut and bury myself in the skins we sleep under on cold nights, weeping as if I have nothing left.

When I come out, Adam is gone. Only when I am nearly overcome with worry does he return. He offers no word of where he has been. No clue to what he is feeling. He reaches for an embrace, but I push him away. Does he expect us to go back to just getting by, never acknowledging that our life is only a shadow of what we shared in Eden? This I cannot do.

Tomorrow morning I will gather a few provisions, along with Abel's precious cloak, and take a half-day's journey to Adam's hunting shelter where he sometimes took Cain and Abel to hunt for antelope and other game. Whatever Adam may say, I will go alone. Suddenly, an image comes into my mind of Adam blocking the door and professing his love for me. How quickly my mind goes to fantasy when pain becomes more than I can bear. *No Adam, you will not stop me. I will stay away until God gives me peace, or I realize that there is no comfort to be found.*

I know in my heart that if I don't find resolution, I'll have nothing to give Adam. Most of all, I have the uncanny sense that he, Jehovah God, has something important to show me. Memories he wants me to revisit. Places that I'm quite frightened to go. The truth is that I'm scared, afraid that my worst fears are true, terrified that I deserve this.

Even my name cries out against me. Eve means *living*.[14] When Adam named me, I marveled at my calling of being mother of all to come. At night, I would lay awake trying to picture a human child, what it would be like to have little ones nestled all around me. Yet death and banishment stole

[14] GENESIS 3:20

the seed God planted before the fruit came to maturity. *Couldn't a real mother save her sons?*[15]

Now the blessing of my name stands far off, taunting me. Mourning surges through my veins like water, into my bones like oil. Abel's cloak has seeped under my skin, binding me to my grief forever.[16]

Adam is right. The only living I know is in deep darkness. I wander in the thorn-filled wilderness of my own sorrow unable to find my way. With my motherhood, the surest sign of my calling, suspended by the barest of threads, I fear I am no longer able to love Adam rightly, to give him my heart. And somewhere nearby, Jehovah waits. He expects me to follow just as he did what seems a lifetime ago. I hear his whisper...

> *I don't willingly bring affliction. I haven't cast you off. Even though you grieve, I long for you to understand my compassion.*[17]

But something blocks his words from finding passage from my head to my heart. To find that closed-off path, I know I must journey backwards—seeking an answer to the question that whispers hope, but also carries my greatest fears...

Can Jehovah God once again bring light after darkness?[18]

[15] *See* 1 KINGS 3:16-28
[16] *See* PSALM 109:17-19
[17] *Paraphrased from* LAMENTATIONS 3:31-33
[18] *"For when I hoped for good, evil came; when I looked for light, then came darkness."* JOB 30:26

PART TWO

Re-Creation

Through the heartfelt mercies of our God,
God's Sunrise will break in upon us,
Shining on those in the darkness,
those sitting in the shadow of death,
Then showing us the way, one foot at a time,
down the path of peace. [1]

LUKE, PHYSICIAN, HISTORIAN
AND FOLLOWER OF THE MESSIAH

[1] LUKE 1:78-79 (MSG)

The Lord your God is with you, he is mighty to save.
He will take great delight in you, he will quiet you with his love,
he will rejoice over you with singing.[2]

ZEPHANIAH, ROYAL PROPHET OF JEHOVAH

[2] ZEPHANIAH 3:17 (NIV1984)

CHAPTER TWO

The Song

RISING BEFORE THE SUN, I MAKE PROVISION for my journey while Adam sleeps. I quickly gather a bag of grain, some dried fruit, a skin for water and some warm clothing. More water, plentiful herbs, roots and berries will be found where I intend to stay. What else do I need? A sudden gust of wind blows in from the open door whispering... *flee, fleeeee.* For a moment I consider slipping out before Adam wakes. As if he discerns my thoughts, Adam rolls over, stretches and sits up on his mat. Looking at me through eyelids heavy from sleep, he motions at the open door, "Going somewhere, my ezer?"

"Please don't call me your ezer. I am not worthy to be called a helper."[3] I take a deep breath, steadying myself.

His eyes open wide in surprise.

"I have no peace, only turmoil inside."[4] I reach for his hand and lay it on my chest for a moment, willing him to understand. "The dreams are worse. We can't get back what we've lost, but I'm standing on a cliff and if I don't do something I'll tumble over the edge.[5]

"It is *only* a dream." The edge in his voice cuts my explanation in two.

19

---

[3] *Ezer is also used to describe God. "We wait in hope for the Lord; he is our help (ezer) and our shield." PSALM 33:20*
[4] *"I have no peace, no quietness; I have no rest, but only turmoil." JOB 3:26*
[5] *"For I am about to fall, and my pain is ever with me." PSALM 38:17*

"My only hope is Jehovah God," I continue. "He has something to tell me. He invites me to the very places I'm afraid to go, places of the heart."

Adam nods at my provisions, "Where will you go, Eve?"

"To your hunting shelter." By lifting my chin a little, I let him know I am not afraid. "I know the way. I'll stay there until I find answers...hope."

"You can't leave," Adam says.

He tells me what to do. His words from the day before bounce around in my skull...*Don't you see that it's time to let go? The darkness hungers for you, but you must refuse it.*

My reply will not be gentle, but I do not care. "Not even once, since the beginning, have I done anything without your knowledge," I assert, making my voice strong.

"Except when you met the serpent without me," he muses.

Ignoring him, I continue, "Just because you were in the Garden first..." Adam touches my lips with two fingers, signaling me to stop before I say something I regret.

"I should be the one to go..." Adam says as he reaches over and touches my hair, twirling a strand around one finger in the way that he knows softens my heart.

"When you offered me fruit from the forbidden tree, you were deceived by the serpent's cunning."[6] Seeing the hurt flash across my eyes, he looks away and quickly adds, "I knew the commandment, yet I was silent. I became a beast of the field, lacking knowledge. Like Jehovah hadn't warned me."

I sigh. I am the one who needs time away. Why should he decide for me?

Feeling my gaze, Adam turns back towards me, "I will take the hardship of sleeping on the ground. After all, I blamed

[6] *"But I am afraid that just as Eve was deceived by the serpent's cunning, your minds may somehow be led astray from your sincere and pure devotion to Christ."* 2 CORINTHIANS 11:3

you, Eve, and I blamed God." His words circle overhead like a falcon seeking its prey. I should be comforted that he admits his anger towards me, but the hurt is too great.

"I've failed you," Adam continues. "I've acted like you were the one who led me astray. I wanted to convince myself that it was more your fault than mine."

For the first time, Adam admits responsibility.

"Perhaps there is hope," I say, not sure whether I'm ready for either of us to leave.

"Yesterday, as I took care of our flocks, I pondered all that we've been through, and how God intended for me to protect you." The ache in Adam's voice catches my breath. "There is more to say, but I'm not ready. I still mourn mainly for myself.[7] I won't cause you more pain."

"So, all this time, even before the boys, you shut me out?" I say. My words are sharp arrows aimed to wound before he wounds me.

He turns his chin downward, away from me. I have shamed him. And now he retreats to some secret place where I can't follow. "Yes, I will be the one to go," he says, speaking to the ground.

"What if we can't move past our grief, Adam?" I continue, letting my pain travel from my stomach to my tongue. "How long must I have sorrow every day? And what if the evil one triumphs over us once again, like he did Cain?[8] What then? What if we are so broken that Jehovah himself cannot mend us?" I lift my eyes above, "Oh Jehovah, my heart is so faint within me!"[9] For a long minute I wait, hoping for reassurance from Adam. When it doesn't come, I go to the root of my fears. "What if Cain is dead?"

---

[7] *"They feel but the pain of their own bodies and mourn only for themselves."* JOB 14:22
[8] *"How long must I wrestle with my thoughts and day after day have sorrow in my heart? How long will my enemy triumph over me?"* PSALM 13:2
[9] *See* JEREMIAH 8:18

"When Cain is ready, Jehovah himself will lead him back."
Adam interrupts. "Cain is alive. I know it!"

Adam speaks of Cain, but he evades the pain—what Cain
did and where Cain is now. Adam can't, won't go there with
me. I nod, mainly to myself, wanting him to leave before I
beg him to stay.

"You can have the provisions I gathered," I say, signaling
that I will accept his way. I wipe away a tear and bite my lip
to keep control. I want to project strength.

"Eve, please don't worry," Adam says, glancing once more
through the door, as if creation calls him away from me, as if
there are more animals to be named. "I won't be far. I will see
to our flocks and take care of our gardens. I don't want you to
be burdened. I may have failed Jehovah God, but I will not
leave you unprotected." Then he turns back to me, coarsely
takes me into his arms, and whispers into my hair, "I won't be
far away....just far enough for both of us to find our way. With
Jehovah's guidance, I may even find Cain."

His words about Cain don't comfort; they sting.

For the longest time after Cain left, I convinced myself
that he was nearby if I could only find him. I would wake up
in the morning, spring out of bed and run through the field,
to the outlook, to the river or to whichever of Cain's favorite
places drew my imagination.

"This is not the way to find Cain," Adam would chide.

I know what Adam refers to. He is thinking of the time
I took off for the hunting shelter by myself. The final time I
searched for my banished son.

My thoughts drift to that day.

THE SONG

IT WAS EARLY MORNING AND I WAS AMBLING towards the overlook. I had no plans of searching for Cain. But then I heard a mockingbird cry out. I could have sworn its high voice warbled, "God boy, God boy." *The bird is telling me that Cain is nearby.* I knew Adam would want me to wait for him, let him decide whether I would go, but my feet knew no waiting, no pause.

Halfway there, Adam caught up with me, frantic and panting. "Eve, where do you think you are going?"

Adam knew where I was going. This was a path we only used to go to the shelter.

"I will go with you," he said, latching on to my elbow as if this were all his idea.

"As you desire," I whispered, feeling ashamed.

After a long, mostly silent walk, we arrived at the last marker that told us we weren't too far from the shelter. My feet took control and I ran ahead. *Cain must be hungry. He needs me.* When I arrived, I pushed aside the door and cried out in disappointment. *No Cain.* Silently I thanked Adam for understanding I needed to find out alone. By the time Adam appeared, I was standing outside. He looked at me and raised his eyebrows in question.

"Something is different," I said. "I think Cain has been here. Was this pile of sticks here? Inside the shelter, there are skins on the floor. We always put them on the drying rack before we left."

"Eve...Eve," Adam said, shaking his head, like he would do when Cain or Abel was determined to get his own way.

"I'm not a child!" I choked out. "I see things you don't see! It is my gift from Jehovah!"

"False hope cannot comfort," Adam said, anxious to leave. "These visions come from your own fear."

Suddenly rage and sorrow exploded within me. I took the sticks, the ones Adam saw as having no meaning, and stepped on them, one by one, snapping them in two. Then, I knelt down and scooped up some rocks from the shelter's base.

"Eve, please."

But it was too late. I backed up a little and threw rocks at the shelter, the shelter that was no longer a shelter. I threw every rock I could find, until I collapsed under the grief. Adam came and put his arms around me, and I finally allowed his comfort. As I wept into his shoulder, I was painfully aware that I was the only one weeping.

We slept there and walked home the next morning. As we neared home, Adam made small talk, as if we had passed some turning point and now all would be restored to his liking.

"Eve you must promise to never do this again."

I chose not to answer. Instead, I pulled Abel's cloak tighter around me. Even if the evil one stole Cain, no one would take Abel from me...even Adam.

MY THOUGHTS RETURN TO THE PRESENT. ABEL IS dead. Cain is banished. My husband is about to walk away, go somewhere to wait while I hope against hope that Jehovah can make sense of all this. I am more than slightly chagrined that I have surrendered my desire to leave. But then I realize, we both can journey. I can take day trips to the places I need to go. Our home will be here for me to return to at night. And Adam won't feel so compelled to follow me if he knows I'm safe at night.

Jehovah, do you have a journey for Adam as well?

A determination washes over me to help Adam remember. Feeling a nudge in my heart, I unwrap the cloak from around my shoulders and extend it towards Adam. "For...for you."

"Abel's cloak? You haven't taken it off. I wouldn't even think of..."

"You must Adam. Wear it and keep him close to your heart, please."

"Are you sure, Eve?"

I nod, unable to say the words. *Believe me Adam,* I say with my eyes.

Adam slings the cloak over his shoulder.

"I will hold you here while we are apart," I say as I tap my left rib.

He places his hand over mine for just a moment.

"What is it, Adam?"

"Nothing. There is nothing."

"Adam, there is one more thing."

He turns his head towards me—gives me his eyes for one last time.

"If you find the serpent, crush him!"

"Eve!"

"We have no children left to crush his head." I reach out and squeeze his arm, urging him to remember his own strength. "Please. For me."[10]

"As you ask," he says with an unconvincing smile, before he turns and walks through the door.

Pacing around our small dwelling, I am unsure what to do next. My every waking moment has been devoted to my husband and my boys. I make a feeble attempt to straighten

[10] *"And I will put enmity between you and the woman, and between your offspring and hers; he will crush your head, and you will strike his heel."* GENESIS 3:15

things, putting everything in its rightful place like darkness hasn't just overwhelmed the light.[11]

With Adam gone, I see neglect all around me.

Blankets that haven't been properly washed.

Clothing that needs mending.

Preparations that need to be made for the colder season.

All at once, I realize I just gave away the one thing that offers any comfort. *Do I have anything left that belongs to Abel? Rummaging through our possessions, I question myself...This blanket. Did Abel ever use it? Did he wrap himself in it? This basket with the shoulder sling that Adam fashioned. Didn't Abel use it to carry lunch with him when he went into the fields to care for our flocks? How I miss you my God boy.*

None of the boys' clothing remains from when they were little. Since skins were difficult to come by, we repurposed everything. It wasn't until the boys grew almost as tall as me that we began to experiment with making cloth from the fleece of sheep and the cotton boils that grew wild in the fields surrounding our home. Then, after Abel died, Adam insisted that we give Cain his clothing.

At first, I protested, but Adam's logic prevailed.

"Cain and Abel shared so many things," Adam said. "Cain won't notice whether it belonged to Abel or him. And what does it matter? Abel is gone and Cain needs these things."

Later I wondered whether Cain threw it all away as soon as he had a chance. Did Adam really believe Cain could wear what had touched his brother's skin? Were we trying to clothe him with shame?[12] Force him to take responsibility?

We also sent Cain with Abel's bow and arrows. Adam and Abel spent many long hours crafting the yew bow with flax

[11] *"That day—may it turn to darkness; may God above not care about it; may no light shine upon it. May gloom and utter darkness claim it once more; may a cloud settle over it; may blackness overwhelm it."* JOB 3:4-5

[12] *"Your enemies will be clothed in shame, and the tents of the wicked will be no more."* JOB 8:22

bowstring. After the bow was finished, they made arrows from hazel wood. Cain didn't like to hunt as much as Adam and Abel did, but we knew Cain would need to provide for himself.

The night that Cain left, I slept fitfully, dreaming in the early hours of the morning that Cain took Abel's bow and arrow and smashed it over his knee, burning it in the fire he built to warm himself. I woke up with my heart fluttering like the small bird Abel found. The bird who didn't make it.

Suddenly, the desire for my husband washes over me like a stream caressing river stones. There may be deep waters between us, but I still need him. I run outside looking in every direction. Adam said he wouldn't be far off. Maybe I can get the cloak back. Surely he will understand. I silently curse myself...*foolish, foolish, so foolish. Why didn't you watch to see where Adam went? Maybe if you run and explain how much you need him, he'll make it as if none of this ever happened.*

Jehovah God's words come rushing back to me from the Garden. There is no mistaking the pain in his voice...

I will make your pain in childbearing very severe; with painful labor, you will give birth to children. Your desire will be for your husband, and he will rule over you.[13]

Was this what Jehovah meant? That my only desire would be for Adam? That he would rule my heart? That I would have nothing without him? With one hand I push Adam away and with the other one I seek to pull him back towards me. Perhaps the intimacy Adam and I have, devotion without the deep places, is better than no intimacy at all.

[13] GENESIS 3:16

"Jehovah, why did you give me children and then take them away? And now, does Adam leave me?"

I put on the elk hide sandals that Adam lovingly fashioned, throw a cape around my shoulders, pick up the edge of my garment and begin walking quickly, calling out for him.

"Adam! Where are you?"

I plod until my legs refuse to take me any farther, disheartened that I've gone the wrong way. Exasperated, I stop and lean against a large tree. *Breathe.* I chide myself. *Calm down, Eve. You've been alone before.* I decide to head uphill to the cliff where Adam and I sat together in better days, watching the hills turn gold right before the sun slipped underneath the horizon. As I wander over to rest on a boulder a couple of feet from the edge, my foot hits a loose place, and rocks go scurrying over the edge. *Who would know or care if I fell? At least the numbness would be gone…I would feel something. And perhaps Jehovah would allow me to be with Abel again.* I imagine myself sliding over the edge just like in my dreams, only refusing to grasp for something to break my fall.

Then I hear the evil one's whisper, the serpent who visited me in the Garden…

Then you'll know whether the Sovereign One will catch you. You'll learn whether he guards you or whether he only teases you with false hope.[14]

I recoil in horror. "No, not you!" I hear a noise to my left and see the striped tip of a snake's tail disappearing behind a rock. *Does he mock me?* My knees feel a little weak.

A vision appears…a piece of fruit glowing as the sun casts its final rays on it. Without thinking, I run my tongue over my lips.

[14] *"For he will command his angels concerning you to guard you in all your ways; they will lift you up in their hands, so that you will not strike your foot against a stone."* PSALM 91:11-12 *Also see* LUKE 4:9-12.

"You would do it again wouldn't you?" The voice isn't going away.

Longing washes over me, mixed with remorse. *Is he right?*

"Away from me!" I cry. "Help me, Father...please."

I turn and begin walking and then running back towards home, the wind at my back urging me along. Tears come quickly. Running through the slippery damp grass, it seems that the earth itself cries out against me. That its furrows are filled with tears.[15] I begin to pray, choking out the words...

My life slips away,
Suffering steals my strength.
Darkness clutches my feet,
Sorrow squeezes my chest.
My safety vanishes like a cloud,
Accusations overwhelm me,[16]
All I should have done, could have said.
Jehovah, defeat every wrong desire,
Bring me back to the land of the living.
Become a cloak that surrounds me,[17]
Lest I return to dust.[18]

When I arrive home, I secure the door and throw myself on the bed. I think back over the many years since the Garden. Now it seems they have fled quicker than the spring torrents that come coursing down the side of the mountain. Exactly when did darkness overtake me?

Then I hear Jehovah's voice...

Walk with me back to the very beginning.

29

[15] JOB 31:38
[16] JOB 30:15-16
[17] *"In his great power God becomes like clothing to me..."* JOB 30:18
[18] *"He throws me into the mud, and I am reduced to dust and ashes."* JOB 30:19

Suddenly, I feel very sleepy. My arms and legs feel heavy.

"Jehovah, would you walk with me through a dream?" I ask out loud. "Are the days of walking with you in the cool of the day, like we did in the Garden, forever ended?"

> *Come with me to seven memories, those that shine*
> *like the sun and those in the shadow of death.*

"Seven memories?" I whisper. The number seven is familiar but I can't quite remember why.[19] "Where else can I turn but to you, Jehovah? Purify me seven times over."[20]

As I drift into a deep sleep, the first memory comes flooding back, as swift as the Tigris in the season of floods.

The first memory with Jehovah

When I opened my eyes for the first time in the Garden of Eden, my head was drenched with dew, my hair damp. My hands dripped with a rich and earthly aroma. I was lying in a bed of spices—the aroma of sage, thyme and lemongrass swirled around me filling me with sweet sensations. Was I dreaming? Where was I? I woke with one memory, a song, rising up from the ground, descending from the sky and embracing me in its warmth.

I reached over and touched my left side. I felt a faint yearning for something, someone beyond myself.[21] And then I heard a whisper, with thunder's strength and the warmth of sunlight's first rays...

> *Place me like a seal over your heart, my*
> *precious daughter.*[22]

30

[19] *"By the seventh day God had finished the work he had beeen doing; so on the seventh day he rested from all his work."* GENESIS 2:2

[20] *"The words and promises of the* LORD *are pure words, like silver refined in an earthen furnace, purified seven times over."* PSALM 12:6 (AMP)

[21] *"Then the Lord God made a woman from the rib he had taken out of the man, and he brought her to the man."* GENESIS 2:22

[22] *See* SONG OF SONGS 5:5, 8:6

Although I didn't fully understand the words, I longed for the one who spoke them. After the whisper, the melody came again. Was it the same one I heard in my sleep? Although the song was new, the voice was familiar. I lay there mesmerized as Jehovah sang over me…

Nature prepares for the sound of my steps.
Mighty trees stretch gnarled arms upward.
Joyfully, they herald my presence.
Flowers timidly open their buds.
For the season of singing.

Blossoming vines burst with flavor.
Flocks of birds break into chorus.

The fig tree forms its fruit,
Ready to bestow blessing
On all who taste.

Cooing of doves is heard in the mist,
While the sheep climb to the peaks,
Beckoning to see who will follow.
Take your hand in mine.
Walk with me.

Look in my eyes and see my favor.
Feel my heart beat in longing.
Hear the whisper of my love.
Do you see my face shining?
With you alone in view?

I betroth you to me in righteousness.
I betroth you to me in faithfulness.
I betroth you to me in justice and love.
I will be your God.
You shall know me.[23]

Peace washed over me, cleansing me from the dross of birth. The sun came through the trees, caressing my shoulders. I held my hands out and turned them from side to side, opening and closing my fingers, while I marveled at their dexterity. Who was I? Why was I here? Where had I come from? I had no answers, but only an assurance it was all supposed to be. It felt as natural as if it had always been. As new as if a world of discovery lay before me.

I turned over and yawned and stretched, testing each joint, rolling my head from side to side, extending my arms up over my head and back again, bringing my knees up to my chest and feeling the pull in my back. I took a deep breath, feeling my chest rise and fall. As I lifted myself to sitting, I was greeted by dizzying colors, sounds and smells, beckoning me to come and see. I stood up and tried my legs for the first time. And then He spoke...

I am Jehovah, God Almighty, the one
who is and was. Your Father.[24]

Of all the words he offered, the last resonated with some unknown place...Father. He added that I could also call him *Abba.*[25] Abba rolled easily off my tongue like it was meant to be my first word. I laughed in delight.

[23] *Inspired by* SONG OF SONGS 2:13; HOSEA 2:19-20
[24] *"We give thanks to you, Lord God Almighty, the one who is and who was, because you have taken your great power and have begun to reign."* REVELATION 11:17
[25] *Abba would be closest to our "daddy." "For you did not receive a spirit that makes you a slave again to fear, but you received the Spirit of sonship. And by him we cry, 'Abba, Father."* ROMANS 8:15 (NIV1984)

My Abba introduced me to the Garden, taking joy in pointing out an elm tree, mastik bush and cornflowers. Vistas of glory shimmered into view as each new sight and sound spoke to my soul. According to my Father, this was the Garden of Eden, my home. It was enclosed by mountains and embraced by four rivers meandering into lands I couldn't yet imagine.[26] The ground was moist from the waters that seeped up from deep within the earth to water the land. Fruit trees were plentiful, mature, and drooping with mature fruit. Berries grew without briars and crept up the side of trees—raspberries, blackcurrant, mulberries, blackberries and more—all plentiful, beautiful to look at and easy to pick.

Jehovah offered me pomegranates. The sweetness swirled around my tongue, the juices bursting in my mouth. Afterwards, he took me to a small pond where I could cleanse my hands and face from the sticky redness. I drank from a stream, cupping my hands to scoop the cool liquid into my mouth. I even caught a glimpse of myself in the water.

Father and I spent what seemed liked an endless day together. As we explored, he told me a story about seven days, as old as eternity, wider than I could fathom.

He introduced me to the great light that gave warmth to my skin. He explained my need to walk in the light.[27] How the light would feed my soul and cleanse my eyes.[28] I laid in a meadow under an azure sky and felt the sun's warmth blanket my body.

Father told me about the dark hours when I would rest, watched over by a lesser light. After we climbed a hill and gazed over the countryside, Abba God explained how he separated sky and earth, and then set a boundary between the darkness and the light.

[26] *Eden (gan in Hebrew) means "walled garden." This could indicate that the Garden was surrounded by mountains.*
[27] *"If we claim to have fellowship with him and yet walk in the darkness, we lie and do not live out the truth."* 1 John 1:6
[28] *"But if your eyes are unhealthy, your whole body will be full of darkness. If then the light within you is darkness, how great is that darkness."* MATTHEW 6:23

As we paused at a creek and I watched the water dance over the rocks, he told me of separating water and land. How the sea was shut behind doors, and then burst forth at his command, until he told it...*Here and no further.*[29] As we walked through the Garden, he spoke of vegetation and plants. Of legions of fish that filled rivers, seas and oceans. Of millions of birds, swooping, singing and inhabiting the sky. Of animals— livestock that graze the fields and animals that roam the earth to search for their food.

He led me into a forest where we crept in close to watch three baby foxes emerge from their den, and laughed out loud as they tumbled in play.

In the afternoon, I rested. When I woke up, I instinctively reached out for him. *Abba. My Abba.* I didn't see him, yet sensed he wasn't far away. I simply had to listen for his voice, follow his melody. I found him singing by the springs...

Eons pass, yet it is the beginning,
My spirit hovers in anticipation.
Darkness flees from the light,
The pillars of heaven quake,
As the dividing line draws.
It is good.

The earth suspends over nothing,
Northern skies over space.
I wrap the water in clouds,
Yet they dare not burst,
As land and sea separate.
It is good.

34

[29] *"Who shut up the sea behind doors when it burst forth from the womb."* JOB 38:8

I cover the moon with clouds,
Breathe a backdrop of blue.
Mighty fish fill the waters,
Winged birds, the air,
As all look to me.
It is good.

I search the river's sources,
Measure winds and waters,
Bring hidden things to light.
Above gold, resin and onyx,
My wisdom reigns.
It is good.

Goodness surrounds me,
Exults in my presence.
Adorned with glory,
Clothed in honor,
Ever rejoicing.
I am good.[30]

As he sang, I sensed how little I knew and how much more I wanted to know. My questions ran so deep that I couldn't verbalize them, but my curiosity filled me with anticipation. Later that day, I asked him to explain more about the seven days.

Jehovah paused for a long moment, before explaining...

Think of it as seven days of filling incompleteness. The
light longed for something to nurture. Plants, flowers, fruits

[30] *Inspired by* JOB 26:8; 28:11, 25; 40:9-10; PSALM 75:3

*and vegetables awaited someone to draw life from them.
Land and seas awaited dominion by fish, birds and great
creatures of the deep. Birds sought someone to marvel at
their songs. Animals begged someone to laugh at their
antics. Mountains cried out for someone to climb them.*

*The Garden of Eden awaited someone to till it and
partake of its delights. Yet all of creation looked with
anticipation toward a final moment—a final stroke of
creative love.[31] A deep sleep, bone and flesh, my breath,
the energy of all creation all led to the crowning moment.
The angels held their breath, ready to shout for joy.*

Finally, I gushed, "What was it Abba? What did you create last?"

*You, Eve. You are the final moment of creation. The most
complex of my creation. When you took your first breath the
angels shouted for joy.[32] You have been equipped to carry life.
You will help fill the earth with my likeness. Walk before me
with all your heart and soul, you and all who come after you.*

The Song

Suddenly, a noise outside jerks me back to the present. I
stretch, a little disoriented, yet with a mustard seed of promise
in my chest from the sheer beauty of the first memory. I still
cling to the hope that Jehovah is good, but I am not good.
This I have proven. Yet Jehovah visited me. He called me on
this journey. He sang a love song over me. He told me I was
the pinnacle of creation. But that was...

36

[31] *The created world itself can hardly wait for what's coming next. Everything in
creation is being more or less held back. God reins it in until both creation and all
the creatures are ready and can be released at the same moment into the glorious
times ahead....*" ROMANS 8:19-21 (MSG)
[32] *See* JOB 38:7

Before the snake.

Before the fruit.

Before the banishment.

The sun is already high in the sky. Is God calling me to walk with him now? Or was that just the memory from the Garden? And where will I find him? Where are these places he has promised to take me?

Come to the springs, my daughter.[33]

I sigh. I haven't been to the springs since Cain left. Throwing my cloak over my shoulders, I make the short hike. When I arrive, I kneel and scoop some clear, sparkling water for a drink. I want to call for my Abba, but the desire sticks in my throat. More often than I'd like to admit, I haven't called on him at all.[34] I'm not worthy of the intimacy of Abba.

The quiet is deafening.

"Father," I call with more than a little uncertainty. "Are you there?"

[33] *"I will make rivers flow on barren heights, and springs within the valleys. I will turn the desert into pools of water, and the parched ground into springs."* ISAIAH 41:18

[34] *"The people I formed for myself that they may declare my praise. Yet you have not called on me, Jacob, you have not wearied yourselves for me, Israel."* ISAIAH 43:21-22

Passing through the Valley of Weeping...Baca
They make it a place of springs.
The early rain also fills [the pools] with blessings.[1]

THE SONS OF KORAH, SINGERS OF PSALMS

[1] *Revised from* PSALM 84:6 (AMP)

CHAPTER THREE

The Springs

THE PLACE OF SPRINGS IS WEDGED BETWEEN two small hills, amplifying the smells and sounds. As my senses fill with the song of trickling water and the aroma of balsam trees, I am reminded why the springs used to be one of my favorite places. I see no sign of Jehovah, but I hear the murmur of memories, glimmers of our family's story that I have buried away in a storehouse of dark earth.[2] Unlike the Garden of Eden where the springs ran day and night, we have come here every morning by necessity, since by afternoon the scorching sun withers any hope of water. Autumn has been the exception. When the sun cools, the springs overflow into pools, making for wonderful possibilities. In the fall months, Adam punctures the balsam trees with a sharp stone to harvest a healing balm we use year round for cuts and scrapes. From the time Cain and Abel were little, the pools' appearance was one of the season's markers. As the boys were growing up, the springs were not only our source of water, but also one of their favorite places to play.

"How soon will it be, Mother?" Cain begged one year as he shifted from one foot to another, with Abel beside him. "When will the pools come?"

[2] *"I will give you the treasures of darkness, riches stored in secret places, so that you may know that I am the LORD, the God of Israel, who summons you by name...I summon you by name and bestow on you a title of honor, though you do not acknowledge me."* ISAIAH 45:3-4 (NIV 1984)

"When Jehovah God blesses, my sons," I replied.

"I can't wait for the springs of blessing," Abel said earnestly, looking to his brother for approval.

Cain rewarded him with a snicker. "Springs of blessing? Let's jump in the blessings when they come, Abel," he teased.

But the name stuck. I had to agree it was a good name, since the pools seemed to appear miraculously overnight, bubbling up while we slept. My boys couldn't wait to revel in the blessedness—where they'd first learned to hold their noses and put their heads under the water. Where they tested their growing strength, finding larger and larger rocks to build entrances to imaginary caves for their elaborate games. I worried for their safety.

"Eve, they are little men," Adam said with a glint of pride in his eyes, hands on his hips, his stance wide. "Let them be."

If the boys had it their way, Adam would have come with them every day. But it was rare for Adam to take leave from his work. He came home from the fields exhausted and ravenous, and the boys fought for his attention. It seemed from the time Abel was small that he fancied himself just as old and capable as his brother.

"I SEE HIM," CAIN SAID, LATE ONE AFTERNOON AS Adam emerged from the brush near our home.

Abel, smaller and more nimble, jumped up, ran towards Adam and flung himself into his father's arms. Close behind, Cain arrived and launched himself onto Abel's back, throwing his arms around Abel's neck and using his weight to pull Abel off. As they started grappling on the ground, Adam pushed his way in, trying to pull them apart.

"Boys, stop!" I yelled, putting aside my work to run towards them. "Give your father a little time to rest."

"Abba Lion needs no protection," Adam roared, throwing his arms open wide.

I smiled, softened by the allusion to Abba. Calling Adam Abba was our boys' idea when they heard us refer to Jehovah as our Abba.

"Big Bear is taller than Abba Lion," Cain shouted, raising his hands up high, like claws.

"And I, Golden Eagle, soar over both of you!" Abel stuck his arms out, and ran a circle around Adam and Cain.

With that, both boys jumped on Adam and the wrestling began in earnest. When Adam pinned Abel on the ground and nuzzled his neck with his beard, Abel yelled, "Help me, Cain!" Launching himself into the air, Cain dropped knees first onto Adam's back.

"Careful, boys!" I wasn't afraid for the boys. I was afraid for Adam.

Adam roared again and turned towards Cain, pinning him on the ground and tickling him. Cain shrieked with joy, even as Abel tried to pull Adam off of him.

Finally, to my relief, Adam said, "Enough!"

The boys rolled over, panting with exertion.

"Golden Eagle was the strong one today!" Abel boasted.

"Tell him Father. Big Bear won today!" Cain shouted.

"You are both strong," Adam said, as he scooped up Cain with his right arm, and then Abel with his left. "But neither of you are as strong as Abba Lion!"

Later, after dinner, Adam went outside and sat on a stool he had fashioned from a tree stump to work on a new tool for the garden. Although they knew their father wanted time to rest, Cain and Abel sat at his feet. Cain didn't have the patience for this. He fidgeted the whole time but he wasn't about to let Abel sit there without him.

Even in the early days, Cain sought to protect his position as the firstborn son. He resented Abel's insistence on proving he was just as capable. To help ease their rivalry, Adam gave them separate duties based on their natural inclinations. To Cain, who loved to dig in the dirt from the time he first sat up by himself, Adam gave the task of working in the garden. Adam would train Abel, with his sensitivity, to take care of the flocks. When Adam wasn't around, Cain and Abel argued about which task their father enjoyed more—tilling the garden or keeping the flocks.

I rejoiced in both my sons, loving them in their differences. Their man-ness intrigued and fascinated me. When Cain and Abel were young, I made up man songs to sing to them here at the springs. Their favorite song went like this...

> Little men, strong and brave.
> Leaping like locusts in the wind.
> Rejoicing in strength,
> Buzzing with joy,
> Keep your hearts near mine.
>
> Little men, running with the wind,
> Charging as horses into the fray.
> Pawing at the ground,
> Laughing at fear,
> Keep your hearts near mine.

Little men, joyful and true,
Flapping with the wings of storks.
Protecting your treasures,
Buried in the sand,
Keep your hearts near mine.

Little men, wise and bold,
Soaring like hawks in flight.
Exploring far lands,
Building new nests,
Keep your hearts near mine.[3]

Oh my little men, so fair and fine,
Please keep your hearts near to mine.[4]

Cain and Abel crouched and leapt like locusts, galloped like horses running in circles, flapped their wings, then jumped on a rock with their chests thrust out proud. At the end of the song, they both threw their arms around me, which was my cue to tickle them until they begged for mercy. We spent many delightful hours at this very spot.

It was here at the springs in the lingering warmth of early autumn, as Cain (not even twelve months old) lay sleeping on a blanket, that I first told Adam I was carrying our second child. Overjoyed, Adam swooped me up, and, ignoring my protests, carried me into the pool.

"Quick, hold your breath, Eve!"

Before I could ask him why, he surprised me by falling backwards taking us both completely under the water. When I came up sputtering, wondering if Adam had misplaced his

[3] *Inspired by* JOB 39:13-30
[4] *Thanks to John Eldredge for his thoughts in* Wild at Heart *on how Job 39 mirrors the heart of a man.*

good sense, he announced with water streaming down his face, "To celebrate another child given by Jehovah."

I looked into his eyes for a moment and then burst into laughter. Never wanting to totally concede his strength, I wrapped my arms around his head and tried without success to bring him under the water. After we frolicked a little, we both relaxed on our backs in the water, floating and talking about possible names for our new little one.

Afterwards, as we let the sun dry us, with our young son between us and our clothes hanging from a nearby bush, I thought back on the day when Cain emerged from my watery womb, his small, red body covered in blood, how Adam cut the cord that bound him to me with a sharp piece of flint, and my cry, "With the help of the LORD, I have brought forth a man."[5] So we named him Cain, our *brought forth* one, marveling at his head full of dark red hair and blue-gray eyes.[6] Knowing I had another child already growing inside of me filled me with wonder.

NOW ALONE AT THE SPRINGS, THE PLACE I HAVE avoided, I wonder whether Jehovah will appear or whether my feet simply took me where I thought I needed to go. All I have left of my boys is a searing pain in my chest and a burning in my womb.[7] *Instead of the springs of blessing, you have become the springs of tears.*

With one son returned to the dust, another wandering far from home, no Adam and little sense of Jehovah God, my life has fled like the grasses that sprout up every morning but dry up by afternoon. The mouth of the earth has swallowed God's creation, leaving me worthless.[8]

[5] GENESIS 4:1
[6] GENESIS 4:1 *is footnoted in the NIV: "Cain sounds like the Hebrew for "brought forth" or "acquired."*
[7] *"...there is no soundness in my flesh. I am benumbed and badly crushed; I groan because of the agitation of my heart."* PSALM 38:7-8 (NASB)
[8] *Read* PSALM 90, *a prayer of Moses that beautifully expresses the anguish of being human and the beauty of God's unfailing love.*

I kneel down and swirl the sparkling water. "Oh, if you could just talk to me, sweet spring that swells with light.[9] Would you chastise me for neglecting you? Would you tell me about how many times Adam came here alone, wanting to spare me the pain? How he sat here lost in his own thoughts? How he longed for me? For our life to be restored?"

I cup my hands and dip them into the water, as my eyes well up in regret. "And what have I gained? Moving through my days without thought? Keeping busy to ensure the world is in a haze?"

As I lift the sweet substance to moisten my lips, I realize how unworthy I feel. "Why did you call me here, Jehovah?"

*When you believe in me, springs of living
water will flow from within you.[10]*

I hear Adam's voice in my head, explaining how springs come from a source of water beneath the earth. Is it possible that even though I have seen little evidence of Jehovah since my boys departed, that he has been nearby all along? Has he been waiting for me to be ready?

I lick my lips. The springs might dry up soon. I came without a skin for water. With Adam gone, I need to provide for myself. It will only take a short walk back to get the skins. Instead, something inside urges me to linger. Spreading my cloak beneath me and looking to the heavens, I ask for a small miracle…"All my longings lie open before you, Father. My sighing is not hidden from you.[11] Surely, you are bigger than the pain I fear. Is there a balm for the heart?[12] A living water I can drink? Help me remember what it is to walk with you."

[9] *"For with you is the fountain of life; in your light we see light."* PSALM 36:9
[10] JOHN 7:38
[11] PSALM 38:9
[12] *"Is there no balm in Gilead? Is there no physician there? Why then is there no healing for the wound of my people?"* JEREMIAH 8:22.

And then, knowing Jehovah awaits my invitation, I say, "Take me to the second memory."

Come with me and remember the roots of blessing.

Another memory comes gushing up from the ground to quench my thirsty soul.

The second memory with Jehovah

I awoke full of anticipation for my second day in Eden. As the sky barely began to redden with the mounting dawn, I mused that my first day with God seemed endless. Although the small tree above me was dark, it seemed to burst with the song of birds, already my favorite part of creation. As I lingered there, bathed in song, I recalled what Jehovah God told me when I asked him why the birds sing.

> *At the dawn of each new day of creation, I sang with joy at what was to come. The birds sing because they imitate their creator. Birds are my gift to you to remind you that joy is your legacy, your way to overcome the darkness and usher back in the light. Listen carefully and you'll notice that the birds' song sounds like laughter. The birds laugh at the dawn because they've forgotten the day before. They simply take up the tasks of a new day trusting that everything will be provided. And so they sing, no matter how dark the night before has been.[13]*

When I rolled over ready to rise, the tree shook as hundreds of purplish black birds lit into the sky. I marveled

[13] *"But no one says, 'Where is God my Maker, who gives songs in the night, who teaches us more than he teaches the beasts of the earth and makes us wiser than the birds in the sky?'"* JOB 35:10-11

that a small tree could hold so many.

It was then that I heard God singing in the distance. His song beckoned me, giving me a trail to follow straight into his presence. The song grew louder as I neared the springs, and deep in my gut I felt a thirst, different than the thirst for water I had the day before after climbing a hill or running through a meadow. I was thirsty for him. Eager to embrace his song...

Bring sacrifices of righteousness,
Welcome a day of blessing.
Bathe your hands and feet in oil,
Then listen to instruction,
In the ways of love.

My children rest in my hands,
Kissed by heaven's dew.
Enjoying grain and wine,
My love poured out,
The land blessed.

With choice gifts of the mountains,
They celebrate my favor.
Fruits bursting with fullness,
The best the sun brings,
A life of abundance.

Today I join three strands,
Two learn the language of love.
Unquenched by many waters,
Rivers cannot wash it away,

It is stronger than death.

Choose me as your dwelling,
My arms as your strength.
Put your roots deep in blessing,
The eternal God your refuge,
His spirit your guide.[14]

As I listened, I wondered about the meaning of the song. "Lord, what is the cord of three strands?"

Eve, I have a blessing for you today.[15] *You are not alone.*

"Of course, I'm with you." I replied simply.

Before you came to be, there was another. A man. His name is Adam. I have walked with him, preparing him for you. Adam longs for you. He is waiting. He reflects my image, my strength, and my courage. You will trust him with your heart and he will give you his hand. And you will be his help, his ezer, standing by his side to strengthen him.

"Where is he?" I ventured, curious to see this man.

Soon you will meet him. "You bear bone and flesh from under his heart. Now you both will be more like us.

"Us?"

I am not alone, Eve. From the beginning, I have been in

[14] *Inspired by* DEUTERONOMY 33, ECCLESIASTES 4:9-12
[15] *"This is what the Lord says—he who made you, who formed you in the womb, and who will help you...For I will pour water on the thirsty land, and streams on the dry ground; I will pour out my Spirit on your offspring, and my blessing on your descendants."* ISAIAH 44:2-3

*relationship. Although you don't see or understand, they
are with me now. Yet we longed for you. One day when
you hold a little one in your arms you will understand.*

Then I saw him. Standing off in the distance. Like me, yet
so different. He strode with a smile and then hung back just a
little, unsure what to do. Father motioned for him to join us,
for us to join hands, and then he uttered a blessing...

*Be fruitful and increase in number, fill the earth and
subdue it. Rule over the fish in the sea and the birds
in the sky and over every living creature that moves
on the ground. I give you every seed-bearing plant
on the face of the whole earth and every tree that has
fruit with seed in it. They will be yours for food.*[16]

The tenderness in Adam's golden brown eyes brought a
flush to my cheeks. With a squeeze of my hands, he whispered,
"This is now bone of my bones and flesh of my flesh; she shall
be called woman for she was taken out of man."[17]

After hearing about my first day with God, Adam began
telling me stories from his time with God before I arrived.
Adam explained how, on his first morning, he woke up
clothed only in the mist rising from the earth. After he tried
out his legs for the first time—as Adam described it, like a
young buck quivering with effort but ready for action—he
and God began an adventure that lasted for untold time.

"Did I ever tell you?" Adam asked as we lay together on
the soft grass watching wispy white clouds pass overhead.
Rising and stretching, he paused, at a loss for words. "Come,"

49

[16] GENESIS 1:28-29
[17] GENESIS 2:23

he said, motioning and smiling. With mischief dancing in his eyes, he led me near the shore of the Tigris to a small inlet where the water was still. There, Adam explained "laying on the water." He first demonstrated with a leaf, then with a branch. Then, wading into the water, he knelt until he only showed from the waist up. After he tossed a quick glance over his shoulder to make sure I was watching, he suddenly threw himself downward, disappearing. I gasped, unsure where he had gone. When I was almost frantic, he popped up, shook the water out of his hair, rolled over and extended his long frame until his toes poked out of the water, with a little moss dripping off of one toe. "It's simply wonderful, Eve, you must try it!"

Always a little more cautious, I nudged up closer to the river's edge, and swirled my finger in the water. I poked a toe in, watching magical rings shimmer outward from wherever I touched. I sat on the shore, swirling my feet in the water, getting used to the liquid caressing my feet.

"Sit and talk with me." Adam smiled and held out his hand, his eyes pleading for me to trust him. With my hand in Adam's, I eventually waded in, and with time we learned to float side by side. Adam taught me that new perspectives come through trusting another's lead. Floating on the water, the clouds were glorious. The trees reaching over us were mighty guardians pointing our hearts to the heavens.

God was everywhere around us.

We'd hear him walking in the forest in the early dawn. The sound was a rhythmic rustling echoing through the trees, a shuddering that carried to the ground beneath us—so mysterious, yet familiar to me as the sound of my own breath.

Jehovah described it as the rustle of thousands of wings.[18] I was comforted by his presence—knowing that he was as close by as the breeze on my cheek or the sunlight on my face. I heard him in the cicadas buzzing at night, and in the sparrows singing in the early morning, as they joyfully flitted from branch to branch by the waters.[19]

Jehovah was also above us, in the stars. They appeared to be close enough to reach out and touch them; yet according to God they were farther away than the highest mountains. Even from the top of a mountain, it would take a river of mountains to get us even one step closer to them. One night as we sat on a rock waiting to welcome the stars, Adam explained, from his conversations with Jehovah, how the stars sang at creation's dawn, while the angels shouted for joy.[20]

It was important to Adam that I try to understand his relationship with his Father and the joy he felt as God unveiled his creation to just him, him alone, one small part at a time. To Adam, God was not only his Father; he was his partner in adventure. I had so many questions about their relationship.

"Weren't you lonely without me?" I asked, wanting to hear that his long wait for me was at least a little difficult.

"God tells me that I was lonely in ways that I didn't fully understand,"[21] Adam replied softly. "Every moment I had with God alone was an adventure. I felt so alive. Like I was exactly where I was supposed to be. Each morning I woke up looking forward to new things to learn, new places to explore and conquer."

"And you've only begun to show me these places," I whispered.

"One of the first things that God told me," Adam

[18] *"When the creatures moved, I heard the sound of their wings, like the roar of rushing waters, like the voice of the Almighty..."* EZEKIEL 1:24
[19] PSALM 104:12
[20] *"On what were its footings set, or who laid its cornerstone—while the morning stars sang together and all the angels shouted for joy?"* JOB 38:6-7
[21] See GENESIS 2:18. *It was God, not Adam, who first noticed that it wasn't good for Adam to be alone.*

continued, "was that he wanted me to rule over the animals, to subdue them. That meant studying the animals, their habits, where they lived and what they ate."

I smiled at the thought of Adam scaling a tree to get a glimpse of an eagle, climbing up the side of a mountain to watch a baby mountain goat play on the edge of a cliff, or even swimming up to a beaver's dam to inspect the use of twigs, rock and grass. I knew from my own time with Jehovah that even one of these would be no small task.

"That's why you know so much about the animals," I offered playfully.

"Eve, imagine it. The God who created the universe trusted me to name his creation. This became my daily work—to choose a name that somehow showed which animals were alike and which were different. And Father was pleased. He said that what I was doing was good."

"As he is good," I ventured.

"Yes, that's it, exactly!" Adam said. "And it was this process that brought me to you. I started seeing that nearly every animal had a partner, a companion. I saw them come together and bring new life into existence. I saw animals build a den in which to birth and nurse babies. I saw them gather food and take care of their young. I saw them running through the woods together..." Adam stopped midsentence and chuckled under his breath. I followed his eyes to see a pair of small birds flying in circles around each other.

"Some birds have interesting mating habits," Adam teased.

"And that's when you realized you were lonely?" I said, needing to hear the words.

He squeezed my hand, then we sat silent for a few minutes.

He sighed softly. "I'm not always good at this, am I?"

And then, turning towards me with a sweet shyness, he offered, "It's just that I knew I was missing something. Someone. Someone I needed. You."

Adam and I compared everything from our elbows to our big toes. The back of his hand was covered with soft, black hair, whereas mine was smooth and clear. His stomach was flat and hard, as smooth as the river rocks Adam loved to skip across the water. I loved to place my hand on his stomach and feel the strength. Mine was a soft mound of flesh that jiggled when Adam would playfully poke it. His ears poked out at a jaunty angle, whereas mine were small, close to my head—a work of genius, as Adam said, as he traced the curves with his finger. Adam especially loved for me to touch his arms. He showed me how he could make his muscles bigger by pumping a fist or lifting his arms in the air. I bit my lip so I wouldn't laugh as he struck amusing poses! Sometimes when he didn't know I was looking, I would watch as he would lift boulders and observe his own strength from the corner of his eye. Adam confided that at the beginning he could only lift small stones, but now was able to lift a boulder that weighed almost as much as I did. Sometimes when I'd walk in the Garden, he'd spring from behind me and swoop me up over his shoulder. While I was screaming, partially in protest and partially in glee, he'd take off running through the forest, whooping at the top of his lungs.

The first time we consummated our marriage was by one of the springs in the Garden of Eden. We were there together talking, resting on the soft grass, both on our sides facing each other.

"I'm ready," I said, moving close into his arms.

Although we were both unschooled in love, our first time together was tender, as natural as if it had always been meant to be. Afterwards, we lay close to each other not wanting to disturb the oneness. As I stroked his back, I could have sworn it was my own.

"Bone of my bones, flesh of my flesh," I mused.

"God has provided the most beautiful of gifts," Adam replied. "Let's find him and share our joy."

As the three of us walked together in the Garden that afternoon, I thought my heart might burst. "Thank you Father," I said. "Thank you for giving me Adam."

Looking at us with great pride, our Father exclaimed,

*I am your provider. Trust that I will always give
exactly what you need, even before you ask.*[22]

The Springs

Stirring from the second memory, I see that the afternoon is practically gone and the spring has dried up for the day. The second memory still swirls around me. I am warmed by it. *Thank you Jehovah that you created me to be in relationship.* Although I am hungry, thirsty and lonely for Adam, I feel comfort. Didn't I linger at the springs, instead of going back home to retrieve a skin for water? It seems such a small step forward, but points to the possibility of hope.

When I finally arrive at home, I am thrilled to discover two skins filled with water and a basket filled with vegetables hanging on the tree. Did Jehovah God stir Adam's heart to provide for me? Jehovah's words from the memory ring in

[22] *"Do not be like them, for your Father knows what you need before you ask him."* MATTHEW 6:8

my ears...*I will always give you what you need.*[23] Moved, I place my hands on the vegetables, much like we did when we sacrificed, and pray, "Jehovah please let the three of us walk together again, just like in the Garden. And thank you for this abundance, for stirring Adam's heart to provide."

As I eat, my thoughts stray back to the Garden of Eden. There, we never questioned where the fruit trees found their fruit. Or how the ground was able to bear delicious vegetables—yellow squash, white turnips, orange peppers, red potatoes. Adam cultivated the Garden, pruned as Jehovah God instructed and then picked the harvest for us to eat. But the Garden of Eden was planted, watered and grown by our Father's hand. When we were banished from Eden, we were forced to provide for ourselves. And it was far from easy. Adam fought stony hard ground, thorns and thistles, and insects that seemed determined to take our crops. At night, I plucked the pesky thorns that dug themselves under his skin and treated his many stings and insect bites. It pained me to see Adam's once soft hands become as coarse as the bark of a tree. Sometimes I cringed a little when he ran them over my skin, although I was careful to never show Adam.

Loss wells up within me, "Jehovah, how can I trust you as my provider when the path you've given has caused us so much pain? Why would I hope for good from you? Why should I pray to someone who did not protect me?" A wail rises up from deep in my chest, as I clench my fists and cry out, "I'm angry with you Jehovah, so angry!"

Moments earlier I prayed with gratitude. Now I overflow with rage. These words must pain Jehovah's heart, but I am not sure if I care. "I've lost one son through his own brother,

[23] *"The LORD will guide you always; he will satisfy your needs in a sun-scorched land and will strengthen your frame. You will be like a well-watered garden, like a spring whose waters never fail." ISAIAH 58:11*

water spilled on the ground never to be recovered.[24] And now, I'm far away from my firstborn who is banished after being taken captive by his own sin and the same enemy that stole our life in the Garden of Eden. What hope does Cain have, now that his life has been swept away by his sin?[25] What living water can he look forward to?"

I use my sleeve to wipe my eyes. I am ashamed at my outburst. "You told me I was created to live in relationship, just as you are more than one. But now loss has stolen my ability to love. And hope is too painful to embrace."[26]

After I eat, I cocoon myself in blankets like a caterpillar hoping for a transformation. I tuck the blanket beneath my knees, under my shoulders, up around my neck, so that nothing is exposed to the chilling air. I pull and tug until every part of my body feels sheltered. Then I allow myself to mourn. My sobs cause my cocoon of blankets to tremble, like life within is hungering to be unbound...to be free.

Even as I mourn, I know that this is different from when I was wrapped in Abel's cloak. His cloak was a hedge to keep pain out. This cloak, or at least the way I used it, stole my life essence. Although the cloak offered a semblance of protection, at least when I was awake, it also kept me stagnant, prevented me from mourning so that I could move forward. Adam's voice comes back to me, talking to our sons...*Stagnant water isn't safe to drink, boys. Look for flowing water.*

My life's flow swirled around Cain and Abel. Now I am stagnant, not really sure *who* I am. Then it occurs to me... Jehovah is the only one who can tell me.

"Father, how I long for the closeness I had with you, and with Adam, when there were no barriers, just complete

56

[24] *"Like water spilled on the ground, which cannot be recovered, so we must die. But that is not what God desires; rather, he devises ways so that a banished person does not remain banished from him."* 2 SAMUEL 14:14

[25] *"For what hope have the godless when they are cut off, when God takes away their life?"* JOB 27:8

[26] *"Hope deferred makes the heart sick, but a longing fulfilled is a tree of life."* PROVERBS 13:12

nakedness." The deep waters of our losses bubble up into my throat. "My life is in ruins. Time has passed, but I have stood still, unwilling to let any more distance come between me and my boys. Give me strength to go where you want to take me. Please, please hold on to me and never let go."[27]

But still I'm afraid. *Is it safe to feel, to let sorrow in? Or do I set myself up for more disappointment, more grief?* Then I remember Jehovah's song about love, about Adam and me…

> *Unquenched by many waters.*
> *Rivers cannot wash it away.*
> *It is stronger than death.*

"Jehovah, you sang these words over us when you brought us together. But what about you and me? Is your love for me able to overcome death? A son I haven't seen for a year? A husband who struggles to understand? Another son who passed from life to death, far, far too early?"

Slowly, I unwind the blankets from around me and get up to splash some cool water on my face. Prayer has circled my thoughts back to Abel.

"I know that Abel is with you even now. He is dead yet he lives. But I am alive and part of me has died." Then remembering my name, I ask, "How can I be the mother of the living when I am the mother of the dead?"

---

[27] *"But you Sovereign LORD, help me for your name's sake; out of the goodness of your love, deliver me. For I am poor and needy, and my heart is wounded within me."* PSALM 109:21-22 *Also see* JOHN 6:35-38 (MSG)

But his bow remained steady,
his strong arms stayed limber…
because of the Shepherd, the Rock of Israel…
who blesses you with blessings of the skies above…
blessings of the breast and womb.[1]

JOSEPH'S LONG-AWAITED BLESSING FROM JACOB,
AFTER HIS BROTHERS SOUGHT TO KILL HIM

[1] GENESIS 49:24-25

CHAPTER FOUR

The Shepherd

A HOWLING WIND COMES THROUGH IN THE night, roaring like a hungry beast, cracking branches and threatening to pull up our home by the roots. As the wind shrieks, a wolf pack comes near yowling with displeasure at the interruption of its hunting. Listening to the cackles and wails of wolves and wind, I break into a cold sweat that sops my forehead, the back of my neck, under my arms, the palms of my hands and the tops of my feet. It seems that evil has not only seized my children, but seeks to steal my faith as well. I can't help but think that the wolves' song is personal—a narration of my fall. My heart flails against my chest, keeping rhythm with the wolves' song.

"Do you pursue me with your tempest? Terrify me with your storm?"[2] I am not certain whether I speak to the serpent or to Jehovah, or both.

A puff of dust blows from under the door. Rising from my mat, I stuff skins in the gap between the door and the floor, not wanting to allow the serpent even a wisp of control. To keep panic from overtaking me, I sing one of Jehovah's verses from the second memory, amazed that the words are still imprinted on my heart…

2 *See* PSALM 83:14-16

Choose me as your dwelling,
My arms as your strength.
Put your roots deep in blessing,
The eternal God your refuge,
His spirit your guide.

As quickly as the storm and the wolves came, they depart. As the storm subsides to a whisper, I allow sleep to come—a deep dreamless sleep, a mercy from Jehovah.

Waking up the next morning chilled to the bone, I roll over and reach for Adam. As the separation washes over me, I pull the soft skins close, counting the days since Adam left. *Has it really been only two days?* I feel like I've hardly slept.

"Who will rescue me?" I whisper out loud as the mid-morning light streams in. As if in reply, a pang of nausea rushes from my head, swirls in my stomach and then inches its way down to my toes. I rub my stomach and realize there are other clues—tender breasts and exhaustion, moods wavering between hopeful and heartbroken. *Am I carrying another child?*

My mind flits from place to place seeking other explanations, counting off the weeks since I last bled. Even though I have lived and slept in Abel's cloak, I laid it aside for intimacy with Adam. Though I received little pleasure and struggled to keep my thoughts with him, I feared that without this connection I would lose what I had left of him. *Something is better than nothing.*

Almost as quickly as the nausea, conviction comes. *I am with child.* I want to laugh. *A little lamb is coming into our fold.* But just as quickly comes the urge to weep.

"Now, Lord? Now? Another child to lose?"

Drawing a circle on my stomach with my finger, I imagine the secret place where two children have grown within me. I am terrified to hope for good but unable to drown out the yearning that has been buried so long. The loss of Abel rolls over me, taking my breath away. Will every step forward remind me of what I've lost?

Come Eve, to the place where Abel kept his flocks.

"Lead me, Jehovah," I whisper. "Give me the courage to follow."

I get dressed, eat a little bread to settle my stomach and pack a small lunch. Thinking of Adam, I also leave some bread in the basket for him to find, wrapped carefully with leaves and tied with twine for safekeeping from animals and insects. I urge myself not to think it through, just go. *Walk past the garden, through the fields.*

Glancing up, I see a bird in the distance, soaring in circles high in the air. Is it an eagle? As I continue walking, I urge myself to look around, really see. See the yellow wildflowers lifting their head regardless of whether anyone sees. Hear the birds chattering back and forth, telling their own stories. When I see my destination ahead, I take a deep breath. For a short moment, I see my son sitting there, legs crossed, staff across his lap, his head cocked confidently towards our flocks. Secured around his neck, his cloak billows behind him, lifted by the breeze. His face radiates pure rapture.

"Abel," I whisper. When I run towards him, the vision shimmers away like a mirage on a dust-drenched summer day, taking my heart with it.

Lumbering the rest of the way up the hill, I look out over the pasture land. This hill is home to a single oak tree, with branches lifted high into the sky and three trunks joined at the base. As I stand there breathing in the aqua-tinged morning sky while wiping away tears, my thoughts are less of Adam and more of Abel. Realizing I'm tired, I sit down by the tree and close my eyes. "Please bring him back, Jehovah." With no answer from Jehovah and not sure I'm ready to go where he bids, I let my heart drift to Abel.

"MOTHER, FATHER, I'M TWELVE YEARS OLD," ABEL said, reaching his arms upwards to demonstrate his growing strength, "I'm old enough to handle the flocks by myself."

Seeing my frown, Adam laughed, "You certainly are my young shepherd...soon you'll be as tall as my staff!"

"Adam, don't you encourage him!" I said, giving Abel's arm a quick squeeze and a kiss on the ear, which he promptly wiped off with the side of his arm.

Later, as Adam curled up next to me, nuzzling the back of my neck with his rough lips, he whispered, "Our boys are growing up, my ezer." Reading my thoughts, he continued, "Don't worry, I'll find a way to protect them."

A few months later, Adam found Abel a companion, a wolf dog with a hurt leg. Abel named him Zayeb[3] and nursed him back to health. Then, aided by his father's knowledge of animals, Abel trained him to help with our flocks.

"Abel, you still have to be alert, even with Zayeb," I chided him gently. And then thinking of the blistering sunburn on his cheeks that took several days to heal, I added, "Zayeb can't protect you from the sun's heat. As a shepherd, our sheep

[3] *Wolf in Hebrew.*

count on you to keep them and you safe."

"I have an oak tree I sit under during the heat of the day. It's on a hill where I can easily watch our flocks," Abel said. And then he added with a smile, "Come and see. We can spend the day together."

"Abel, you don't understand how much I have to do at home," I said, hesitant.

"Please, come."

Looking into his innocent gaze, I knew I couldn't refuse him.

The next morning, as the sun came up to kiss the sky, I walked with Abel as he took our flocks out to pasture.

"How does Zayeb know how to herd the flocks?" I asked.

"A wolf's natural instinct is to bring the sheep to the pack's leader so that a kill could be made," Abel replied with pride in his eyes. "When Zayeb nips at the rears of the sheep, he is nudging them to me."

"Ah, Abel...so, you lead the pack," I teased. "I think your father might say that he leads both you and Zayeb."

"See how gentle he can be, yet so bold," Abel continued. "Although they don't like Zayeb pushing them around, they trust that he won't hurt them."

I thought to myself...*Gentle yet bold, like you, Abel.*

"Father says that if Zayeb hurts one lamb, even once, we will remove him...But don't worry Mother, he won't hurt them."

While I watched, Abel demonstrated how he taught the dog basic commands with his staff—the most important being, "Stop!" so that Zayeb didn't overexcite the flocks. I took note of my son's firm touch with the dog.

"Cain is jealous of Zayeb," Abel announced, when we sat down to rest. "He says it isn't fair for me to have a companion, while he works in the garden alone. Could he come help me here?"

"Let me talk to Cain," I said as I ruffled my son's hair. "Are you hungry?"

As we ate lunch under the cool shade of the tree, Zayeb asleep at our feet, Abel told me how he talked with God under this tree. Later he shared a simple song he sang to his sheep as he took them to the watering place.

> Grazing sheep,
> God has given,
> Enjoy the pasture,
> Where you're living.
>
> Sweet flock I embrace,
> Don't forget your watering place.[4]
>
> Hear my voice,
> When you're alone.
> Let me guide you,
> Direct you home.
>
> Sweet flock I embrace,
> Don't forget your feeding place.
>
> Romp freely,
> Within these grounds.
> Then follow me,

4 "...and you who walk along the road, consider the voice of the singers at the watering places. They recite the victories of the LORD." JUDGES 5:10B-11A

Where grass abounds.

Sweet flock I embrace,
Don't forget your resting place.

Between my shoulders,
Within my pen,
For you are mine,
And I am His.

Sweet flock for whom I long,
Don't forget where you belong.[5]

At the end, he looked at me with a deep dimple in his cheek that reminded me of Adam, and said, "Have you ever thought about that, Mother, how we are Jehovah's sheep and he is our shepherd?"[6] He paused, deep in thought. "And do you believe that when the darkness comes that he looks after us? That when danger threatens, he rescues us?"[7]

"Yes, son. I do believe that."

"To be protected, the sheep must stay within the pen; they must stay near the shepherd." As he spoke, Abel looked at me, his brown eyes brimming with trust. "Only when they run away from the shepherd, can the wolves attack."

I AM JERKED BACK TO THE PRESENT WHEN A LARGE branch tumbles through the limbs above me, making a swooshing noise as it brushes against other branches on the way down. The larger end lands on the ground with a big thud just a few footsteps away. Catching my breath and

---

[5] *Inspired by* PSALM 23:1-2, DEUTERONOMY 33:12, JOHN 10:1-18.
[6] PSALM 100:3
[7] *"As a shepherd looks after his scattered flock when he is with them, so will I look after my sheep. I will rescue them from all the places where they were scattered on a day of clouds and darkness."* EZEKIEL 34:12

willing my heart to slow, I urge my stunned legs to push me to standing. Cautiously, I move away from the tree where it can't harm me. *Where did that branch come from?* It is twice as tall as me and full of green leaves. Shielding my eyes from the sun, I locate where the branch tore off—high above me. *What caused the limb to fall?* I feel no wind.

"Stay near me Jehovah," I pray, realizing why Adam didn't want me out here by myself.

A swarm of small black bugs appears out of nowhere. As I swat the pesky creatures away, my thoughts gang up on me as well. *Our boys ran free in the wilderness. They needed protection. Abel needed a companion to protect him in case of wolves. And Jehovah blessed us with Zayeb. But what of Cain? Would it have been so difficult to find an animal for him as well?*

"Let the boys work it out, Eve," Adam had told me. "Zayeb belongs to the family, not just Abel."

Recognition comes with a sharp pain in my side. The garden belongs to the family, yet Cain felt the sting of our losses far more than Abel. Cain bore Adam's grief over the garden—the way it reminded Adam of the Garden of Eden, far easier to tend. The words of God after we sinned...

> *Cursed is the ground because of you; through*
> *painful toil you will eat food from it all the days*
> *of your life. It will produce thorns and thistles for*
> *you, and you will eat the plants of the field.*[8]

NOT TOO LONG AFTER MY TIME WITH ABEL, CAIN and I went together to survey the garden and pick vegetables. Beyond spending time with him, I planned to talk to him

[8] GENESIS 3:17–18

about Zayeb and pray with him over the garden.

As Cain walked me through the rows, showing me the beautiful hues of the newest crops of tomatoes, I could tell something was bothering him. Thinking it might be Zayeb, I said, "Cain, my firstborn, I'm so proud of your work here. But something weighs on your heart. What is it my son?"

Cain paused for a moment, picked up a tomato and examined it from every angle. He sighed. "Mother, why did Abel get the better job?"

"What makes you think his job is better?" I asked, surprised at my son's indignation. I glanced at the tomato he held. It had a small split on one side, but other than that, the tomato appeared to be perfect.

"Why didn't I get to choose?" Cain asked. "Shouldn't the oldest choose?"

"Cain, you've always loved the soil," I replied. "When you were a little boy, you were always digging in the dirt."

"I was too little to understand," Cain mumbled, taking the tomato and flinging it far from him.

"And the soil responds to you, like it does for no one else, not even your father. It's like the plants and vegetables recognize your voice, your touch."

"It's just that I'm protecting our carrots from rabbits, while Abel protects the flock from wolves."

"Cain," I said, touching his cheek and looking into his eyes, "You are my firstborn, my brave one. The thorns we fight are worse foes than even the wolves. Without you, birds or rabbits could steal our crops."

"I am Cain the brave one," he said with a smirk and a smile, waving his hands in the air. "Fear not spinach and squash, beans and berries, the slayer of thorns and thistles, birds and rabbits, is here. I will save you from them!" With that he picked up two loose sticks, and swung his arms to and fro, as if he were in a great battle with thorns, birds and rabbits, causing me to laugh and shake my head.

"Brave man, you have slain the thorns in this field! Have you vanquished birds and rabbits? Could you come fight the thorns all around us?"

"If you feed me, I might," he said with a laugh.

"Let's finish picking first," I said, throwing my arm around him in a loose hug, the only type I knew he would allow.

During lunch, I decided to wait for both the conversation about Zayeb and the prayer. *There will be more time to talk and pray.* At that moment, the curse seemed far away.[9]

"JEHOVAH, WHAT ELSE DID I MISS?" I CRY, LIFTING my arms to the sky and then lowering them slowly. My eyes go once more to the branch that fell from the tree...surely Jehovah prevented it from reaching me. Still not ready to go with Jehovah to the third memory and no longer feeling safe under the tree, I decide to walk to the very places I have avoided. I trudge down the hill into the valley where our sheep graze. Next, I go to the river to stroll by its banks and soak in the trees' reflection in the water. When I see a shadow flit across the water, I lift my eyes to the sky. There I see a lone eagle. Is it the same bird I saw earlier near the tree? With its wings spread wide, it makes a large circle above me, not even needing to flap a wing. My spirit lifts. The enormous bird, with a white head that appears to glow against the afternoon sky, makes increasingly larger circles until it disappears.

---

[9] *"Cursed is the ground because of you; through painful toil you will eat food from it all the days of your life. It will produce thorns and thistles for you, and you will eat the plants of the field. By the sweat of your brow you will eat your food..."* GENESIS 3:17B–18A

By the time I arrive home, the sky blushes with the approaching sunset. Adam has taken the bread and put a bouquet of purple cornflowers in its place. Instead of going inside, I climb up into the tree to the very spot where I once found Adam in the early morning. Held by the tree's branches, I pull the flowers to my chest and breathe in their peace.

Even as I recall the beauty of the two memories Jehovah has given me—the first memory, the bed of spices where he sang a love song over me, and the second memory, my first days with Adam—I know there will be pain in the memories to come. Pain that I must face in order to move forward.

A snake called Serpent convinced me that I needed more. He seduced me with the very gifts God gave me for my enjoyment, whispering that I could no more trust the Father of light than the shifting shadows.[10]

A second-born son was found dead in a field, after his brother, the firstborn I mothered from his very first cry, struck out against him in jealousy.

Will the heavens expose my guilt?

Will the earth rise up against me and replace me with another woman made of bone and dust?[11]

Come with me.

"Jehovah, the first two memories were so beautiful. Yet I fear the memories to come...the memories in the shadow of death. I have no one but you. So take me where you will."

In answer, the third memory pushes itself up through the tree roots into the branches that cradle me, and seeps into my pores as if the tree and I are one.

[10] *"Every good and perfect gift is from above, coming down from the Father of the heavenly lights, who does not change like shifting shadows."* JAMES 1:17
[11] *"The heavens will expose his guilt; the earth will rise up against him."* JOB 20:27

The third memory with Jehovah

It was a glorious day in the Garden of Eden. Earlier, Father and I had walked together, talking about the flowers and the bees. Without bees there would be no flowers. And we wouldn't enjoy the fruit God placed in the Garden.

Now alone, my thoughts were still full of bees. Did bees carry pollen from the tree of the knowledge of good and evil to other trees? Would that make them unsafe? God told us that we may eat of every tree except *the tree* (as Adam and I sometimes called it). Not even saying the tree's name seemed, well...safer. Then it came to me. Perhaps God carried pollen to *the tree* himself, instead of having the bees do it.

Wondering about these things, I took a different way home, the path that led to the tree. For the longest time, I mostly avoided the tree. But on this day, I took the way not allowed. I reasoned that as long as I didn't eat the fruit, I wouldn't be in any danger. As I walked, I gathered a bouquet of brightly colored flowers to take home to Adam.

Once I came near the tree, I stopped and circled it slowly, watching for danger. I didn't see any bees.

"Beautiful, isn't it, Eve?"

I looked around, startled.

"Look, up in the tree, above you. Here I am," he said, lifting his head and exposing his forked tongue. "Yes, it's me talking to you."

The snake didn't appear to be talking out loud, as Adam and I did. Unlike the growls, barks, whines, clicks and chatter of the other forest creatures, I could hear *and* understand him. The snake's voice had a slow drawl, almost mesmerizing.

"Well, hello," I said, uncertain.

"I am Serpent, the whisperer. I live here in Eden. I've been waiting for the right time to introduce myself, waiting for you to choose this path."

I looked up, squinting as sunlight shafted through the branches. A chill snaked down my spine, as I saw his scaled skin shimmering in the light.

"Whisperer?" I said, thinking to myself that this is why I couldn't see his mouth move when he talked.

"I have many names. Diviner. Enchanter. Diligent Observer. Shiny One.[12] You can call me Serpent. Don't be afraid," he added. "I'd like to be your friend."

Part of me wanted to run quickly and find Adam. Another part of me wanted to be brave. After all, Adam wasn't the only one who could connect with the animals. And surely Adam would have told me about Serpent if he knew him.

"You are curious about this tree," Serpent offered with a slip of his tongue.

"Oh, I know God doesn't want us to eat the fruit of this tree," I replied, feeling a little tug of conscience. "I wouldn't even think of eating it. I was just looking to see if any bees are nearby."

"Odd name for a tree, if you ask me." He slithered up the branch a little to take a position in the sunlight. "The tree of the knowledge of good and evil. Now what do you suppose that means?"

"If we eat it, we will die," I offered solemnly, taking a step back from the serpent and the tree. The light reflecting off of his shiny skin was blinding.

"Now what do you suppose the Great One is trying to protect you from?"

---

[12] *Whisperer, Diviner, Enchanter, Diligent Observer and Shiny One are all possible meanings of nachash, translated serpent.*

I was stumped. "I, I'm...not quite sure what you mean?"

"You'd like to touch the fruit, wouldn't you?" Serpent slithered a little bit closer.

"Oh, no!" I stuttered, embarrassed.

"My understanding is that you weren't told you couldn't touch it. Only not to eat it," he coaxed.

Seeing my hesitation, he wove himself in and out of the branches, touching piece after piece of fruit. "See," he said. "You notice I'm still here, the same as I was before. There's nothing to hurt you."

I looked at the fruit. Each piece was well formed, pleasing.

Then Serpent's tail swung around, knocking a piece of fruit from the branch. It fell to the ground and rolled close to my feet.

Could one piece of fruit harm me? I rummaged through my memory. Had God said anything about touching the fruit?[13]

"You used to be afraid to just look at the fruit, didn't you?"

I shivered. *How does he know my thoughts?*

"But now you've looked and the fruit almost touches your toes. You seem to be quite fine," he quipped. I could have sworn there was a smile at the corner of his mouth. Was he mocking me? I felt my cheeks flush with some unknown desire. I came here today, hadn't I? Without Adam, without God, I chose my own path, followed my curiosity, tested out my own thoughts.

I sighed, laid my flowers carefully on the ground and picked up a branch. I knelt down and gave the fruit a little push, examining it from every side. I sensed Serpent watching me. His eyes were bright red, remarkably close to the color of the fruit he teased me about.

[13] *"But God did say, 'You must not eat fruit from the tree that is in the middle of the garden, and you must not touch it, or you will die."* GENESIS 3:3

"You yearn for beauty," Serpent interjected. "The Creator himself gave you that desire."

Adam and I observed the animals. But, I never considered the possibility that they observed us. I glanced around the woods. Was something else watching? Mocking us, like this snake?

"With my form, I move very slowly." He haltingly unwound himself from a branch to demonstrate. "But this gives me time to understand the Garden in ways that perhaps you and Adam haven't considered."

I felt a bit dizzy, so I sat down, carefully distancing myself from the piece of fruit. I laid my flowers tenderly on the ground beside me. I could feel my heart banging against my chest. Was this fear? Or excitement? Maybe Adam felt this way when he discovered something for the first time. The piece of fruit glistened a little in the sunlight. I was surprised at my courage to be so close.

He began to whisper, as if only I was worthy of his confidences. "I too once held reservations. But then I came to understand that the One from Ancient Days,[14] the one whom you walk with, doesn't explain things very well. His wisdom is so all-encompassing, that he loses touch with his own reasoning."

"I'm not sure you should talk of him in that way," I said softly.

"Oh, let me assure you that I, of all the animals, respect the Eternal One." I rubbed my ears. Now it seemed he was too loud, even angry. "I have known him from the beginning of the ages. Let's just say that he prides himself on having a secret sort of wisdom."[15]

---

[14] *"Yes, and from ancient days I am he. No one can deliver out of my hand. When I act, who can reverse it?"* ISAIAH 43:13
[15] *"No, we declare God's wisdom, a mystery that has been hidden and God destined for our glory before time began."* I CORINTHIANS 2:7

A little sadness washed over me realizing that even Serpent had known Jehovah God longer than I had. Was Father keeping secrets from us? Surely Jehovah would explain.

"Eve, if you don't mind, I'd like to offer some advice," Serpent interjected. "This is not something you should talk to the One in the Heights about just yet.[16] Give it time. Figure out what you really want to know."

I sighed. I wanted to say something. Something that showed how much I already did know, but I could find nothing.

"Do you think Adam has told you everything that he knows?" Serpent wove himself around a branch.

"He walked with Father long before me...he couldn't possibly tell me all."

"Perhaps you're on the short end, when it comes to knowledge." Seeing me lower my eyes to the ground in chagrin, he added, "Oh, but you mustn't worry. There is always time."

My stomach rumbled a little. Suddenly, I wanted nothing more than to get out of there and be with Adam.

"I must go," I whispered under my breath. "I really must go."

"No hurry," Serpent whispered. "No hurry."[17]

I wasn't sure if his words were for me or for himself.

I collected my bouquet of flowers and walked off, not wanting to show Serpent that I was more than a little unnerved. When I was certain I was out of sight, I began to run. Having done something that Adam didn't know about, I felt a new emotion. Was it regret? Was it excitement?

I went to the pond to freshen my face and calm myself

[16] MICAH 6:6 *Elohay Marom, The God of Heights*
[17] *"When the devil had finished all this tempting, he left him until an opportune time."* LUKE 4:13

down. I dropped the flowers on the pond's bank, distracted by my thoughts. *Did I imagine all of that? Perhaps I am making something out of nothing. I'll wait awhile before I talk to Adam. I need to understand this better first.* Then it occurred to me that for the first time I had something that only I knew.

When I turned to pick up my flowers, they were all completely wilted. I recoiled in shock. Did I press them too hard to my chest? My thoughts raced. I threw the wilted flowers in the pond and watched sadly as they sank. Looking around, I saw some purple flowers growing nearby. I quickly gathered some to take to Adam.

When I returned, Adam looked up and smiled. "You were gone longer than usual."

"I explored a little," I said, mustering a smile. I wondered if he could see through me. Would he be able to read my thoughts?

"Ah, my love... without me?"

I sat down next to him, put my head on his shoulder and raised the flowers to his nose. "Smell," I said.

After Adam inhaled deeply, I showed him how the little stems could be pulled out so that the little drops of sweetness landed on his tongue.

"Adam," I asked, gathering my courage. "Do you ever wonder if there is anything God isn't telling us?"

Adam smiled and shrugged. "From all the time I've spent with Father, I've found that his timing is perfect." Adam gave my knee a squeeze. "He who formed the mountains, reveals his concern for us through his many good gifts."[18]

And then turning to face me, he said the words I never grew tired of, "Just like when he gave you to me."

---

[18] " *He who forms the mountains, who creates the wind, and who reveals his thoughts to mankind, who turns dawn to darkness, and treads on the heights of the earth—the* LORD *God Almighty is his name.*" AMOS 4:13

The Shepherd

As I slowly wake from the third memory and come back to the present, I find myself cradled by the tree's branches, shrouded in the shadows of a moonless night. I take a deep breath, climb down carefully with the purple flowers and hurry into our home, securing the door behind me with the cords that Adam wove out of bamboo stalks. After sticking the flowers in water, I feel my way to my bed and get in with all my clothing on. As I pull the covers up to my neck, I think back through the third memory. *I chose to go outside of Jehovah's boundaries.* Abel's words come back to me with a sting of conviction, "To be protected, the sheep must stay within the pen; they must stay near the shepherd." My thoughts race. When I walked with Jehovah, I was within his pen. My own wandering stole my protection. My secret from Adam gave the father of lies a place to slither his way in, climbing into my reservations, my secret fears, almost as if I were a tree.[19] I shudder. Then Abel's words come back to me with such clarity that I wondered if he were sitting next to me. "Do you believe that when the darkness comes he protects us? That when dark clouds come he rescues us?"

"Did Jehovah protect you?" I ask Abel. My heart isn't to accuse Jehovah. I just want to know how Abel would see it. I want truth. As if Abel himself was there to gently nudge me, a day comes back to me. The day Cain was the protective one. The day he rescued his brother.

CAIN CAME RUNNING, COVERED IN SWEAT, "Mother, Abel fell from the oak tree by the flocks," he blurted out. "He's hurt!"

[19] *"Whoever conceals their sins does not prosper, but the one who confesses and renounces them finds mercy."* PROVERBS 28:13

"Why did you leave him there alone?" I said, panic pushing over me. "What if a wild animal attacks him? You are the oldest. It is your responsibility to watch out for him."

Shame darkened my son's face. "I wasn't sure if I should move him," he murmured. "Zayeb will protect him."

"Cain, get the healing balm," I instructed, while I gathered some water and rags, refusing to let the fear welling up inside overcome me. Since Adam was hunting, Cain and I made the trek to the tree, half walking, half running. When we arrived, Zayeb stood erect, ears up, sniffing the wind for danger.

"Good dog. You guarded him well," I whispered, giving him a quick pat, grateful to see my son's chest rise and fall.

"Abel, your ankle is twice its usual size," I said, giving him a gentle nudge to wake him.

Abel opened his eyes, looked at me with a sleepy, yet sheepish grin, then winced in pain.

"Son, how far up were you in the tree?" I asked as I attended to his scrapes.

"Near the top," Abel boasted. "The highest I've ever climbed. A small branch broke underneath my foot."

"Where? Show me?" Cain piped in.

Abel grimaced as I dabbed at the small cut on his cheek. "There was a golden eagle circling overhead and I wanted a better view," Abel explained. "He was enormous!"

I wrapped his ankle with a straight stick and some cloth to secure it, shaking my head at my son's foolishness, yet proud of his courage.

"Abel, we need to get you home. Let's see if we can help you walk."

After trudging along for a bit with Abel between us, his arms over each of our shoulders, Cain stepped in, "Mother, this is too slow. I will carry him home."

I glanced at Cain. Tilling land and clearing rocks had made him quite strong. And I heard authority in his voice, of a boy turning into a man. I nodded.

"Abel, put your arms around my neck," Cain instructed.

Cain hoisted Abel onto his back as if he weighed very little.

"Thank you, my strong one," I added, rubbing my shoulder, already sore from the attempt to help Abel walk.

On the way home, Cain told funny stories to lift Abel's spirits. Abel told us how the golden eagle hovered over him while he waited for us, making sweeping circles and even landing on the top of the tree. "Did you know that the golden eagle has two chicks, and often the older one will eat the younger?"

"How do you know this?" Cain asked.

"Father told me," Abel said simply.

"Your father shouldn't tell you such stories!" I chided.

"I'll believe that when I see it," Cain said.

THE BITE OF CAIN'S WORDS BRINGS ME BACK TO the present. *How could a boy who saved his brother also slay him?* I pat my stomach. "Little lamb, you will have no brothers nearby to watch over you, but I promise to protect you." As soon as the words leave my tongue, I realize that I have no right to make such a promise. I couldn't protect my first two children. How will I defend this one?

I begin to talk out loud.

"Jehovah, the loss of my boys tore my heart out by the roots, ripped it into shreds and scattered it over the ground," I cry out. Remembering a fallen tree the boys found, I continue. "Now my roots lie exposed, unable to nourish or be nourished. How will I protect a new little one?" Suddenly I realize that my instinct to protect is alive and well.

"Why would you give me the desire to protect without the ability to carry it out?" I cry out in frustration. My accused mind answers...*I am like the fallen tree. And a tree dies if it loses all that it has to nourish.*

I curl up on my side into a tight ball. A hiss comes under the door in a long, slow drawl, like the sound of water putting out a fire.

Hissssss love has left you. He promises to protect, but doesn't deliver. I put my hands over my ears, but the whisper continues...*We have more to consider, Eve.*

"Leave me, wayward one!" I cry, afraid his venomous lies are already seeping into my veins.[20]

Then I feel something like the brush of Abel's lips against my cheek, like the flutter of a child growing in the womb. *Does he kiss me goodbye?* Putting my hand to my cheek, I find a small leaf. Rolling onto my back, I hold the leaf on my chest, knowing that Jehovah seeks entrance to my heart. Believing that he is the only one who can protect me from the evil one, I finally find the courage to say what is needed.

"Father, I am weak. I am the sheep in need of a shepherd. I will go wherever you lead."

---

[20] *"Their venom is like the venom of a snake; like that of a cobra that has stopped its ears, that will not heed the tune of the charmer, however skillful the enchanter may be."* PSALM 58:4–5

In your anger, do not sin;
when you are on your beds,
search your hearts and be silent.
Offer right sacrifices and trust in the LORD.
Many are asking, "Who can show us any good?"
Let the light of your face shine upon us, O LORD. [1]

KING DAVID, A MAN AFTER JEHOVAH'S HEART

[1] PSALM 4:4–6 (NIV 1984)

CHAPTER FIVE
The Sacrifice

I N THE MORNING, I WAKE UP SORE. MY BACK hurts from falling asleep in the branches. My heart hurts from the third memory, my first encounter with Serpent, who also calls himself Whisperer, Diligent Observer and Shiny One. I use my fists to dig into the painful lumps in my lower back. Then, I stretch my arms upwards, trying to pull my ribs off the sore muscles in my hips, wishing there was a simple way to release my accused heart. Walking outside, I notice that the sun is already high overhead. I can't resist checking in the basket on the tree, hoping that Adam brought some fresh game for a savory stew with rosemary and onions from the garden. Or anything to indicate that Adam is thinking of me—Eve, the mother of deceit, the one who decided not to tell what happened at the tree. I'm disappointed to only find a few leaves and wisps of purple pedals. I wander back inside to check Adam's bouquet that I stuck in a gourd of water late last night—still holding their heads high. I sigh in relief. If my flowers can live on, perhaps I can too.

Then as quick as the breeze that rises to whip the fields without warning, nausea sweeps over me. Unable to restrain it, I run out into the fields behind our home where the nausea throws me on my knees, and I empty the little in my stomach onto the ground. Crawling a bit farther, seeking a place to lie down, I prick my hand.

"Wicked thorns! Messengers of Whisperer! Why do you torment me so?"[2]

I roll onto my back steadying my throbbing right hand, while I gently extract the thorn with my left— a hooked thorn that has to be taken out carefully, consciously. Accusation sees the opportunity to visit...

You are a thorn, rejected by Adam and the One on High.

I suck on my hand for a second, seeking to soothe my pain and the harsh reality that I am with child, sick, scared and alone. As my pricked thumb throbs in rhythm with my pounding chest, it strikes me that perhaps nausea is the thorn and this child is the small flower bud it protects.

When I was pregnant with Cain, the nausea was so unexpected. After all, God's prediction was that *giving* birth would be painful. And once the nausea started, it seemed my constant companion—it came in the morning, revisited me in the afternoon and sometimes came by for another visit in the evening. Even as my belly swelled into a mound of firm flesh, the nausea lingered. And just as sickness began to recede, other ailments stood by, ready to take its place. Sometimes eating would set my chest on fire—a burning I learned to quell by soaking peppermint or elm bark and then drinking the water. Other times my ankles would swell so large, it was almost as if they were carrying their own children.

But with all the discomfort of bearing Cain, there was joy. His first butterfly-like flutters, which later turned into kicks so hard I thought he might punch his own path out. The way

[2] *"To keep me from becoming conceited because of these surpassingly great revelations, there was given me a thorn in my flesh, a messenger of Satan, to torment me."* 2 CORINTHIANS 12:7 (NIV1984)

Adam would lean over my belly and talk to him at night, whispering great adventures they would share and singing him impromptu songs about Jehovah God. With the miracle of Cain's birth, joy took the place of pain. Adam's first words of awe, "It's a man-child!" And mine, "With the help of the Lord, I have brought forth a man!"[3] How I marveled at his perfect little head covered in the softest of red hair, his furled brow and insistent cries when he was ready to eat, and how after he ate, his mouth would relax in contented bliss as a little drop of milk ran down his cheek.[4] I heard his every sigh in the night. Sometimes I slept with a hand on his chest, so that his heartbeat could echo through my veins as well as his own. Is this what Jehovah meant when he said I would understand him better, how he is more than one, once I had a child?

A FEW MONTHS AFTER CAIN WAS BORN, ADAM woke me early in the morning. Cain was nestled next to me. "Let's go," he whispered. "Bundle up Cain."

I rubbed the sleep out of my eyes, "Where are we going?"

"Come," he said. "We need to honor Jehovah, thank him for Cain."

I got up and quickly gathered some bounty from our garden. After I swaddled Cain in a soft cloth, I threw a skin around my shoulders. When I came outside, Adam was leading a small lamb on a rope. Soon after the lamb was born, her mother died. On more than one occasion, Adam slept with her to keep her warm. He teased that just as Cain was his son, the lamb was his daughter.

Now seeing the question in my eyes, Adam quipped, "Trust me, my love." Always considerate, he reached for the

83

[3] GENESIS 4:1
[4] Traditionally, it is thought that Cain had red hair. Hence, Shakespeare's nod to the "Cain-colored beard" in The Merry Wives of Windsor (Wilkepedia).

bag of vegetables, knowing I would prefer to carry Cain.

Noting the direction we were headed, I asked Adam, "To the overlook?"

Adam nodded and smiled, and began softly singing a song of thanksgiving to Jehovah God, a song he prepared for this occasion.[5]

> Come, let us bless the Lord,
> Offering thanks to him.
> He injures and heals,
> He tears and binds up,
> Lending hope of new birth.
>
> Come, let us honor the Lord,
> Offering thanks to him.
> As the sun rises and sets,
> He redeems and restores,[6]
> Promising hope of new birth.
>
> Come, let us praise the Lord,
> Offering thanks to him.
> As dawn kisses the west,
> The spring rains appear,
> Granting hope of new birth.
>
> Come, let us praise the Lord,
> Offering thanks to him.
> Fruit of his love,
> Through a firstborn lamb,
> Growing hope of new birth

[5] *"But I, with a song of thanksgiving, will sacrifice to you. What I have vowed I will make good. Salvation comes form the* LORD.*"* JONAH 2:9 (NIV 1984)
[6] *"Come, let us return to the* LORD. *He has torn us to pieces but he will heal us; he has injured us but he will bind up our wounds. After two days he will revive us; on the third day he will restore us, that we may live in his presence."* HOSEA 6:1–2

Come, let us wait for the Lord,
Offering thanks to him.
Maker of heaven,
Creator of earth,
Proving hope of new birth.

When we arrived, Adam secured the young lamb to a nearby branch, placing the offering from our garden next to her. Then he took Cain from my arms and laid him gently on a large rock. He encircled Cain's small head with his large hands, calloused by his hard labor in the fields, and began to pray, his voice choked with emotion,

"Jehovah, our Father, from whom all life springs, we thank you for this son you knit together in Eve's womb."[7]

After leaning over and kissing Cain on the forehead, he handed him back to me. Cain rooted around on my chest, insistent on his milk. As I opened my tunic to satisfy his hunger, Adam gently bound the lamb to the rock, speaking softly to her, the lamb strangely silent. As he worked, I mused that the first time I ever saw a mother nurse an infant was a sheep nursing a baby lamb. I marveled at the way the lamb eagerly took his mother's teat and how fast he grew with his mother's milk.

Adam encircled the lamb's head gently with his hands, much like he did with Cain...

"Jehovah, our Father, I thank you for allowing me to become a father. And we thank you for opening Eve's womb to birth this strong and healthy son, given by you. Today, we devote Cain, joy of our hearts, represented by this young lamb and this bounty from our fields, to you."[8]

[7] PSALM 139:13
[8] "As it is written in the Law of the LORD, every [firstborn male] that opens the womb shall be set apart and dedicated and called holy to the LORD." LUKE 2:22-24 (AMP)

Later as we walked home, Adam gently bouncing Cain on his shoulder, we were quiet, each in our own thoughts. I was touched by my husband's faith. But even though we did eat lamb from time to time, it seemed cruel to leave the lamb to die. As if he heard my thoughts, Adam looked at me and then wiped a tear from the corner of his eye. "God will deal gently with the lamb. Did you see how the lamb gave herself?[9] Jehovah himself prepared her."

But all I could think was that we gave a female instead of a male, a lamb that would have grown into a sheep that could bear more lambs. When we came back to the rock after a week had passed, the rope that bound the lamb was still there, but no trace remained of the lamb. I smiled at Adam, my concession that he was right, that his heart of sacrifice ran deeper than mine.

As time went on, our yearly offerings changed. Adam began to slaughter an animal first, to give the most select parts. Only afterwards would we prepare the rest of the meat for the family. Lamb was a precious commodity—Adam would roast it with garlic pushed underneath the skin, and for a very short time, thorns and thistles would seem far away, as we reveled in God's provision.[10] We sought to use everything the lamb gave us, from the fat in the tail—especially precious as an oil or seasoning—to the skin. Other times Adam would choose special fruits and vegetables to offer to Jehovah, like a squash that grew larger than any other. Or, from a small plant, he would give the sole piece of good fruit. From the time our boys were small, they participated in our annual offering. And as the boys matured, they had many questions.

Cain asked once, "Father, why would Jehovah give us

86

[9] *"He was oppressed and afflicted, yet he did not open his mouth; he was led like a lamb to the slaughter, and as a sheep before her shearers is silent, so he did not open his mouth."* ISAIAH 53:7
[10] *Read* NEHEMIAH 9:25

something and then expect us to give it back? When we give to each other, you tell us it's not right to take it back."

Abel added, "And, how can we know what makes Jehovah happy? How can we know what is most important to him?"

Adam patiently addressed both boys with a simple wisdom that touched my heart. "It is to thank God for what he's given, and show that we depend on his good gifts."[11]

Adam smiled and then squeezed Cain's arm affectionately, "Cain, can you make a seed grow? Abel, can you weave together a baby lamb in its mother's womb?"[12]

Cain piped in, "The seed won't grow unless I put it into the ground."

"But Cain, when you put the seed in the ground, it is still hard. The seed is still holding on to its own life," Adam explained patiently. "But when the seed dies inside of the ground, only Jehovah can bring it back to life. And that one little seed becomes many."[13] Motioning around him, Adam added, "Every plant that pushes its shoots up out of the ground towards the sun is a miracle, just like God creating all of this. He drenches our garden's furrows and then helps our crops go from seed to full kernels that we grind into flour for bread—the garden grows while we sleep."[14]

Adam nodded towards Abel, signifying that the next words would be for him. I'm not sure if Abel understood, but I would ponder these words, wondering at their meaning again and again...

"We simply do our best to make him happy; every time we give to Jehovah, like the seed, we let go of a little bit of ourselves. We commit our harvest, our herds, even our very lives to him."

[11] *"Every good and perfect gift is from above, coming down from the Father of the heavenly lights, who does not change like shifting shadows."* JAMES 1:17

[12] *See* PSALM 139:13

[13] *See* JOHN 12:24

[14] *Read* PSALM 65:9-11

My thorn-pierced, throbbing hand suddenly pulls me into the present. Then, I hear Jehovah's call...

*Come and eat what is good. You will
need strength for the journey.*[15]

When I return to our house, the basket holds a portion of roasted lamb prepared just the way I like it. The aroma sends a chill down my spine, making my jaw ache in anticipation. Amazed that I could be so ravenous after being so sick such a short while ago, I muse how God once again moved Adam's heart to provide. After I attend to my hand, coating it in the healing balm and wrapping it with a small cloth, I nibble on the roasted lamb, thanking Jehovah for each juicy bite. When I am finished, I wrap up the leftover lamb to protect it from insects and put it in a cool place. Seeing the beautiful day outside, and drowsy after eating, I take a blanket outside to rest in the sun. Hiking my garment up around my knees and taking off my outer garment, I imagine the sun permeating my skin and warming my very soul. I ask Jehovah, "Why do you bring these memories when I am still?" I am so weary that the words barely leave my lips.

Come. The fourth memory is prepared for you.

As I drift towards sleep, I rehearse the first three memories.

The first memory...the glory of exploring creation with Jehovah.

The second memory...the light-filled days frolicking with Adam in the Garden.

[15] *"Listen, listen to me and eat what is good, and you will delight in the richest of fare."* ISAIAH 55:2

The third memory...Whisperer convincing me to deceive my husband.

Sickness, a sore hand and a weary heart recede into the background as another memory springs up from the ground and wraps itself around me like a vine.

The fourth memory with Jehovah

I was sitting outside in the sun, when I saw Adam approaching, his feet slamming into the ground like he had some kind of grudge against it...with Cain following close behind. The lingering heat seemed to radiate around Adam's head, while sweat and dirt splayed across his face, broken only by tracks of tears. Cain's arms were crossed so tight he was digging his fingers into his arms. His eyes were downcast.

"Birds destroyed our harvest. A huge swarm of tan birds with red bills. I've seen their woven nests in the trees near the river more and more often, but never knew there were so many." Adam's voice choked with emotion, "We've lost everything, Eve."

"I wish I could have saved you from this," I said to both of them, as I went over and put my arms around Cain. He allowed the closeness for only a moment before he shrugged off my embrace.

"It's been so dry this year. I'm guessing the weaver birds couldn't find grass seed to eat," Adam continued. "Cain and I have been fetching water from the springs for our garden. I'm afraid we created a feeding place for the birds...like they thought we did all this for them."

"Show me," was all I could manage. I didn't want to add my fear to theirs.

"I want to see too," Abel piped in solemnly.

As a family we walked to the garden to inspect our crops. All of our wheat and millet had been completely ravaged. Our vegetable plants looked like someone had pulled them apart and thrown them into the dirt, sampling and then rejecting some vegetables, while eating others. The foliage was shredded. I had to agree that the field looked unsalvageable.

Disregarding us, a weaver bird lit back into the field determined to find yet another tidbit. Adam went running toward the bird, flailing his arms with rage, "Away from here, you cursed bird!" Walking back towards us, Adam's rage exploded, "It is like these crazy birds cannot hear!"

"How could this have happened?" Abel asked as he began to cry.

"I prayed over this field," Cain finally said, his voice trembling. "I prayed that God would show himself through this harvest."

"Cain, I'm so sorry," I murmured. My mind raced ahead. *Such a harsh awakening—seeing his hard work destroyed in one swift blow.*

I gave my son's arm a squeeze. "This has nothing to do with you, Cain." And looking at my husband I added, "None of us could have prevented this…and it doesn't mean Jehovah has left us." I hoped not only to reassure them, but also to convince myself that there was hope.

While the boys walked back and forth surveying the damage, I whispered in Adam's ear, "Your sons, Adam…" wanting to remind him to help the boys see hope.

But Adam could barely contain himself. All he could see was disaster.

"I was nearby when they came. It was unreal. Every inch of air was full of hungry birds, making it hard to see. The noise of their wings was deafening. Everywhere I looked all I saw was birds, swooping, squawking, gorging themselves."

I reached over and brushed his hand with mine.

"At first I was frozen in shock, and then I started running, yelling, 'Stop! Stop!' I waved my arms, jumped up and down, but it was too late. I've never felt so helpless."

As Adam spoke, I could picture him running and yelling and the wildness in his eyes as the birds attacked. If he had possessed a way to do it, I had no doubt he would have destroyed the birds before they destroyed us.

"Where were you Cain?" I asked, seeing his downcast eyes.

"I was...asleep under the tree. I only woke up when I heard Father yelling."

"It wouldn't have mattered, son," Adam said, shaking his head and crossing his arms.

"Either I matter or I don't!" Cain howled, wiping his running nose with his sleeve. "You can't have it both ways!"

"Of course you matter, son," I responded, jerked out of my own shock by Cain's outburst. "Your father is just saying that one more person couldn't have stopped the weaver birds."

Cain was silent. Did he want Adam to tell him that he could have made a difference? But wouldn't that have caused Cain more shame? I could see Cain's point...he prayed over these fields. I desperately wanted Adam to tell Cain something, something wise about why Jehovah would allow this. But then I noticed an ugly gash over Adam's left ear. I reached out to touch it and Adam winced in pain.

"From the birds?" Abel asked.

"It's nothing, Abel," Adam answered. "As they were flying off, one flew by and pecked me."

"Like the bird won," Cain offered, his voice now lower, full of resignation...or something else, something dark I couldn't decipher.

"Where was Jehovah's protection?" Abel mused, the only one willing to say what we were all thinking, yet still managing hopefulness—like God's protection was there if we could only find it. "After all, Jehovah created these birds."

I looked around the field and reached deep for my faith. "See boys, there is still some grain that can be salvaged." I continued, "We'll make it, Adam. It will stretch."

"But we fought so hard this year," Adam said with a deep pain in his eyes. "We labored to find and bring additional water. Even though our crops were meager, they were enough. Just enough."

"Thank Jehovah we still have the flocks," Abel said quietly.

"I don't want to work in the garden, ever...ever again." Cain took off ahead of us running home. I promised myself I would talk to him later, after he'd had time to grieve.

Later, when Adam let me minister to his cut, I prayed silently that the birds wouldn't steal our faith as well.

For the rest of the day, all of us were quiet. I saw Abel out back still wiping away some tears, as he played with his turtle, Nod.[16] Abel had named Nod for the way he swung his head about and how he always wandered off, at least until Abel built him a little cage he made out of willow branches. Cain hid away, not wanting to talk to any of us.

Adam had little to say. Finally, when I asked him how he

[16] "So Cain went away from the presence of the Lord and dwelt in the land of Nod [wandering] east of Eden." GENESIS 4:16 (AMP)

was doing, he replied, "Jehovah said that I would rule over the birds. Did eating the forbidden fruit in the Garden take that away?"

My knees suddenly felt weak—like a weaver bird had taken a bite out of each leg, giving me no place to stand.

Early the next morning, Abel came rushing in, waking the rest of us. "Father, one of our sheep is ready to give birth!"

Adam and Abel rushed out.

After they left, I thought to wake up Cain. *We can't leave him out.* By the time Cain found his way out of a deep sleep and walked over to see, the birth was over. When Cain arrived back home, he announced flatly, "It was over."

"But did you get to see the little lamb?" I said, coaxing Cain to see good.

Cain nodded and then went outside. I found him a little later curled up asleep next to Nod's cage. Guilt washed over me that I hadn't sympathized more with Cain.

Later that day, Adam announced that the mourning was over. "Enough time crying over our fields," he said. "We need to focus on what is ahead."

I knew in this moment that this was not good…that we needed more time to grieve. But it didn't seem worth it to question him, at least out loud. *I don't understand you Adam. And in this moment, I don't even like you.*

Since I knew my own need for forgiveness and since there was no time for bitterness, I moved on. As a family, we leaned more heavily on the berries, roots and plants that grew wild in the fields, eating more wild game the boys brought home.[17] With fewer healthy plants in the ground, the thorns and thistles attacked our garden with renewed vigor.

[17] *"It will produce thorns and thistles for you, and you will eat of the plants of the field."* GENESIS 3:18

"It's like we are being attacked twice over," Adam said one evening over dinner, as he eyed our meager meal. "I'm thinking about letting the sheep have the garden and starting over again with new ground. They won't mind the briars."[18] Adam looked out past us, his eyes far away, "But what will prevent this from happening again?"

"Perhaps, it's most important that we guard our souls,"[19] I offered. "Keep bitterness from taking root."

"Guarding our souls won't fix this problem, Eve!" Adam finally mumbled in a prickly tone.

I held my tongue. When Adam only saw despair, pressing on him could push him further away. Yet, I wished Adam could have looked deeper. Like him, I saw the difficulty of making do with so little. But it seemed to me there was a worse danger, the danger of drifting from Jehovah and each other. We'd already been launched into the wilderness because of our sin. Would we forget all we learned from those hard years of adjustment to harsh new realities?

"Jehovah won't forget us, will he, Father?" Abel looked towards Adam with trusting eyes.

I stifled a small smile. Could Abel read my mind?

"Easy enough for Abel to say," Cain interjected, ever the practical one. "He didn't lose his flock to birds."

"Cain, the flocks and the garden belong to all of us." Adam paused as if saying the words needed would take all the strength within him. "Your mother is right."

Several months later, when the time rolled around for offering, Adam was silent.

When I brought it up to him, Adam said, "Not now, Eve...not now." The rawness in his voice made me wonder

[18] *"As for all the hills once cultivated by the hoe, you will no longer go there for fear of the briers and thorns; they will become places where cattle are turned loose and where sheep run."* ISAIAH 7:25

[19] *"In the paths of the wicked lie thorns and snares, but he who guards his soul stays far from them."* PROVERBS 22:5 (NIV 1984)

whether I injured him by asking. After waiting and realizing that *now* wasn't coming, I decided to quietly take the boys and let them give an offering at the springs, something small enough that Adam wouldn't mind.

Cain and Abel were sad when they learned that their father wouldn't be coming.

"But Mother, if Father thinks we don't have enough to give this year, perhaps he knows best," Cain said. "Father said that God shouldn't take when he hasn't given."[20]

I was surprised that Adam let Cain so deep into his pain, further than he let me in.

"There is always something to give. The crops aren't the only thing Jehovah has given us," Abel offered, always the peacemaker, earning him a harsh look from his brother. "Do you remember the story about Father sacrificing the little lamb after you were born?"

Thinking of Cain's position as the firstborn, I said, "Cain, why don't you lead our sacrifice? You can offer the prayer for us." Seeing the objection in Cain's eyes, I added, "We need to give your father time to work through his feelings about this year's harvest. When we sacrifice to God, we'll sacrifice for him as well. Why don't you each choose one thing to give, and we'll go down to the springs."

Then, thinking about how we could make the most of the circumstances, I offered, "We can take our lunch with us and we can eat there afterwards."

Cain shrugged and went for a small orange squash, one that he had already picked.

Jehovah, forgive his indifference. Cain has no way to process our heartaches.[21]

95

[20] *"He also who had received one talent came forward, saying, 'Master, I knew you to be a harsh and hard man, reaping where you did not sow, and gathering where you had not winnowed [the grain]. So I was afraid, and I went and hid your talent in the ground.'"* MATTHEW 25:24-25 (AMP)
[21] *"A happy heart makes the face cheerful, but heartache crushes the spirit."* PROVERBS 15:13

When we arrived down at the springs, I was surprised to see that Abel brought his turtle. For just a moment I wondered whether giving away his comfort was a good thing.

"Are you giving Nod because there is nothing left to feed him?" Cain asked.

"I'm giving him because he is close to my heart," Abel answered without hesitation. "For you Jehovah…from me, from Cain, from Father, from all of us."

Then Abel leaned over and gently released Nod into the water. The turtle swam halfway out into the pool, cocked back his head as if to say goodbye, and then dove underneath.

"Mother, could you say the prayer instead?" Cain said, suddenly embarrassed.

After our sacrifice, when he thought I wasn't looking, Cain gave Abel a shove and said, "You should have asked me before you gave away Nod."

The Sacrifice

A small animal scurries through some dried leaves, pulling me out of the fourth memory. When I open my eyes, a hare sits nearby, looking at me with one bright eye surrounded by dark brown, shiny fur. Adam once explained how the vision of the rabbit is a marvel, extending all around him and far into the sky to sight hawks or eagles, but with a small blind spot right in front of him. I can still hear him explaining to our boys, "That is why Jehovah placed the rabbit's eyes high on the sides of its head."

Suddenly, it occurs to me that the rabbit has a gift similar to what Jehovah told me about being an ezer…*Your vision ranges all around you to help you see danger.*

When I yawn, the rabbit spreads his long legs and hurls himself into the bushes. *Oh, to have your energy, little hare! I am past the end of my strength, of my ability to be strong.*

Thinking back through the memory, I say out loud, "Cain, you are not the only one to wander. Adam and I have been wandering since the Garden." And then thinking of the rabbit, I add, "Maybe I've have a blind spot, too. I struggle to see what is right in front of me."

I sigh. Feeling reality slipping away, I glance at the ground and see my shadow spread before me. *A shadow is something to thank God for, a sign that I live on.*[22] I take a deep breath and then continue talking, this time to Adam. "I think I understand a little better now, my strong one." I close my eyes, picturing my husband. *When I am out of sorts, Adam is so kind, so quick to offer compassion.*

I continue, "Adam those crops were an extension of you. After the weaver birds, it seemed nothing was sacred, nothing was enough. All your hard labor was destroyed. Your faith left on the wings of those belligerent birds, the very birds that Jehovah gave you to rule over."

I continue, groping my way along a rocky path that leads to who knows where.

"I think we are the same, Adam. You gave birth to our garden, planting seed and sheltering it until it burst forth in life. You fought for those fields, because they could sustain and nourish us. And then you were forced to let thorns and briars take the fields. You had to create a whole new garden, like your work on the other garden no longer mattered."

Emotions swirl around me like a flock of birds writhing in one black mass. I cannot tell one from the other.

[22] *My eyes have grown dim with grief; my whole frame is but a shadow.*
JOB 17:7

97

"I birthed and then lost two boys. I know you miss them just as much as I do. Yet both of us live like we have no eyes to see, like the possibility of God's goodness is too much to hope for.[23] You've hidden in silence. I've hidden in a cloak."

I begin to chuckle. The thought of a garment of clothing made with my own hands protecting me seems laughable, almost as strange as me talking to Adam without him here.[24] First the fig leaves. Then the cloak.

A resolve arises within me. A determination to give this new little one the benefit of what we've learned from losing what was precious to us, from falling hard, but somehow still living on, still loving. How I wish Cain had fallen towards us, let us help him in his time of need, instead of falling away from Jehovah and away from us. Yet, I can only help Cain if I fall towards Jehovah, rather than away from him.[25]

"Jehovah, how can I show you how grateful I am for this blessing of the womb? What sacrifice would please you?"

Come. Come with me.

I'm not sure how, but I know immediately where he wants to take me. "No Jehovah, please," I whisper, my willing spirit vanishing. "Not there. I'm not ready."

I sit on my blanket for what seems the longest time, my arms wrapped tightly around my knees, as if I can prevent my legs from taking me where Jehovah wants me to go—from giving the sacrifice I know Jehovah really wants. Knowing that Jehovah hears my thoughts, I say them out loud.

"Jehovah...Father, I'm not strong enough for this." And then feeling anguish rush from the top of my head to my

[23] Read ISAIAH 59:9-15
[24] "In his great power God becomes like clothing to me; he binds me like the neck of my garment." JOB 30:18
[25] "Let me fall into the hands of the LORD, for his mercy is very great..." 1 CHRONICLES 21:13A

feet, I add, "How much hardship can one person handle? How many thorns can one heart bear? This role you've given, being the first of all women to come, it is too much for me!"

Then all at once I know what I want—an earthly parent here with me now. A mother to cradle me in her arms and tell me I am beautiful.

I haven't forgotten my promise. Your offspring will crush the head of the evil one. Rest in my arms.

"Jehovah you are my mother and father," I say. "Teach me how to rise above my loss." Sadness washes over me. Although I call to him, something holds me back from his comfort.

Then I remember the eagle from the day before—how it lifted high with so little effort, trusting the wind to support its wings, to guide it. What would it be like to live without flailing against the currents that toss me?[26] I still remember Adam's words about the eagle… "Her huge wings will tire quickly if she stays too close to the ground. And then how would she build her nest? Provide for her young?"

My thoughts go the day when Adam and I sat enthralled, watching from a safe distance as a protective mother eagle trained one of her little ones. With her eaglet resting on one of her wings, she lifted him into the air, teaching her babe that he could rise upon the currents of air, just like her. Once again, I can almost hear Adam's voice as he explained…

"When it is time for her eaglets to leave, their mother takes all the padding out of the nest, leaving bare branches and thorns. The thorns urge young eagles towards horizons

[26] *"But those who wait for the LORD [who expect, look for, and hope in Him] shall change and renew their strength and power; they shall lift their wings and mount up [close to God] as eagles [mount up to the sun]; they shall run and not be weary, they shall walk and not faint or become tired."* ISAIAH 40:31 (AMP)

beyond the nest, far more beautiful than they could fathom."

"Ah thorns, you have so many purposes," I say to myself, "far more than helping eagles learn to fly. You help protect some of my favorite things." I think of blackberries, raspberries, hawthorn and rosehips (the tasty fruit of the rose plant that I cook with and brew into tea, the very tea I gave Abel for his swollen ankle after he fell from the Oak tree) and how the thorns keep animals from poaching my beloved fruit. I muse how each bush snags me in different places. The raspberry bush grabs at my legs and middle. The blueberry bush aims higher, tangling into my hair and scratching my arms. The hawthorn plant has stiff bristles like a porcupine; bristles I must go past to pluck the leaves for their healing. The rose bush will pounce at whatever part of my body I bring near.

And some thorns simply refuse to let go, until I acknowledge them by gingerly disengaging my garment, one thorn at a time.[27]

A banished child may be the worst thorn of all. There is no way to pull it out—it has to work itself out. The loss of Abel tore me in two, yet Adam tells me he is with Jehovah. Cain is another matter. Will he be lost to Jehovah and to us forever? Or could this thorn be a type of guard, ensuring that the most tender part of my desires and longings stay entrusted to Jehovah, lest Serpent seeks to steal them?[28]

The evil one pushes into my thoughts...*"Haven't you learned yet that the One on High offers you nothing but thorns?"*

I take a deep breath and exhale, hoping my breath will push his ugly whispers far from me. I say out loud, "Jehovah, you are my only safe place. Search my anxious thoughts and

[27] *Thanks to Jim McDonald, Herbalist for his musings on thorns at http://www.herbcraft.org/thorns.html.*
[28] *"That is why I am suffering as I am. Yet this is no cause for shame, because I know whom I have believed, and am convinced that he is able to guard what I have entrusted to him until that day."* 1 TIMOTHY 1:12

show me what you want from me."[29]

Then Jehovah's words come to me, the very same words he gave me in the very beginning, swelling with pride....

Be fruitful and increase in number;
fill the earth and subdue it.[30]

In Father's words, I see a new possibility. Serpent would have me think that the earth has subdued me, rather than me subduing it. But if I will look past the thorn's bite to see Jehovah's good gifts, I can help put the earth in its rightful place—under my feet instead of looming over my head. The question is...can I do this?

I'm not yet sure, but this I know. I can't have Jehovah in my life unless I am willing to follow him. I can't ask for his help and then refuse him in the same breath.

"You want my trust." I whisper.

I kneel and then on a whim throw myself facedown on the ground. "Without you, I have nothing. I will go where you lead. I am the sacrifice you require."[31]

Suddenly, I want nothing more than to be in the spot where Abel left this earth. Perhaps there is something there that will remind me of him. Something to mark his abrupt leap from life into death.

I start running.

---

[29] *See* PSALM 139:23-24
[30] GENESIS 1:28
[31] *"Therefore, I urge you, brothers and sisters, in view of God's mercy, to offer your bodies as a living sacrifice, holy and pleasing to God...."* ROMANS 12:1

If you take your neighbor's cloak as a pledge,
return it by sunset, because that cloak is the only
covering your neighbor has. What else can they sleep in?
When they cry out to me, I will hear, for I am compassionate.

JEHOVAH, MY COVERING[1]

[1] EXODUS 22:26-27

CHAPTER SIX

The Skins

A S I RUN INTO THE MARSH, DARK LIQUID spatters up onto my garment—yet I thank Jehovah that the ground is just solid enough for me to keep moving. Halfway through the marshland, not watching closely, I step in mud. The dark cool stickiness oozes in between my toes and swallows my foot. I stop for a moment to wipe my toes and my sandal with a handful of tender marsh grass I yank out of the ground. The last thing I need is to slip and fall, turning an ankle out here alone. Stopping for a moment to catch my breath, I urge myself to continue. *It would be so easy to turn back.*

Now being careful to stay on solid ground, I step into some brush where a thorn bush catches my dress, forcing me to untangle myself. I should take the time to free myself one thorn at a time, but instead I reach down and pull so hard that the edge of my garment rips. At least it is only my clothing, not my flesh that the thorns tear. Then I hear a whisper, barely audible, thrusting evil towards me, demanding entrance into my thoughts...[2]

Nothing but trouble! And do you really think you'll find what you're searching for? Turn back. Abel isn't there. Adam isn't there.

[2] *"His mouth is full of lies and threats; trouble and evil are under his tongue."*
PSALM 10:7

The All-Sufficient One won't be there either. No one sees. No one hears. You should have thrown yourself over the cliff.

"The Lord has heard my weeping!" I exhale, pushing the dark whispers away.[3] Shiny One's familiar, though inaudible voice lures me toward self-pity and doubt as if there is comfort and resolution to be found in these feelings.

The hill seems steeper than I remember. My legs are heavy like a garment soaked in water. A cloud passes momentarily overhead, obscuring the sun from view. A wind seems to come up out of nowhere, whipping my hair around the front of my face and into my eyes. I take the skin of water that I am carrying and place it between my knees, so that I can use both hands to gather my hair to the right side of my neck, twisting it into a knot I can hold with one hand. A fresh wave of nausea sweeps over me. *No, not here...please.* I cry out, "Lord, why is this so difficult? I'll never regain what I've lost!"

Not your strength, Eve. Not your power. My strength.[4]

I gather courageous thoughts. I can look for reasons to turn around and go back, hoping that Adam will find a way to rescue me from my pain. I can resign myself to a lifetime of loneliness. Or I can look for evidence that Jehovah is here with me, now, in the midst of my pain. I look around me. I am so empty, the wind could easily whirl me away. Losing Abel and Cain drained an essential part of my being, like the sweet, sticky sap of the maple tree Adam harvests each year. Abel's question to Adam, when Abel was just a small boy, now seems like a prophecy... "Abba, is the tree bleeding?"

The wind at my back reminds me that Jehovah urges me

[3] *"Away from me, all you who do evil, for the LORD has heard my weeping."* PSALM 6:8
[4] *"He gives strength to the weary and increases the power of the weak."* ISAIAH 40:29

forward. I take a deep breath and press on. When I reach the top of the hill, the very sight of the field and the river weaving through it bring a flood of fresh grief. This has always been one of my special places—a place I sometimes come to meet with Jehovah. As I look down, the tall grasses, dotted with yellow and white flowers, tremble. When the sun pokes its head out, the field and the river light up, glowing as if nothing has changed, nothing has been taken. But when dark shadows sweep the field like waves whipped by the wind, the river becomes a dark snake claiming the field as its own.

Wiping my running nose and eyes on my sleeve, I make my way down the hill carefully, remembering the precious cargo I am carrying—the tiny seed of hope that Jehovah has given. How can life and death be so close together? How can compassion for this child still survive when my face is covered with darkness?[5] Is it a betrayal of Abel to long for another child? *What do you want to show me Jehovah?*

Arriving at the field and looking around, my heart sinks. *Where did it happen?* I know I need the very bit of earth where Abel left us, the place where the essence of him departed before Adam carried his empty body back to the house to bury him. Something catches my eye—a stick standing above the grain. I push my way through, ignoring the burrs fastening to my cloak. There, in a bare spot, is a branch shoved into the ground, surrounded by a mound of rocks. A marker. Gratitude washes over me. Adam has been here. He knew that one day I would need to know the exact spot. I fall to the ground as a scream catches in my throat. As hard as I have fought for control, I can no longer hold back the pain.

"Oh Abel, my Abel," I mutter to the empty ground. "If

[5] *God has made my heart faint; the Almighty has terrified me. Yet I am not silenced by the darkness, by the thick darkness that covers my face.* JOB 23:16-17

only you were here. You would see light in all this darkness."
I press my forehead to the dark dirt in front of the marker, and
spread my arms, as if I can somehow find him, embrace him
for just a moment. For a second, I press my lips to the earth.
I savor the bitter flavor of dirt mixed with tears…somehow
now the taste of my son. I inhale the earthy aroma, the smell
of my boys.

How many times in the past, in my motherly fear, have I
rehearsed all manner of ways my sons could get hurt? But this,
I never could have imagined this.

Jehovah, where is he? Where did you take him? The words stay
lodged in my head. Even if I can bring myself to say them, I
am not expecting an answer. Looking around, I notice the
wind has settled down. The clouds above move slowly, the
sun nowhere to be found.

"Do you cover yourself with a cloud, so that my prayers
don't even reach you?"[6] I cry aloud.

Then it comes to me. Since God created Adam out of
dust, he can also recreate Abel. With my bare hands, I claw at
the ground, trying to break up the earth. Frustrated, I find a
stick nearby and use it to dig up a few clumps of dirt. After I
break up one of the clumps, I hoist a palmful of soil towards
the heavens.

"Jehovah, please breathe life into this dust. Bring back
Abel." As my arms shake, I am showered with dirt, as if in
preparation for my own burial.

Then his voice comes…

I have him, Eve. Abel is with me. I carry him close
to my heart and he is rejoicing in my presence.

[6] *You have covered yourself with a cloud so that no prayer can get through."*
LAMENTATIONS 3:44

Undeterred, I continue, "Put me to sleep and take one of my ribs, part of my flesh."

Eve, you are precious in my sight. I've called
you by my name and created you for my glory.
Follow me to the places you are afraid to go.

His call resonates through my entire being. It is a call of love. Jehovah is fighting for me, not warring against me.[7] I think back to a day when I walked with Jehovah through a verdant paradise, every leaf shimmering with possibility as sunlight streamed through the trees.

I will never leave you nor forsake you.[8]

His words wrap around me, filling every crevice of my being. I roll onto my back and place the other clump of dirt right above my heart. Closing my eyes, tears still streaming down my cheeks, I want something, anything, to happen other than what I fear God wants. Anger, fear and sadness immerse me, as the heaviness of grief presses my back into the dirt. A shudder passes from head to toe. My bones tremble, barely able to contain my broken heart.[9]

"Would you have me give up Abel?" I whisper, afraid that letting go means losing him forever.

Then I remember the little lamb, our sacrifice for Cain's birth, stretched out on the altar. Bound by a few simple cords that he surely could have broken, the lamb looked at us with dark, trusting eyes, resting in whatever Jehovah brought. And somehow, I am sure that Abel went to Jehovah willingly.

[7] *"Read* JOSHUA 23:9-11
[8] DEUTERONOMY 31:8
[9] *"My heart is broken within me; all my bones tremble. I am like a drunken man, like a strong man overcome by wine, because of the* LORD *and his holy words."* JEREMIAH 23:9

Abel would have given his very life if he knew it was what Jehovah desired.

I know hiding, like I did from Jehovah in the Garden, or hardening my heart to the pain won't honor Abel's death, redeem my God boy's murder. From my years of walking with Jehovah, I know that he doesn't take what isn't offered. He won't push through a door unless I open it. Even more so, I know the yearning in my chest will not be satisfied by anyone but Jehovah, God. But am I ready to trust him?

"Am I the sacrifice you really want, Jehovah? I whisper, even though I already know the answer. "Then, Father, please help me."

I spread my arms wide on the ground, willing myself to relax, to trust. I breathe in and out deeply, watching my own chest rise and fall. Again, I rehearse what I've learned from the memories, knowing somehow they hold the path to life, to healing, to hope.

The first memory...coming to know God as my Abba.

The second memory...rejoicing with Jehovah after Adam and I consummated our marriage.

The third memory...allowing Whisperer to get me to hide from Adam and to distrust Jehovah.

The fourth memory...God calling me to sacrifice my very will after weaver birds destroyed our fields.

"Show me what you want me to see, Abba," I pray. "You are my protection against the foe. I give myself over to your will." Although I'm tempted to flee like a bird to the mountain, Jehovah's answer is tender, full of mercy.

Let me carry you. Come.

"Be my refuge, my Abba," I whisper as the fifth memory has its way with me.[10]

The fifth memory with Jehovah

It was an average day in the hot season, and our annual day of sacrifice. This year was special, the first time Cain and Abel would offer sacrifices on their own, and Adam had spent time alone with each of them in preparation. My heart was full of anticipation. Adam and I would offer Jehovah a grain offering of thankgiving. After the boys finished their offerings, I would prepare a meal of lamb and vegetables with bitter herbs.

Mid-morning, Abel came home with blood on his garments from offering the fat portions of a lamb. He gave me the meat, already skinned, so that I could prepare it.

"Abel, can you take your garment to the river and wash it?" I asked, glancing at the grisly mess on his tunic, not even acknowledging his sacrifice. I'd always had a weak stomach.

"There's no time right now, Mother. Besides," he said with his eyes smiling, quick to forgive my oversight, "there is something comforting about being covered in the blood of a sacrifice to Jehovah. Like it really should be me on the altar instead of the lamb."

"If you don't mind, I think I'll keep you here with me," I said with a smile.

"I'll change before dinner, Mother," Abel said over his shoulder as he turned and left.

"I'll look forward to hearing more about your sacrifice then," I called as he left to attend to the flocks, still wondering at his words.

[10] *"For you have been my refuge, a strong tower against the foe. I long to dwell in your tent forever and take refuge in the shelter of your wings."* PSALM 61:3-4

As he walked away, I wondered about Cain. Since his offering was simpler, I had expected him to come first to bring some tender, young vegetables for our meal. Assuming Cain was distracted by his chores, I went to the garden. No Cain. As I picked purple eggplant, orange peppers and yellow tomatoes, I reminded myself how self-sufficient the boys were and how grown-up they must feel, now that they have offered their own sacrifices. *No doubt, Cain went to help Abel with the flocks.*

The afternoon sped by as I prepared our sacrifice feast. By the time the light began to change, and dinner neared completion, I began to fret. *Cain, whatever adventure you've led Abel on, please come home. Abel, I would have glady washed your garment myself, or even slaughtered the lamb myself, just to have you here now.*

"Adam could you go look for the boys?" I said. "I can't imagine why they are so late."

"They'll come when they get hungry," Adam said, with a forced smile that betrayed his concern.

Then we heard Zayeb barking outside.

"Zayeb, shush," Adam yelled.

Zayeb's barks became insistent—faster, louder.

When we walked outside, Zayeb started running in circles.

Adam leaned over and spoke firmly to him. "What is it, Zayeb? Where is Abel? Where is Cain?" he asked.

Zayeb pulled back on his haunches and whined. His dark eyes begged for our trust. He barked in indignation.

"Show us boy, show us," Adam said.

"If this is a trick the boys are playing on us..." I said,

trying to convince myself that nothing was wrong, trying to push back the panic quickly rising in my chest.

We followed Zayeb through the marsh and up the hill. Looking down into the field, we saw no sign of the boys. We considered turning back, but Zayeb still seemed to want us to follow—running ahead of us into the field and then circling back to make sure we were coming.

"Why don't you stay here and wait," Adam said. "I'll see what has Zayeb so worked up. I'm guessing there is an animal he wants to chase." Touching my cheek, he added, "Perhaps the boys are already back home by now."

I sat down for a moment on a boulder, watching my husband and Zayeb make their way down towards the fields. By the time Adam was at the bottom of the hill, I knew I couldn't stand not knowing. Wild animal or no wild animal, I needed to be there.

When I reached the field, I saw Adam stop in his footsteps far in front of me and then fall on the ground, partially hidden by the tall grasses.

"What is it, Adam?" I yelled, moving quickly towards where I saw him disappear.

When I came upon him, Adam was kneeling in a small clearing, tears streaming down his face, Abel in his arms. Zayeb was right beside him, ears down, lying with his face to the ground, whimpering.

I fell on the ground beside him. "Abel! What's happened to Abel? What's wrong?" I cried.

"He's dead," Adam choked out, barely able to speak through his tears. "He...he's gone. There's no more breath in him. His heart has stopped beating."

"No," I whispered. "No! It can't be," my voice getting higher. "Do something, please do something."

Adam turned Abel's head to examine him, "His neck is black and blue. A wild animal must have attacked him." Then looking closer, he choked out, "I don't see teeth marks, but there's a cut on his head...and blood on the ground."

"No...no, Adam. This is just a nightmare. I'm going to wake up and then everything will be as it should. Abel, we are here. Mother and Abba are here."

"His body is cold," Adam said, shaking his head sadly. "I've seen this with our flocks...Jehovah said that once the spirit is gone, nothing can be done."

I laid my hand on Abel's forehead as I did countless other times when he complained that he was hot or cold. Frantic, I examined his arms, his hands. They were cold, clammy, lifeless. Suddenly faint, I sat back, stunned. My head was spinning.

Laying him tenderly on the ground, Adam put his head on Abel's chest and began to weep, his shoulders heaving. Fear overwhelmed me. I could hardly breathe. I fell to my knees, still dizzy, and then wailed with my hands lifted toward the heavens, "Did *you* take my son, Jehovah?"

Then it came to me. My other son. I stood up and began calling, choking out the words through my tears, "Cain, where are you Cain?"

Zayeb growled and then bounded just beyond us into the brush, barking.

"Eve, listen to me. I need you to stay here with Abel," Adam said hoarsely. "I'm going to find Cain." He gently lifted my chin and looked into my eyes to make sure I understood.

I scooted over and put my son's head in my lap, and began to stroke his hair. "Abel, I'm here," I said. "Your mother's here. Wherever you've gone, you can come back now." My tears ran down my cheeks, dropped off my chin and landed on Abel's face. I leaned over and brushed his cheek with my lips, tasting the salt of my own tears.

"He's here," Adam shouted from a short distance.

When Cain and Adam appeared, I wanted to run to Cain, but I couldn't let go of Abel. That would mean acknowledging he was gone, and that I was not ready to do. Cain stood there stiff and awkward, his eyes downcast.

"Thank Jehovah, you're safe," I cried out.

"I should have been my brother's keeper,"[11] Cain murmured under his breath. "His blood cries out against me."

"Whatever happened, Cain, we don't blame you," I said, unable to peel my eyes away from Abel.

Cain crumpled onto the grass, his head hitting the ground with a dull thud.

"No...no, not Cain too," I blurted, my heart pounding.

Adam quickly knelt down. He listened for his breath and then gently shook him. "Cain, Cain, wake up, son."

"Where am I?" Cain said as he came to. "What have I done?"

Adam checked his head to make sure he wasn't bleeding. "Just be still, Cain. Let the dizziness pass. We can talk later."

As soon as Cain could stand, we made the trek back to our home, wanting to get there before sunset. Adam carried Abel. I offered Cain my arm but he refused it.

"I deserve nothing from anyone," he whispered, his eyes still fastened to the ground.

---

[11] *"Then the* LORD *said to Cain, "Where is your brother Abel?" "I don't know," he replied. "Am I my brother's keeper?"* GENESIS 4:9

I was stunned by his shame, wanting to stop right then, right there, find out what happened. *Follow Adam's lead*, I told myself.

When we arrived home, Adam instructed Cain to lie down. "We'll talk soon, son."

Together, Adam and I wrapped Abel's body in skins. I took a cloth and cleaned the dirt off of his face, tended to the cut on his head, smoothed his hair and talked softly to him. It didn't seem possible that he was gone. I half expected that he would open his eyes at any moment, and say sleepily, "Where am I?"

"I will find a place for his body later, a special place," Adam announced. "He should be buried so that the animals can't get to him."

"In the ground?" I gasped, horrified at the thought of my son covered in dirt. "Abel didn't love the dirt like Cain did. Surely, there is another way."

"Just as we came from the soil, Abel will return to it," Adam murmured sadly. "Do you remember what Jehovah said to me after we sinned in Eden?"

"I do, Adam," I said softly as the words came tumbling back—a prediction I had pushed far back into my memory.

> *By the sweat of your brow you will eat your food until*
> *you return to the ground, since from it you were taken;*
> *for dust you are and to dust you will return.*[12]

"Did we cause this?" I blurted out. "Is this yet another consequence of eating the forbidden fruit?" I clutched my chest as if I could stop fear, guilt and regret from coursing

[12] GENESIS 3:19

through my body. As I turned my head away from Abel, away from Adam, I noticed that Cain was standing nearby.

"My son," I said.

"I'm leaving," he replied gruffly, eyes on the ground.

"No, Cain, don't leave," I said. "You can talk to us… please. Please son, don't do this to me!"

"Jehovah has banished me," he said, catching my eyes for a few seconds, suddenly looking very much like a frightened little boy.

"What happened, son?" Adam spoke firmly, yet kindly.

"I did it," his voice broke. "I stole Abel's life."

"What do you mean, Cain? You don't know what you're saying," Adam pleaded.

"The bruises on his neck are from my hands. I was angry. Jehovah liked his sacrifice better than mine. What I gave wasn't enough. It's never been enough."[13]

Sadness, despair and rage swept over Adam's face.

"I threw a rock at him and hit him right in the forehead," Cain continued, his voice shaking, "Then I shook him like I have seen Zayeb shake a bird."

"But you didn't mean to do this," I said, panicking. "Surely Cain, you didn't mean to do this! Remember how you helped him when he fell from the tree? You saved him!"

"Over a sacrifice?" Adam's voice was cold as he shook his head in disbelief and motioned towards Abel. "How could you?"

"Jehovah said I'll be a restless wanderer, forever," he sputtered, fighting back tears. "That the ground will never yield for me again.[14] I wish I were the one dead. I wish Abel had killed me."

---

[13] GENESIS 4:3-5
[14] GENESIS 4:10-12

Suddenly a determination rose up within me. No matter what, I wasn't going to lose two sons. "Surely, this can wait for the morning. It's nightfall. You'll be in danger from wild animals." If I needed to I would get on my knees and beg.

"Jehovah put a mark on me. He said that no one would kill me because of my guilt. Don't you see? I'm banished. My life is over. You will be better off without me."

"Cain, please wait." I pleaded. "Let us talk to Jehovah on your behalf."

"Jehovah may strike me dead if I stay. I must go."

"Tell Jehovah how sorry you are...tell him, Cain, tell him!" I begged, tears streaming down my face. "He is merciful."[15] I glanced at my husband, "Tell him, Adam. Please tell him."

"Let him go, Eve," Adam whispered, not even looking up. "You know as well as I, that Cain cannot resist God's judgment."[16] And then looking up and catching my eyes for a second, he added, "We know this all too well." In Adam's eyes, I saw untold accusation.

"Mother, I must...I *will* go tonight."

In Cain's voice I heard the hardness of resignation. He would not be swayed. I forced myself not to think, not to feel. My son was leaving and I needed to make sure he took what he needed to survive.

"You just go and stay somewhere for a while. Work things out," I said to Cain. "Give us some time to grieve. And then come back. No matter what, this is your home."

I still couldn't believe that Cain meant Abel harm.

Adam watched as I searched for provisions, finally mumbling, "Send Abel's clothing with him. He'll need it

15 "By your Spirit you warned them through your prophets. Yet they paid no attention, so you gave them into the hands of the neighboring peoples. But in your great mercy you did not put an end to them or abandon them, for you are a gracious and merciful God." NEHEMIAH 9:30-31
16 "For with fire and with his sword the LORD will execute judgment upon all people, and many will be those slain by the LORD." ISAIAH 66:16

and we have no use for it."

I threw together some clothing, both Cain's and Abel's. Then, thinking he would need some way to protect himself, I added Abel's bow and arrows. Lastly, I wrapped some of the lamb that Abel had brought earlier and added a skin of water I had set out for the evening meal.

Cain watched through lowered eyelids. His posture, the strain in his face all said...*I'm not worthy of this. Why are you bothering?* When he saw the lamb, his eyebrows arched in surprise and distaste. He reluctantly took what I offered.

Adam, say something, anything.

It was then I noticed a faint reddish stain on Cain's tunic. *The lamb's blood...from Abel.* In my mind's eye, I saw Cain tackle Abel, grab him so tight that the lamb's blood from Abel's tunic smudged Cain's garment.[17]

Suddenly, I wanted to grab Cain. Shake him. Beat him with my fists.

He turned to leave.

"My firstborn," I cried.

He turned back momentarily, holding his hand up, lest I try to force him to stay, giving me his eyes for the briefest moment.

"Mother, I want you to know that Jehovah tried to prevent me from doing this. He warned me.[18] He said that if I did what is right, he would accept me." And then murmuring under his breath, just loud enough that I could make out the words, he said, "I don't understand. How could he say he would accept me after he rejected my offering?"

With that, Cain turned and walked into the wilderness, leaving us barren.

[17] *"Why are your garments red, like those of one treading the winepress? I have trodden the winepress alone.... I trampled them in my anger and trod them down in my wrath; their blood spattered my garments..."* ISAIAH 63:2-3

[18] GENESIS 4:6-7.

The Skins

Hoisting myself out of the fifth memory, I find myself back in the present, still lying on the ground in Abel's spot—the very place where his soul departed his body. "Banished," I whisper softly to myself. The word judges my thoughts and lays me bare. I sense that the sixth memory is also nearby, clutching at the edges of my mind as if Jehovah's breath, the infusion of his nature that brought life to dust, is taking down my carefully built wall of denial to expose secrets deep within.[19]

"No more memories!" I say. "I will not go with you." Then remembering my surrender to Jehovah, my heart gives a little, "Please, just a little more time."

I am reluctant to leave, but I must go. I cannot bear another memory in this place. I want it to be Abel's place alone. I stand up, brush the weeds off of my garment and silently thank Jehovah for his protection. Then, after putting my fingers to my lips, I kneel and touch them to the ground. "I will always love you Abel," I say. "Always."

As I walk away, I turn on my heel. There is one last thing I must tell Jehovah, Abel and myself. "From this day on, I am a stranger on this earth. I will never be completely at home until I am with Abel again."[20]

As I make my way through the field and up the hill, I am lost in my thoughts. I know that I brought death to the earth. Serpent's cruel lie still bites me to this day, "*You will not certainly die.*"[21] But although the pain of Abel is as fresh as the day I lost him, I feel lighter.

Now I see that my banished son Cain was trying to protect my faith. His words, "Jehovah tried to warn me," console me. Even though Cain felt less than a mustard seed of hope

[19] *See* PSALM 18:15, HEBREWS 4:12–13.

[20] *"All these people were still living by faith when they died. They did not receive the things promised; they only saw them and welcomed them from a distance, admitting that they were foreigners and strangers on earth."* HEBREWS 11:13

[21] GENESIS 3:4

for himself, he didn't want me to give up on my faith. And then Cain's other words, the ones I barely heard, "How could he say he would accept me after he rejected my offering?" Somehow I hear myself in those words. I hear my own striving. My hiding. My worst fears. How can Jehovah love me after he allowed such distress?[22] For that matter, how can Adam love me after he has shut me out for so long?

Back home, as I prepare for the night I know there might be a nightmare, like my nightmares of forgetting I have a child or falling off the cliff into the arms of the tree. But I also realize that the walls around my heart can no longer hold. I am weary of holding them up, weary of going through life's motions with my heart disengaged. Sure enough, sometime in the night, I am transported back to a moment I stuffed away, never to be remembered. Only instead of being in the dream, I hover over top, watching from the outside...

A man runs, with a woman in hand. He is panicked, running like the ground is seeking to swallow them. He tugs her hand so hard, I wonder if he'll pull her arm out of its socket. Under his other arm, he has a lamb—shaken to its core, legs flailing in all directions, paws up in the air, fear in its eyes. The woman looks frightened at the man's roughness. Even in her fear, she is very beautiful.

What are they running from?

The Garden they run through is mesmerizing. Yellow, red, orange and purple fruit hang low and burst with juice, while flowers abound in an extravagant display of different designs and colors. They charge past a tall cliff as water bursts over the top and plummets into a crystal clear pool.

---

[22] *"In all their distress he too was distressed, and the angel of his presence saved them. In his love and mercy he redeemed them; he lifted them up and carried them all the days of old."* ISAIAH 63:9

"Stop and bathe," I urge them. "Let the water cleanse you."

They reach what appears to be the only exit from the Garden. There are trees tightly bunched together as far as the eye can see, with only one opening. As they push through the gap, the man drops her hand and she falls on the ground, the fig leaves barely covering her nakedness. Everything is different here. Darker, bare, dusty, desolate.

The woman is now weeping into the earth. He, too, weeps silently into the lamb's fur, grasping the animal as if it is his only hope. The wind whips in. They look so cold and frightened. Jehovah speaks...

You may never return to Eden again, lest you
take the fruit of life, eat it and live forever. I
offered you life, but you chose death.

Sternness, yet such kindness.[23] They sit with eyes fastened to the ground. The voice continues,

Let me cover you.[24]

They both look up. Draped over a bush are the hides of two animals.[25] The man gets up, slips on the larger one and motions for her to take the other. She is reluctant.

Suddenly an angel appears. His sword flashes over his head in blazing light, guarding the opening. With panic in his eyes, the man motions for the woman to follow. His eyes say, "We must leave now." As he drapes the other animal skin over her shoulders, I'm filled with overwhelming love.

[23] *"Consider therefore the kindness and sternness of God: sternness to those who fell, but kindness to you, provided that you continue in his kindness..."* ROMANS 11:22A
[24] *"I have...covered you with the shadow of my hand—I who set the heavens in place, who laid the foundations of the earth, and who say to Zion, 'You are my people.'"* ISAIAH 51:16
[25] GENESIS 3:21

As they walk away, I cry, "Let me help you, children of Jehovah…"

I JERK OUT OF THE DREAM IN THE MIDDLE OF THE night, roll over and pull my knees to my chest, my face wet. *I am the woman in the dream.* Jehovah gave me the dream so that I can understand how he felt when Adam and I rebelled, when we were so lost yet lamenting our mistake, so wayward yet so weak.

Then Jehovah's voice comes, breathtaking in its kindness.

Could you forget Abel? Even if you could forget, I could never forget you. I breathed myself into you.[26]

"But in the Garden everything was so simple," I cry out. Rolling over, I find myself moved to my knees. With my hands clasped and head to the ground, I begin to pray…

"Father, the weight of my sorrow is more than I can bear. I thought that you rejected me, when it was I who ran from the pain, hiding behind walls of my own making. Please take down my defenses to the ground.[27] Help me to find a place of rest. *Your* place of rest." Jehovah speaks again…

Take refuge under the cover of my wings.

"Please be my only covering, Jehovah," I whisper.

As I drift back to sleep, I picture myself in a soft nest, padded with feathers and leaves and warmed by a blanket of downy feathers. *Bring the next memory when you know I am ready, Father.*

121

[26] *"But Zion said, 'The LORD has forsaken me, the LORD has forgotten me. Can a mother forget the baby at her breast and have no compassion on the child she has borne? Though she may forget, I will not forget you!'"* ISAIAH 49:14–15
[27] *"He will bring down your high fortified walls and lay them low; he will bring them down to the ground, to the very dust."* ISAIAH 25:12

My tent is destroyed; all its ropes are snapped.
My sons are gone from me and are no more;
no one is left now to pitch my tent or to set up my shelter.[1]

THE WEEPING PROPHET OF JEHOVAH

[1] JEREMIAH 10:20 (NIV1984)

CHAPTER SEVEN

The Shelter

I T IS MORNING AGAIN, THE FOURTH DAY without Adam. I yearn for him, yet he cannot satisfy my truest hunger. My stomach grumbles and loneliness gnaws at my bones. The physical hunger is easier to remedy. Keeping something in my stomach helps to keep the nausea at bay. When Cain and Abel were in my womb, I reminded myself...*nausea is Jehovah's reminder to keep replenishing the small life growing within.* I took to keeping a little food by my bed, a little bread or meat, so that I could eat a little something before I rose. Now stumbling around lightheaded and sick, I wish I'd thought to do the same. Having eaten the rest of the fresh lamb last night, I gather some dried meat and a few nourishing wild roots and sit down until the nausea recedes. Willing my jaws to move up and down and the food to stay in my stomach, I urge the babe within, "Eat quickly, little one."

Since my dream and prayer to Jehovah last night, I've felt several faint flutters in my womb, like a tiny butterfly looking for a place to alight. Can one who is desolate once again hope?[2] I sigh. The whispers of a child cannot mend the loss of two boys I've spent eighteen years loving. How I miss their bright eyes, sparkling with mischief. How I long for the

[2] *"Though you were ruined and made desolate and your land laid waste, now you will be too small for your people, and those who devoured you will be far away. The children born during your bereavement will yet say in your hearing, 'This place is too small for us...'"* ISAIAH 49:19-20

banter of their voices, the rise and fall of their laughter and the shy way they offered the words I never tired of, at the most unexpected moments, "I love you, Mother."

As much as I want the suffering gone, I fear the love will depart as well. Pain preserves the memories of my loved ones. Love and suffering are woven tightly together with threads into a covering more powerful than Abel's cloak. My love for Abel is a gaping hole in the fabric, one that will never be repaired. And Cain is the ragged edge, quickly unraveling as the days pass. I cannot, no I *will not* stop loving Cain even after he took my other son's life. Even when anger overwhelms, love whispers, *Cain is just a boy.* Picturing Cain wandering alone, struggling to survive on his own with the burden of his brother's death on his back, makes my heart as heavy as a piece of overripe fruit, ready to burst and stain the dust with its lifeblood.

I take a minute to straighten our bed, shaking out the covers and then tucking them in. With loss hovering over my every movement, I miss the physical comfort of Adam at night. The way I would carefully press my chest against his back, bury my knees into the crook of his, push the front of my feet to his soles and then press my nose against his neck to breathe in his strength and physicality. Only when he sleeps can I do this without guilt that I am not giving enough back.

I look around me, satisfied that everything is in its place. *Jehovah said he wants me to make him my shelter.* Somehow I understand this is a call to the hunting shelter—the very place I determined to go before Adam made the decision to leave instead. As I start looking for provisions, I talk to Adam out loud to steady myself.

"Adam, what would you say if you knew that I am going to the shelter by myself...with child?"

Adam's likely reply echoes through my veins, circles around the lone rib, my inheritance from him, and then quickens my heartbeat...

I was put here to protect you, Eve. Stay where I can see you. I would wrestle a snarling wolf to the death before I'd let him touch you. See? I keep my arms strong for you.

I continue the conversation. "I must go Adam. Just as I couldn't prevent Abel's spirit from departing or breathe the breath of life back into his body, I cannot give you what Jehovah alone can show you. I can only walk my own path. As God promised to protect Cain from harm, he will protect me as well."

I allow my heart to drift for a moment to the thought of Adam—the substance of him, and how just a touch of his hand calms me, reassures me. I turn and speak one last time into the home we have made together..."Jehovah will be my dwelling place.[3] The very wild animals that could harm me will protect me instead. Jehovah will keep our home secure until I return. Not one thing will be missing."[4] And then I utter a silent prayer...*Guide Adam, even as you instruct me.*

When I step outside to check the wind and see what garments I need for my walk, the basket draws my eye. Inside I find wild berries, apples and pears. My eyes become dewy. *Adam came.* Did he hear me talking to him? Glancing around, I see no trace of him. I carefully divide the fruit in half, take my half and leave the rest for Adam. Knowing I should let him know where I am going, I fetch a single arrow and wedge it in the basket so that its feathers jut out of the top.

125

[3] *"In your unfailing love you will lead the people you have redeemed. In your strength you will guide them to your holy dwelling."* EXODUS 15:13
[4] *"You will laugh at destruction and famine, and need not fear the wild animals....You will know that your tent is secure; you will take stock of your property and find nothing missing."* JOB 5:22, 24

I draw my cloak around my shoulders, put the fruit, more dried meat and a skin of water in my basket and begin the long walk. To keep from bemoaning my weary feet, I recount the way in my mind.

The first time I journeyed to the shelter was right after the boys completed building it. Before the boys, Adam never felt a need for a permanent hunting shelter, just a place to sleep. After both boys reached what Adam declared hunting age, he took them to one of the spots he liked to hunt and guided them in the building of a more sturdy structure. We never discussed how (with my womb still empty) there were no wives for the boys, no one for them to build a home with. The boys told me later that when they asked their father where they would find wives, Adam told them, "Jehovah will provide."

To ready them to hunt, Adam instructed Cain and Abel how to track an animal, stoke a fire, and make their way safely through the wilderness. Remembering Jehovah, Adam taught the boys to pray over a kill. When they were away for their day hunts, I would picture Adam, Cain and Abel bowed over a mighty elk, now stilled, all with a hand on the animal, as Cain prayed, "Jehovah, we thank you for this elk that gave its life to nourish and sustain us." Adam would never kill an animal just for its skin. He only took the few animals we needed for nourishment.

Once the shelter was built, I took to accompanying them, never liking to be alone overnight. While they stalked their prey, I tried to domesticate the shelter, adding practical touches they declared unnecessary, but secretly appreciated.

Eventually, Adam declared that the boys were old enough

to make their way to the shelter alone. To answer my protests, Adam taught them a rhyme to help them remember the way. When I told the boys I was worried, they looked at each other, grinned with boyish conspiracy and repeated the rhyme…

> The place where you can stand on a rock.
> The grassy field where our sheep flock.
>
> The bush that seems to be on fire.
> Along the river to ground that's higher.
>
> The spring in the ravine with a rocky shore.
> The tamarisk tree where the eagles soar.
>
> And when the olive tree shakes hands with the sun.
> Thank Jehovah that your journey is done.[5]

As the words skitter through my mind, I see my boys as clearly as if they are back with me again.

Abel spreads his long arms in the sunlight. Cain's cheek holds a single dimple, one that only appears when he is amused. Grinning, they shake hands with each other exactly four times, and then, still grasping hands, see who can wrestle the other onto the ground first, laughing.

The first night Cain and Abel went to the hunting shelter without Adam and spent the night there alone, I didn't sleep. I can't remember a happier moment than when they returned safely the next morning. They came bearing a couple of snipe (or flying goats as the boys liked to call them for the bleating noise made by their tail feathers) ready for a stew.

127

[5] *All are analogies for seeking and enjoying God's presence. See* EXODUS 33:21; PSALM 23, 46:4, 52:8, 104:10, ISAIAH 40:31.

BY THE TIME I REACH THE GRASSY FIELD WHERE
we pasture our sheep, the lump in my throat barely allows a
swallow of the cool water I carry. My tears remind me that
this will be yet another memory wrought with pain. How
I long for relief, to be covered by Jehovah himself. Letting
me know he can see into the depths of my soul, Jehovah
responds. His words tenderly probe and expose the thoughts
and purposes of my heart.

I have always covered you.[6]

I begin to speak out loud, wanting to be sure Jehovah
hears.

"No, Jehovah, you haven't always covered us. Remember
how hard we've worked to make clothing and cover ourselves.
Remember how many shelters Adam built that didn't quite
work, until he figured out how to build a sturdy, warm home
for us?"

Bitterness swirls in my stomach like a sour root, looking
for a way to move from my stomach, up to my head and back
to my heart. Stopping to rest for a moment, I finally voice my
real complaint with boldness that surprises me.

"And did you cover our boys? Where were you when Cain
was plotting to kill his brother? Did you even care? Where
was our shelter then! And who put the tree in the Garden, the
one that stole everything from us? You made it impossible for
us and then blamed us when we fell!"

Jehovah is silent. He feels no need to make a defense.

My faithlessness hangs there in its ugliness, daring me to
face the real reason I am hiding from Adam and, even more

128

[6] *"You forgave the iniquity of your people and covered all their sins. You set aside
all your wrath and turned from your fierce anger. Restore us again, O God our
Savior, and put away your displeasure toward us."* PSALM 85:2-4

so, from Jehovah. Along with my own anger and fear comes a greater danger. The evil one lurks at the edges of my mind, seeking a foothold to climb into my thinking and move in once and for all.[7] Images of our encounters in the Garden rise up in my mind like an early morning mist, obscuring my faith. Will I sink into the depths?[8]

Is not your wickedness great? Are not your sins endless? Who could love such a woman?[9]

"Away from me, evil one!" I say, exhaling sharply and imagining the evil one being swept away by the breath of Jehovah. Perhaps Jehovah breathed himself into me for such a time as this.

I arrive at the river. As much as I want to run home and find Adam, I am exhausted. I need sleep. Walking along the riverbed, I discover a soft bed of green moss inviting me to rest. I take off my sandals and step into its cool squishiness.

"Did you prepare this for me, Jehovah?" I say, now ashamed of my outburst. "For one that accuses you?"

Come with me Eve to the place you dread.
Yes, come make peace with me.[10]

With his words, my lower lip begins to tremble a little. As much as I want peace, I'm still afraid. I think back through the five memories Jehovah has given. Two were full of life...my first day and meeting Adam. Three were heavy with pain... the tempter pushing his way into my thoughts, the birds stealing our crops, Zayeb leading us to our murdered son. Yet somehow all were meant to lead me towards Jehovah. Even though I am still unsure of all the lessons, I am grateful

[7] *"In your anger do not sin. Do not let the sun go down while you are still angry, and do not give the devil a foothold."* EPHESIANS 4:26-27
[8] *"I sink in the miry depths, where there is no foothold. I have come into the deep waters; the floods engulf me."* PSALM 69:2
[9] *"Is not your wickedness great? Are not your sins endless?"* JOB 22:5
[10] *"Or else let them come to me for refuge; let them make peace with me, yes, let them make peace with me."* ISAIAH 27:5

that Jehovah took me to these memories *with him.* Rejoiced with me. Mourned with me.[11]

Sensing the darkness of the sixth memory and terrified by the snares around me, I mutter a plea before I fall into a deep sleep. "Stay near me...please.[12]"

The sixth memory with Jehovah
Twilight was nearing in the Garden of Eden. Adam was curled up on a bed of moss, already asleep, tired after climbing up the side of a mountain to spend time with Jehovah. Not at all tired, my thoughts went to the tree of the knowledge of good and evil. Ever since my last encounter with the tree, I'd wanted to go back, just at a time when Serpent wasn't nearby. *Just one more visit, then I'll tell Adam.* Since I first met Serpent sunning himself in the heat of day, I decided to go in the evening light as day was fading, a time when Serpent was unlikely to be anywhere nearby.

When I arrived at the tree, I took one glance and knew I had no good reason to be there. But before I could turn away, I heard him, Serpent.

"Hello, Eve," he said with a slip of his tongue. Again, I saw no indication that Serpent was talking, but I heard him clearly.

"How did you know I'd be here?" I mumbled, embarrassed to have been caught alone at the tree again.

"Why, I came out to meet you, of course," Serpent murmured sadly as if I'd offended him.[13] "The perfume of the tree drew you I see?"

"Perfume?" I asked.

"Yes, the tree is especially fragrant in the evening...a

130

[11] *"Jesus wept."* JOHN 11:35
[12] *"That is why snares are all around you, why sudden peril terrifies you, why it is so dark you cannot see, and why a flood of waters covers you..."* JOB 22:10-11
[13] *"So I came out to meet you; I looked for you and have found you!"* PROVERBS 7:15

sensual smell, like the most fragrant spices on earth, the scent of love. At night I come here to drink deeply of its scent. Sometimes, I linger until morning.[14] Would you like a sniff?"

"No, no," I said, taking a step backwards, even though I did indeed want to smell it. I drew in a breath cautiously, knowing that even the aroma might be dangerous.

"Eve, have you ever wondered why Jehovah doesn't want you to eat from the trees in the Garden? Why he seeks to shelter you so?"

"Actually, we may eat from the trees in the Garden," I replied, still unsure where this was leading, "It's only this tree that God has forbidden, the tree of the knowledge of good and evil. Jehovah said its fruit leads to death."

"Interesting name for a tree, wouldn't you say?" Serpent's brazen eyes sparkled as if they were full of laughter. "There are many trees in Eden, like walnut, apple and peach, and many trees that bear no fruit. But none with a name like this. And such a cumbersome name for a beautiful tree. What do you suppose it means?"

"I'm not sure," I said. I never thought to ask Jehovah the meaning of the name.

Looking closer at Serpent I was momentarily stunned. His colors were brighter and more varied than I remembered, similar to the hues of my favorite flowers.[15]

"Just so you know, you will not surely die," Serpent said, moving closer as if he were confiding in me. "The Lofty One knows if you eat it, you will be like him, knowing both good and evil. I suppose he considers himself the only one worthy of such knowledge. And there are certain pleasures he doesn't want you to give Adam."

[14] *"I have perfumed my bed with myrrh, aloes and cinnamon. Come, let's drink deeply of love till morning; let's enjoy ourselves with love!"* PROVERBS 7:17-18
[15] *Then out came a woman to meet him, dressed like a prostitute and with crafty intent."* PROVERBS 7:10

My cheeks warmed as I lowered my head and whispered, partially to Serpent, partially to myself, "Adam could explain better. Perhaps I should bring him back here with me. He was with Jehovah in the Garden before me."

I didn't want to look at Serpent again. I only wanted to leave, but my feet stayed planted, as if roots were springing all around them, anchoring them to the ground. Did Serpent have power to hold me here?

"At one time I was with the Mighty One," Serpent mused, "but then I learned I was the only one who could shelter myself. Just one mistake and he rejected me. But not to bother you with this. I'm sure your Adam will have an answer...Ah, yes, Adam will enjoy this pleasure."[16]

I turned on my heel and ran. I'd kept this secret far too long. *I will tell Adam everything about my encounters with the serpent. He will have answers.*

When I reached Adam, I nudged him, "Please wake up, my strong one."

He yawned and rolled over, his eyes heavy with sleep, "Now?"

"I have something to tell you," I said with my voice trembling just a little. "Something I should have told you sooner. But first you must come with me."

"Where are we going?" he mumbled, as we trudged along the path.

"Let me show you," I said.

When we arrived at the tree, I was unprepared for the sight. With the yellow-orange of the approaching sunset streaming through the branches, the fruit appeared to glow.[17] Adam rubbed his eyes and whispered hoarsely, "The tree?"

[16] *"'Stolen water is sweet; food eaten in secret is delicious!' But little do they know that the dead are there, that her guests are deep in the realm of the dead."* PROVERBS 9:17–18

[17] *"He was going down the street near her corner, walking along in the direction of her house at twilight, as the day was fading, as the dark of night set in."* PROVERBS 7:8–9

As we stood and looked, a breeze stirred a faint aroma, unlike anything we'd experienced. It was bold and fruity yet wrapped in the richness of the earth. Desire stirred in my stomach, pushing out all thoughts of the conversation I intended to have with Adam.

I took one step forward, then, letting go of Adam's hand, I looked back over my shoulder to reassure him and murmured, "Just a closer look."

I strode up to the tree. As I approached the fruit, the sun cast its last light, illuminating the fruit in one final burst of glory.

I hadn't meant to touch it, but suddenly it was in my hand as if the tree placed it there. It was heavy with possibility. The skin was good to touch. I rubbed it against my chin. So soft.

"Wisdom...Serpent said it offers wisdom," I divulged. "He called it the scent of love."

Adam had a strange look on his face, one I couldn't discern. His eyes were wide open, fastened on me.

Lifting the fruit up to my nose, I inhaled.

"Smell," I urged, holding it towards him. "So pleasing."

Adam took the fruit in his hand and inhaled, his eyes closed with satisfaction.

I reached up and picked another piece to take a closer look. There was a small drop of juice near the stem. I touched it with my finger and lifted it to my mouth, running my tongue over my lips. So sweet. Then forgetting everything but the piece of fruit, I suddenly bit in, chewed and swallowed. The flavor was dizzying. I felt weak in my knees.

Now I was ravenous. All inhibition gone, I plunged into the fruit and watched as Adam joined me. It was as if all the pleasure of the universe was contained in this one small creation. Warmth flooded from the top of my head to the tips of my toes.

We ate until we could eat no more. Wanting to taste the fruit's pleasure and mine, Adam rubbed some of its juice on my skin and roughly took me in his arms. But instead of his usual tenderness, he squeezed me so hard I couldn't breathe.

"Please, not so rough."

I pushed against his chest, wanting him to continue, but wanting him to stop. When I caught Adam's eyes, his look scared me, full of desire and raw hunger like he could no longer control himself. We wrestled for a moment, falling backward onto the ground, Adam's weight knocking the breath out of me. Gasping for air, I looked up and noticed the sky was completely black.

It was then I sensed evil so terrifying that I couldn't move, like something savage and sinister was sitting on my chest. Glancing at the darkened tree, I saw a twisted face in its bark laughing at me. I forced my body into a sitting position and nudged Adam, "Look!" Serpent slid in front of the tree, lifted his head our way and slipped his forked tongue at us, his eyes glowing red in the shadows. *Is he grinning?*

"Come, Eve," Adam shouted in panic as he stood up and turned on his heel. "Follow me!"

I stood up and ran away from the tree, away from what I'd just done. Branches slapped me as I ran by, reprimanding me for my disobedience.[18] When I reached our usual resting place, I fell on the ground weeping. My stomach was churning. What did I just do? What would Jehovah think?

Adam sat with his back against a tree, deep in his own

[18] *"It is shameful even to mention what the disobedient do in secret."* EPHESIANS 5:12

pain, holding his head in his hands, unable to comfort himself or me.

Finally, after a long pause, he looked off into the distance and whispered gruffly, "Why did you take me there, Eve? Why there?"

I wanted to tell Adam how Serpent deceived me, how I hadn't intended evil for us. How all I wanted was to have something to give him. How I knew he would explain everything. But instead, for the first time, I could find no words. We remained in complete silence for the longest time until I dozed off, exhausted.

Sometime in the deepest reaches of the night, the KNOWLEDGE OF GOOD came, seeping into my soul like a mist, wrapping around every part of my being.

EVERYTHING IS COVERED IN DEEPEST DARKNESS. Complete chaos reigns. I'm frightened until I sense I'm not alone. Love is there. She draws me, warms me. Then love bursts into light. Dawn emerges from its abode. Color springs forth. Reds, yellows, oranges, pinks and purples rise from the edges of the earth. Black waters turn blue-green with white foam edges. A voice booms...

It is good.

Good whispers, "Goodness alone can turn darkness to light."[19]

A mighty wind rushes. Seas burst from their Creator's womb. They spread to the farthest reaches, then halt as the voice commands...*Here and no farther.* Faithfulness separates

[19] GENESIS 1:4

the waters from the sky. A chorus of voices swells in perfect harmony. At Jehovah's word, clouds begin to rise. They reveal hills. Great dunes of sand. Purple peaks of mountains carved from mighty masses of rock. Verdant islands rising from the sea. A voice carries over the waters...

It is good.

Good speaks, "The Lord's goodness cannot be shaken."[20] Jehovah stretches a measuring line for the land. He sets the footings of the seas. Plants emerge from the soil—frilly and fuzzy, smooth and spiked, delicate and sturdy. Vegetation covers the mountains. Trees send out roots by lakes, streams, rivers and springs. Some reach towards the sky. Others burst with fruit. Flowers, mosses and vines blanket the hills, a feast of color, texture and beauty. They cry, *touch me, taste me, smell me.* All drip with dew given by the Beautiful One. A wind sweeps the land, causing plants and trees to tremble...

It is good.

Good surrounds me, "All who look to him reflect his goodness."[21] Sunlight spills onto the earth. Every plant lifts its head to receive its warmth. Day turns to night and the stars blaze as the constellations march into their places. At the Gracious Creator's command, the laws of the heavens move into place.[22] The heavens shout their glory as the voice resounds...

It is good.

136

[20] See PSALM 125:1
[21] "And we, who with unveiled faces all reflect the Lord's glory, are being transformed into his likeness with ever-increasing glory, which comes from the Lord, who is the Spirit." 2 CORINTHIANS 3:18 (NIV1984)
[22] Read JOB 38:1 through 39:4

Good confides, "His goodness does not sleep or slumber."[23]
Birds fly across the expanse of the earth, guided by Jehovah
himself. Two eagles take flight, spreading their enormous
wings towards the south. Fish spin upwards from the springs
of the sea. Heaven laughs with joy at each one's colors and
curiosities. Great sea creatures of the deep lift their heads
above the turquoise waters and bellow to the Father with
mighty wails...

It is good.

Good trembles, "No good from the Almighty can be
thwarted."[24]
Animals crouch and bring forth their young. Nourished
by their mother's milk, they grow strong. They squat, slither,
strut and stampede, dancing with their creator. As his voice
travels to the ends of the earth, each animal lifts its eyes
toward the heavens. Adam rises from the dust and stretches.
He laughs with his Creator as he tests his strength. Overcome
with emotion, the voice trembles with giddiness...

It is good.

The voice begins to sing a love song...my song. The
goodness of pure love overpowers me, washing me with
peace. The two become one, a strand of three cords with their
Creator.[25] Then three voices come down from the Heavens,
blending in a mighty chorus of praise...

It is good!

[23] *Read* PSALM 121
[24] JOB 42:2
[25] *"Though one may be overpowered, two can defend themselves. A cord of three strands is not quickly broken."* ECCLESIASTES 4:12

Good boasts, "Goodness only comes from Jehovah."

Men and women accept the mark of Jehovah. A small fire glows in each of their hearts.[26] They refuse to deny him, instead sharing Jehovah with those ready to take their lives. "Snuff out my body," they cry, "so that my soul can live."

As each dies, the fire bursts out of their chest, swirls into brilliant light that rises to the heavens. Moments before a lion leaps for his neck, a man lifts his hands to the sky, smiles and murmurs, "God, you are good."

A woman watches, her little ones tucked under her arms, as her husband is strapped to a tree. Violent men set him on fire for his faith in Jehovah. As tears run down her face, she lifts her head high and says in her children's hearing..."Abba Father, we commit ourselves to your goodness."

Good rejoices, "God's goodness conquers all."[27]

As THE KNOWLEDGE OF GOOD FADED AWAY, I fought to keep it. "Please, let good stay here with me," I whispered. Then feeling it slipping away, I cried out loud, "Jehovah, put your fire in my heart!"

Now fully awake, I looked over at Adam, still in a deep sleep. Did he share the same vision? Realization came—the foolish reasoning that made me crave the forbidden when indescribable goodness had been given. Sorrow washed over me. Love was the reason Jehovah didn't allow the tree. I sinned against the goodness of Jehovah. I am not good.

I'll do better, I vowed silently. *I'll never listen to the evil one again.* For what seemed like the longest time, I was still, silent, sorry, willing myself to always remember the goodness of God. Trying to convince myself that my sin didn't happen,

[26] *See* PSALM 39:3, JEREMIAH 20:9
[27] *"We know that in everything God works for the good of those who love him. They are the people he called, because that was his plan."* ROMANS 8:28 (NCV)

that my fall wasn't as evil as the vision insinuated.

Instead, as I drifted back to sleep, I was jerked awake as if a hand reached into my chest and pulled me upright. "No, please, no," I cried out in fear. The vision would not be denied entry.

The KNOWLEDGE OF EVIL stormed on me in anger, thrusting its grisly images into my soul, challenging the goodness of Jehovah.

DARKNESS SWIRLS AROUND ME AND THEN PARTS IN two. A woman walks in the forest. Her skin is mostly covered. A man waits from behind a tree. His eyes shift back and forth, full of hunger. When she comes near, he pounces on her like a lion, throws her to the ground and rips off her coverings. Now she is naked and panicked. When she pleads with him to stop, he strikes her with such force that she ceases to struggle. Forcing himself on her, he consumes her like a loaf of bread.[28]

Terror rushes from my head to toes, making it impossible to breathe.

"Like you, he desired the forbidden," evil hisses. "Evil is more desirable than goodness!"

With brilliant flashes of light, a cloud descends to the ground, carrying uncountable voices crying out in anguish. A dark child emerges from the cloud. She walks so slowly. She is naked and her ribs protrude like the carved shell of a walnut. Her cheeks sink inwards and her eyes bulge. Her gaunt legs barely carry her...so hungry. A vulture circles over her head, its eyes bright with anticipation. All around her people eat until their bellies swell with food, yet they offer her neither food nor clothing.[29]

[28] *"Don't the wicked understand? They destroy my people as if they were eating bread. They do not ask God for help."* PSALM 53:4 (NCV)
[29] *"Share your food with the hungry and bring poor, homeless people into your own homes. When you see someone who has no clothes, give him yours, and don't refuse to help your own relatives."* ISAIAH 58:7 (NCV)

"They don't even see her!" I cry.

"Oh, but now they have more for themselves," evil laughs. "From evildoers come evil deeds."

A man-child wails in the dark, tiny and defenseless. So that's what a human child looks like, I think, as tenderness rushes over me. Moments later a man screams in rage, threatening the child if he doesn't quiet. The man appears... *the child's father?* He picks the child up and shakes him violently. With a thud, he throws him to the ground. The mother appears, screaming in protest when she sees the child. As her child's life ebbs away, the woman curses the man. He turns on her, kicking her...her stomach, her head, her back, until she is motionless. The blood of mother and child mix and seep into the soil as the man flees.

"Why would he attack a little one?" I gasp.

"Little ones are so easy to prey on," evil confides. "Vulnerability is a curse!"

After that, the horror picks up speed, evil swirling around me like leaves in a sudden wind.

Brothers throw curses and fists at each other with words of hatred. Men leer at naked women. A mother and father lift their infant boy, his eyes full of trust, onto the burning hot arms of a golden statue. As the child shrieks, they pray to the stars, moon and the earth.[30] A woman winks at a man and purses her lips, pushing her breasts towards him. He follows her down a slippery path, giving her his very soul.[31] A man kills his wife because her skin is a different color than his. He lifts an instrument and splits her head in half. Her infant child wanders outside into streets filled with bodies. The child splashes in blood, as if it is water, rubbing it on her cheeks.

[30] *"They shed innocent blood, the blood of their sons and daughters, whom they sacrificed to the idols of Canaan, and the land was desecrated by their blood."* PSALM 106:38
[31] *See* PROVERBS 16:28-30

I scream, "No more, please no more!!!"

"They serve my purposes," evil boasts. "Every inclination of man's heart is evil."

Then a loud voice proclaims...

Woe to those who call evil good and good evil.
Woe to those who exchange darkness for light and bitter for sweet.[32]
Woe to those who take what wasn't provided.
Woe to those who speak what isn't true.
Woe to those who heap insults on what is holy.[33]
Woe to those who sell their soul for pleasure.

A great multitude of men and women turn their backs on Jehovah as he speaks. They walk away from his dwelling place, thirsting to see, touch and taste what is forbidden.[34]

"Don't you see the evil one taunting you?" I cry.

Of those who remain, some use the service of Jehovah for their own gain, to horde things...even stealing the innocence of little ones in their greed.

I look and see no fire in these hearts, only blackness.

Wickedness seeks to overthrow the heavens, but is thrown to earth in the form of a serpent of dazzling colors. A son is sent to make peace, yet people strike him with sticks. They curse this son, piercing his hands and feet. Darkness falls over the land as heavenly beings weep and then rejoice as a great light dawns and Serpent shrieks in defeat.

Many hate the light, fight against the light, hide from the light.[35] Spiritual forces of evil attack Jehovah's beloved ones, seeking to turn their love cold through great delusions.

"Don't follow in my path!" I plead.

141

---

[32] ISAIAH 5:20
[33] "...who has treated as an unholy thing the blood of the covenant that sanctified them, and who has insulted the Spirit of grace?" HEBREWS 10:29B
[34] "For everything in the world—the lust of the flesh, the lust of the eyes, and the pride of life—comes not from the Father but from the world." 1 JOHN 2:16
[35] "Everyone who does evil hates the light, and will not come into the light for fear that their deeds will be exposed." JOHN 3:20 (NIV1984)

Evil floods over me, wanting to claim me for its own…
"You caused all this! Who will protect you now, you who ate
the forbidden fruit! Who will cover you?"

WHEN I OPENED MY EYES, I SAW THAT ADAM WAS
already up, pacing. It was morning. The knowledge of good
and the knowledge of evil had taken me through the night.

"Eve," he said, crouching beside me, "We must hide
ourselves before Jehovah comes."

I looked at myself embarrassed and terrified by the evil
I still felt pressing around me. "We are…naked," I said,
wrapping my arms around my chest and knowing now that
these parts should be covered. *I am dirty, covered in a filth that
cannot be cleansed.*

The thought of giving myself to Adam, as I did before the
fruit, filled me with dread. I feared that with no coverings
Adam would look straight through me, and see me for who I
was, a woman who ruined everything we had with Jehovah
and each other. At that moment I determined that I would
never let Adam in close enough that he could see who I really
am. *Yet I must please him so that he never rejects me.*

We glanced at each other's naked parts and then looked
away. Spotting a fig tree with large leaves, I hid myself in its
branches, wrapped the plant around me, desperately wanting
to hide. Then I remembered the woman in my vision, a
covered woman. "I can make us coverings out of these fig
leaves and this bamboo."

I took some bamboo, began to shred the long stalks into
strips and handed them to Adam, who wove them into a cord.
As we worked silently, one of Jehovah's songs came to me…

Today I join three strands,
Two learn the language of love.
Unquenched by many waters,
Rivers cannot wash it away,
It is stronger than death.

Regret washed over me. Cord that was meant to join us together now would divide us. With a stick, I punched holes in the leaves, the thickest leaves I could find, and began weaving them together. First I covered myself and then helped Adam cover himself.

Is this part of the knowledge of good and evil?

The fig leaves hardly covered, but they were better than being naked. Exposed. Vulnerable.

Adam led me to a grove of trees surrounded by thick bushes. "We can wait here," he announced, "until Jehovah passes by. I've seen the deer nurse their young here."

We pushed through the bushes until we found a spot barely large enough for both of us to squat and wait. Fear washed over me...*Will Jehovah ever want me again?*

"Adam, I will make this up to you," I whispered.

"Shhh," he said. "Jehovah may hear you."

Silently I mouthed the words I dared not utter out loud, "Please tell me you still love me."

Then we heard the sound that was so familiar to us, the sound of the Lord walking in the Garden in the cool of the morning. His voice, the voice that once could lift my heart with a song, now was heartbreaking in its sorrow...

Adam, where are you?[36]

[36] GENESIS 3:9

You have been…a shelter from the storm
and a shade from the heat.
For the breath of the ruthless
is like a storm driving against a wall.

ISAIAH'S PRAYER TO JEHOVAH COMFORTER[1]

[1] ISAIAH 25:4

CHAPTER EIGHT

The Storm

W HERE ARE YOU?" THE SIXTH MEMORY IS
over, but Jehovah's voice remains. As soon as I
wake, I stand up, gather some provisions and
take off into the forest on the path to the hunting shelter. Yet,
I leave the mossy bed by the river with an unseen companion,
Jehovah's cry. *"Where are you?"* When we were hiding in
the bushes after we ate the fruit, all I could think about was
myself. Now, having revisited the memory with Jehovah, I
hear clearly his longing, his love. *"Where are you?"* Jehovah's
words weren't an accusation—they were the plea of a broken
heart. What I feel for my lost son Cain. *"Where are you, Eve?"*
As my head clears, I urge my feet to move faster. Part of me
wants to run from the sixth memory...the pain of breaking
the only boundary Jehovah set. Instead I call out, "I am here,
Jehovah. I am coming to the shelter."

As I push forward towards the ravine where the springs
flow, I urge myself to trust that good conquers evil. "All
that is beautiful looks to you," I whisper as I look around
me. Yet the knowledge of evil struck a blow that cannot be
easily undone, making me wonder if it is possible that evil
is stronger than good, or whether it's just me. Am I just not

strong enough, too quick to give in to fear, too faithless? *Weak. Cowardly. Unbelieving.*[2] The words circle around me like vultures surrounding their prey. If Jehovah were walking with me, I feel sure he would remind me that vulnerability is a gift, something to be embraced. From the sixth memory, I see how Adam and I began drifting away from each other when I decided to hide my tender parts from him—my emotions, my insecurities, my thoughts and my body.

"Keep faith," I urge my battered mind. "God created you to be tender. He will protect." But how can my heart accept this when my head refuses to believe? When my instincts still urge me towards Serpent's whisper...*vulnerability is a curse.*

All at once, I realize that I've lost track of the markers to the shelter. Glancing around, I see nothing familiar. The trees are thicker and more pressed together than I remember. They grasp each other's arms in a tight embrace over my head. Small animals skitter around me—most likely chipmunks, squirrels or moles—snapping tiny branches yet not showing themselves. The sunlight barely peeks through, creating tiny patches of light on the ground. *I know the path, but somehow, I've strayed.* The farther I push, willing the real path to appear, the more flustered I become. I turn one direction and then another, trying to find my way back. "The springs with the rocky shore at the bottom of the ravine...where are they?" I whisper, urging myself not to overreact.

Taking a few deep breaths to steady myself, I lean against a tree, allow myself a few bites of fruit and dried meat, and think through my options. If I don't find my way soon, I may have to spend the night here alone. And since I am off the path and little light remains, Adam may not be able to find

[2] *"But the cowardly, the unbelieving, the vile, the murderers, the sexually immoral, those who practice magic arts, the idolaters and all liars—they will be consigned to the fiery lake of burning sulfur..."* REVELATION 21:8

me. I can hope against hope and wait here for Adam, refusing to move until he comes. Then, seeing a large branch on the ground, I wonder whether I could build a shelter.

I picture our hunting shelter and all the small details Adam and the boys considered when they built it. How it rests against the side of a hill, supported by a wall of rocks. Adam inserted three tree limbs in the rocks that stretch from the cliff to two trees beside the cliff wall, tying bamboo supports to these limbs to create the structure for walls and a roof. How he and the boys padded the shelter with all manner of limbs and pine branches, strapped together with twine Adam made. They finished it with a door and several rough windows. To complete their work, Adam and the boys added a low wall around it made with branches, rocks and mud.

I remember Abel with his foot positioned on top of the wall, with both hands on his hips, eyes sparkling, announcing, "We made this to keep the small animals out, like rats and raccoons."

Then Cain, his reddish-brown hair glinting in the sun, dimples showing as he spread his arms wide (so much like his father) piping in, "We chose the perfect location. If we built the shelter near a ravine, we'd have a hard time staying dry."

The trees rustle above me, jerking me back to reality. Any inclination I had to build a shelter is gone.

"Adam," I call, loud as my lungs allow. "Where are you?"

Darkness is falling quickly, too quickly. When a huge frog croaks beside me, I trip and spin into the side of a tree. Bouncing off, I manage to stay on my feet, but I'm shaken. Black flies swarm around me and land in my ears, on my nose. I swat them away. Crickets warble a song that sounds like a muted scream. With every step, my chest is heavier...it barely rises and falls. *How can this be? I had time to make it to the shelter.*

Just before the sun drops beyond the horizon, I see hope. Just fifty steps beyond me I see what appears to be an entrance to a cave—a possible hiding place until the morning when I'll have light to help me find my way to the shelter. As I get closer, I see a faint glow inside. A fire deep within? My heart lifts. *Adam is here!*

I crouch and move into the cave so quickly that I lose my balance. I catch myself with my hands and tumble from my shoulder to my back, making sure to shelter the little one within. My right shoulder begins to throb. Little dots of bright red blood gather on my palms. I dust myself off with the back of my hands and walk towards the light.

"Adam?" I whisper.

As I turn the corner, my voice lodges itself in my throat. The light comes from the glowing eyes of Serpent. *How can his eyes create that much light?*[3] His body is curled beneath him and his head is lifted in anticipation. *Did he expect me?*

"It's *you*," I say in disgust, not even willing to say his name lest I give him power. Noting his beautiful colors, the hues of my favorite flowers, I wish with all my might that Adam had crushed his head.

"Eve!" he intones with mock tenderness. "You came! Look at you, lost in the dark forest. But not to worry," he quips. "I have a gift for you, a gift of great value."

"Like the forbidden fruit?" I say and immediately regret my boldness. Making him angry may not be a good idea.

"Were you hoping I would offer more?"

"No...no," I say, shaken but trying not to show it. The

[3] *"And no wonder, for Satan himself masquerades as an angel of light."* 2 CORINTHIANS 11:14

fruit's pleasure comes flooding back. My stomach growls and I pray silently that the serpent does not hear.

"I've brought a man to protect you. Isn't that what you've always wanted?"

"Adam will protect me," I say. *Where are you Adam?*

"Oh, but don't you see? Adam is busy protecting himself from those *pesky* thorns, briers and birds."

"Adam needs me!" I say, inhaling sharply. I exhale, "I am his helper."

"Oh, yes, you are so right," Serpent chirps. I could swear he is laughing. Just like in the Garden, I hear his words, yet he gives no sign he is talking. "The question is whether you need Adam. It appears to me that you need someone else, a man who appreciates your courage in eating the fruit."

"Only Jehovah can create a man!" I croak, unsure why I'm even dignifying the snake with a response. I glance towards the black entrance, wanting to flee but feeling like my feet have a mind of their own.

Serpent goes on as if I had not said a word, "He used to be with the Eternal One." Seeing the surprise on my face, the serpent hisses, "Oh, I'm sorry, Eve. Yet another thing the One from On High didn't tell you."

A mixture of desire and regret washes over me. How I wish I'd never strayed from the trustworthy path. How I wish I hadn't gone alone to Serpent and then hid from Adam. It's like Serpent has secured an entrance into my very soul.

"But like you, this man wanted something more," he continues, "something only for himself. He desires you, Eve." The word *desires* lingers on Serpent's forked tongue as if he couldn't let the sweetness of it depart...*desssiresss you, dessssiressss you, dessssssiressssss*…like some kind of ruthless song.

"My, aren't you beautiful tonight,"[4] a man trills in a low voice from the darkness behind Serpent. His words are smoother than oil.[5] His brazenness shocks me, but before I can think, my hands reach up and smooth my clothing over my chest. I stop myself and cross my arms.

"Where did you get this, this man?" I sputter, confused.

"Like you, he used to be in God's presence. His name is Nephilim.[6] Let her see you," Serpent commands.

The man steps out of the shadows, lifting one side of his mouth and then the other to form a smile. He is at least two heads taller than me. His eyes are as black as his garment and his arms ripple with muscle. Somehow he looks familiar, like I have seen him before. Then I realize…he makes me think of the angel with the sword guarding Eden. But instead of streaming with light, Nephilim is full of dark shadows. Mystery.

"Let me help you," Nephilim whispers.

The snake sways back and forth as if he is doing a dance of celebration, his eyes fixed steadily on me. "See, he wants you."

"I carry Adam's child."

"If your Adam cares about you, why does he let you be so…vulnerable?" The way Serpent spits out the word vulnerable makes it sounds like it is an ugly word…something to be avoided.

A vision of Adam staring at another woman slithers through my mind. A naked woman. "Adam would never accept a woman from you," I exclaim. No sooner than I say

150

---

4 *"For such people are not serving our Lord Christ, but their own appetites. By smooth talk and flattery they deceive the minds of naive people."* ROMANS 16:18
5 PROVERBS 5:3
6 *"The Nephilim were on the earth in those days—and also afterward—when the sons of God went to the daughters of humans and had children by them. They were the heroes of old, men of renown."* GENESIS 6:4

the words, doubt comes trickling in. I feel like I've been kicked in the stomach.

"And we can take care of that human child, that remnant of your pain," Serpent drawls. "Just a few herbs and the child will be gone. Adam will never know...and don't worry about pain. We can make you numb, so you won't feel anything."

I look around, startled. I could swear I heard more than one voice. Is there more than one snake? Or does Serpent speak of himself and Nephilim? I wrap my arms tighter around my womb. I turn to run, but Nephilim has moved around behind me to block the entrance. Something prevents him from getting to me but I fear he will break through.[7]

Then, seeing the muscular cut of Nephilim's arms, longing presses on my stomach. A chill snakes up and down my spine as I remember the strong arms of a man, Adam, around me offering comfort, strength and protection. My eyes flicker down to his legs. They seem like stone pillars. My mind and body want to shut down and lose themselves in the suggestion of pleasure. *Perhaps being numb wouldn't be so bad. It might take away all this pain.*

"I must go," I manage with great effort, my voice hoarse.

"A second chance, my tender one. Nephilim will give you a child you won't have to worry about...a mighty man, a hero." Then rising up even higher, he strikes. "I know you didn't mean to, but you murdered him...your precious Abel."

Serpent wants me to deny the truth. He would have me take refuge in a lie and hide behind falsehood, making an agreement with death itself.[8]

"You...you're right," I stutter out. "I didn't mean to, but what I started in the Garden ended in Abel's death. When I

151

[7] *"...and do not give the devil a foothold."* EPHESIANS 4:27
[8] *"You boast, 'We have entered into a covenant with death, with the realm of the dead we have made an agreement. When an overwhelming scourge sweeps by, it cannot touch us, for we have made a lie our refuge and falsehood our hiding place.'"* ISAIAH 28:15

took fruit from the forbidden tree, I introduced death." Tears begin streaming down my face and I wipe them away.

"But can there be life without death?" Serpent asks. "When you took the fruit, you thought of yourself. Is that such a terrible thing? And who could blame Cain after the Holy One rejected him?"

Serpent acknowledges my guilt and then seeks to use it to strangle me. Confuse me. Cut off my airway.[9] He pauses and waves his head dramatically—similar to the way Adam would wave a hand—saying, "Only my plan proposes a way out."

Suddenly I realize the appeal of Serpent's offer. A man without the messiness and demands of true intimacy. Without the heartache and shared pain. I shuffle deeper into the cave, away from the evil one. A high-pitched shriek right outside the cave entrance almost makes me lose my footing on the moist cave floor. *Vultures?* Without warning, two bats come out of nowhere, screeching and circling my head, brushing against my hair with their wings. "Stop! Stop! Please stop!" I cry, covering my eyes with my hands to block out the terror. With a flutter of black wings, one flies up to my face and nips me on the cheek like the weaver bird did to Adam.

"Nephilim will gladly rescue you!" Serpent whispers.

I carefully open my eyes and take a step closer to Nephilim, yet not close enough for him to touch me. *Trust me,* his eyes plead. A small drop of saliva runs down his chin and he licks his lips, moistening them. His aroma wafts towards me, making me feel a little dizzy. The smell is bold and musky, mixed with the earth's richness and the sweetness of fruit.

He wants me.

"I've asked some friends to witness your union," Serpent

9 *"See, the enemy is puffed up; his desires are not upright— but the righteous person will live by his faithfulness."* HABAKKUK 2:4

drawls. Looking up, I see that the roof of the cave is full of unblinking yellow eyes staring at us, mocking me.

I cover my mouth with my forearm, not allowing the scream lodged in my throat to come out. Adam told me never to show fear in front of an animal. "Please!" I whisper to Nephilim, as if Serpent isn't here. "Please take me away from here! Help me find Adam."

"But of course," Nephilim says. As he extends a hand, his eyes urge me to reach for him. I lift my hand slightly, trembling so hard that my teeth chatter. When I hesitate, his dark eyes flash with fury and I suddenly know all he wants to do. He seeks to seize me, seduce me and steal all my vulnerable parts for his pleasures...take my child.

Am I the woman in the vision of the knowledge of evil? The one who had her tender parts, even her life, stolen from her? With great effort, I tear my hand and eyes away. I back up, silently mouthing...*no, no, no!*

Serpent puffs his cheeks and enshrouds Nephilim and me in a cloud of vapor. Fighting the instinct to reach for comfort, I throw my arms in front of my face, careful not to move even one step towards the vile man. At first the smell is tantalizing like the forbidden fruit, but then it quickly begins to change into a musky, putrid smell—like fruit combined with the rotting flesh of a dead animal.

I bend over and heave, but my stomach refuses to release what little is there. As the cloud dissipates, angry sores appear on my arms.[10]

"Will Adam want you now?" Serpent asks. "He likes that you *were* beautiful."

"Look!" he commands, as he glances at the ground.

[10] *"The first angel went and poured out his bowl on the land, and ugly, festering sores broke out on the people who had the mark of the beast and worshiped its image."* REVELATION 16:2

The light rises and I see a small pool of clear water a few steps from my feet.

"Are you afraid to see yourself as I do?" Whisperer sneers. "Are you a follower of Jehovah or a coward?"

I fall to my knees and look into the water. *What will it hurt to look?* As the woman in the water looks back at me, I hardly recognize her, although undoubtedly she is me, Eve, the mother of the living and the dead. A large raw sore blooms on one cheek and then the other. When I touch my cheek, I find a mixture of blood and pus.

"You seek to disfigure me!" I cry, standing up.

"Go to Nephilim and he'll remove the sores," the evil one shrieks. Then lowering his voice into a whisper, he sounds almost tender, "Then Nephilim will comfort you...he doesn't mind a little blood."

"I refuse your mark,"[11] I say, closing my eyes, falling back on my knees. "Sores or no sores, I refuse his comfort!" Lifting my arms up above, I cry, "Save me, Father! I give myself to you and you alone." Then I bow low, touching my forehead to the stony ground, and I pray out loud for the longest time to the only one who can save me. I ask for...

Deliverance from the evil one.

Protection for the little one nestled safely in my womb.

Direction for Adam and redemption for Cain.

Most of all, I pray for myself. I tell Jehovah how frightened I am, how weak I am, how much I need him. I ask him to take over, to win the victory over Serpent and his Nephilim. I beg Jehovah for his forgiveness.

And then I choke out the words that are hardest for me to say, "Thank you for loss...it only comes because I love."

[11] *"...And I saw the souls of those who had been beheaded because of their testimony about Jesus and because of the word of God. They had not worshiped the beast or its image and had not received its mark on their foreheads or their hands..."* REVELATION 20:4

With a shiver, I realize what Jehovah sought to teach me, that my vulnerability is my beauty. And gratitude protects my vulnerable parts. It is my guard.[12] Gratitude allows the past to be a gentle teacher instead of a harsh judge.[13] With that I roll on my side, refusing to give Serpent or his evil man entrance into my eyes, my body, my heart. Instead I thank Jehovah for encircling me with his arms, drawing me under his wings. Warmth surrounds me, as if I'm covered in a cocoon of blankets, safely tucked away from a world of serpents, sores, Nephilim and thorns.

When I lift my head, Serpent, the bats and Nephilim are gone. I am alone in the dark cave and light streams in from the entrance.

Was this all a dream? No, it was just too real.

I check myself for clues. The sores are gone from my arms. I touch my right cheek. It feels supple, flawless. My shoulder aches from my fall when I entered the cave, but when I lift my arm to my nose and inhale, I almost weep in relief...I don't smell like Serpent's vile vapor.

I stroke my womb. *You are safe, my little one. Jehovah has kept us safe.*

Although I don't remember sleeping, when I look outside I see morning has dawned. As I leave, I turn and speak into the now empty cave. I make my voice bold, filled with the confidence of having survived a cruel attack, "I will never take what you offer again. I am going where Jehovah calls."

As I walk into a verdant forest, Jehovah speaks...

*I hid my face from you for a moment, but with kindness
I will have compassion on you. You will teach your sons*

[12] See PHILIPPIANS 4:6–7
[13] "*For everything that was written in the past was written to teach us, so that through the endurance taught in the Scriptures and the encouragement they provide we might have hope.*" ROMANS 15:4

and daughters well. Great will be your children's peace.
Whoever attacks you will surrender to you. This is your
heritage and my vindication.[14] I am your shelter.

Jehovah gives me a promise, his word. Then I realize what
the evil one really fears.[15] He shudders at Jehovah's word, the
curse he would suffer at the hand of my offspring...*he will crush*
your head and you will strike his heel.[16] But the evil one only
pretends to have victory. Abel is with Jehovah. Cain's story is
yet to be told. And I will protect this new little one, him or
her, no matter what I must give, how I will suffer. And to do
that, I will need the help of Jehovah.

I FIND THE PATH AND WALK SLOWLY TO THE NEXT
marker, the spring in the ravine. Ravenous, I eat the rest of
the fruit in my basket, saving the dried meat. I find a small
brook and wash the stickiness off my hands. When I arrive
at the springs, tucked in the rocks I see an enormous feather.
When I pull it out, it is as long as my forearm, a beautiful
golden brown with white stripes and a downy base—the
feather of a golden eagle. Cain and Abel took great delight in
finding one of these.

I kneel in gratitude. I take the feather and lightly skim it
over my eyes. "Lord, may my eyes be full of light."

I let it softly caress each of my ears. "Help me to listen for
your instruction."

Then I press it to my lips. "Please help your words to be
mine."

Satisfied, I tuck the feather into my basket for safekeeping
and move down to the sparkling water. Just as Jehovah

156

---

[14] See ISAIAH 54:8-15.
[15] *"You believe that there is one God. Good! Even the demons believe that—*
and shudder." JAMES 2:19
[16] GENESIS 3:15

provided water in the season of springs and in the long dry summers, he provides now. I refill my skin first, and then bathe away my encounter with the evil whisperer and his Nephilim, as I pray…

"Thank you Jehovah that even after my sin, you find a way to cleanse." I lift the skin of water to my parched lips, hoping for a clean heart.[17]

"Jehovah, thank you for the skins you gave, at the cost of killing an animal, part of your loving creation, after we ran out of the garden covered only by a few fig leaves."

Now that I have washed, I am ready to move forward. Jehovah has one last memory for me to revisit. Somehow, I know that this memory will come as I walk. Perhaps, I no longer need dreams to access my memories. Instead, I can follow Jehovah where he leads, knowing that even in the midst of my worst memories I can find peace, rest.

But before I allow the seventh memory, the last memory, I want to take time to rehearse all that has come before, cherish what I've learned.

The first memory…my first day with Jehovah.

The second memory…Adam and me celebrating our union.

The third memory…my first encounter with Serpent.

The fourth memory…the weaver birds stealing our crops and our faith.

The fifth memory…finding Abel dead, losing Cain.

The sixth memory…the forbidden fruit and the knowledge of good and evil.

The memories have ranged from the glory of the Garden to the terrors of death. From the heights of waking on the

[17] *Who may ascend the mountain of the* LORD*? Who may stand in his holy place? The one who has clean hands and a pure heart, who does not trust in an idol or swear by a false god."* PSALM 24:3–4

morn of creation to the earth giving way beneath our feet. From freedom and a complete lack of shame to a flaming sword warning us that the Garden was no longer ours to tend. From the promise of life to the shadow of death. Yet, I see that each memory held hope, each pointed to a loving Abba who mourned with us, even sacrificed for our best good. I no longer fear where Jehovah takes me, for his mercy is great.[18]

I slow down my pace and utter an invitation, "I am ready for the seventh memory, my Abba. Take me where you will."

The seventh memory from Jehovah

We had just exited the Garden of Eden. Adam and I were stunned when we saw skins hanging from a bush with traces of dried blood on the undersides. We both knew that Jehovah himself had killed and then stripped these animals of their covering. Adam seemed resigned to wear them. As for me, shame came coursing through my veins, bursting out in anger.

"Adam, you can't expect me to wear this. I'd rather be cold than put on this! This bloody thing!"

"But Eve, you are shivering and almost naked. Your lips are turning blue."

"I want no part of them. It was too great a price for an innocent animal to pay."

"I tell you, you *will* wear them!"

"I'm going back into the Garden of Eden. It's warmer there…and I'm hungry."

"Suit yourself."

Adam threw a skin and a cold glance over his shoulders, before he froze in his steps and slowly turned around. Turning

[18] *"Let me fall into the hands of the* LORD, *for his mercy is very great; but do not let me fall into human hands."* 1 CHRONICLES 21:13

to see what Adam saw, I fell to the ground.
"Who are you?" I lowered my eyes, afraid.

I am God's messenger.

His voice echoed with the authority of a forest full of voices, while his presence stretched towards the heavens. Robed in a cloud, his face shone like the sun; his legs pulsated with tongues of fire. With arms streaming with light, he lifted a blazing sword over his head, thrusting his words into our souls...[19]

> The Satan bit the heel of man.[20] Those created sought
> to be Creator.[21] At the command of the Almighty,
> I, Jehovah's messenger, seal the Garden of Eden,
> never to be opened, until the entry of eternity, until
> creation's rightful order is restored! Holy is the Lord!

Seeing Adam beside me, I jumped into his arms, burying my head in his shoulder. I felt exposed—even more exposed than when I discovered I was naked. "Please, take me away from here," I begged.

Adam helped me to my feet. Both of us kept our eyes away from the messenger as Adam took the skin and put it over my shoulders. The bloody smell nauseated me, but I could no longer refuse. I couldn't deny the warmth.

Before we left, Adam and I both took one glance back. As if he knew our longing, the messenger rapidly swung the radiant sword from ground to sky to ground again, hiding our view of the entrance into the Garden and giving us our

---

[19] See REVELATION 10:1–4
[20] Satan in Hebrew is "Ha Satan," the opposer. "Bit the heel of man" is God's prediction in GENESIS 3:15
[21] "They exchanged the truth about God for a lie, and worshiped and served created things rather than the Creator—who is forever praised. Amen." ROMANS 1:25

last glimpse of pure light. As we walked away from our only home, I wept silently, knowing I would never be worthy of the Garden again.

As we faced the difficult years of adjusting to life after the Garden, the skins came to symbolize all that hurt us... Serpent, the forbidden fruit, the nakedness and shame. After we began to make our own clothing, I was anxious to be rid of the skins. I hid them away for a time, hopeful Adam wouldn't notice as he brought new skins to be used for various purposes. One day while Adam was out in the field, I burned them, silently praying the fire would burn away my shame, praying the wretched smell would blow away. When Adam returned, I had a tasty meal cooking, a stew with elk and root vegetables. I knew I was once again covering over my hurt, fear and shame. I knew that Adam might discover what I'd done and be angry or even feel rejected. I could not move on with the skins, so I chose to move on without them.

The Shelter

On the rest of the way to the shelter, the seventh memory gives me much to ponder, much to mourn. By the time I reach the hunting shelter and find it intact, I am overcome with sorrow and gratitude. Sorrow that there is yet another way that I turned my back on Jehovah, chose my way instead of his. Sorrow that I once again deceived my husband and even more so, deceived myself. Is it possible that of all the ways I sinned against Jehovah, that burning the skins was the most painful to him? Was I saying, "No Jehovah. You will not love me in my brokenness. Yes, you helped me cover my nakedness, but now I will cover myself. I want you, but in my own way." Was this born of the seed planted by the forbidden fruit?

But, I am also full of gratitude. I'm grateful to Jehovah for gently leading me to conviction. I'm grateful to Adam for putting a skin on my shoulders even when I didn't understand. How it must have pained Jehovah to kill a part of his creation to cover us. Yet without skins, what would we have slept in? What would have protected us on chilly nights, before we figured out how to make shelter, how to make fire to warm us? How could we have carried water? The skins saved us. "I should have been the one to sacrifice, my Abba,"[22] I whisper. "Please forgive me for despising your gift. Thank you for the seven memories...and for the skins."[23]

I undo the shelter's door and cautiously step aside in case any small animals have found their way in. Pulling open one of the windows to let in the afternoon light, I notice a pile of skins in the corner. I smile. *Thank you Jehovah.* I know from experience that spiders and small insects will join me for the night. I will wrap up tight and hope for the best.

With light flooding the shelter, I allow myself to turn and look around. Glancing in the corner, I catch a familiar sight. Not trusting my eyes, I move closer and find they do not lie. It is Abel's bow and arrows. *Cain has been here! Is he nearby?* Although Adam does not speak of such things, I'm fairly certain that he hasn't been here since the loss of our boys. Surely he would have brought these back for my safekeeping. More hurt surfaces...*my husband and two boys slept here together.*

Wiping away moisture gathering in the corners of my eyes, I stroke the bow, feel the tension in the string, and then hold it to my chest. *My son Abel used this bow.* I lift it to my

22 *"We love because he first loved us."* 1 JOHN 4:19
23 *"He was despised and rejected by mankind, a man of suffering and familiar with pain. Like one from whom people hide their faces, he was despised and we held him in low esteem."* ISAIAH 53:3

nose, hoping to catch a whiff of him. I put down the bow and collapse on the skins, burying my face in one of the hides. The losses that have only been partially mourned burst open and I weep until the sorrow is completely drained. A breeze blows through the partially open door, stirs up leaves and debris from the floor and caresses me. I turn over and allow myself the solitude of the moment. Soon it will be time to prepare to spend the night here alone.

Taking the skins outside, I look for a place with the last remaining sunlight. Adam taught me to soften skins by setting them in sunlight and then rubbing them with a rock. While they warm, I go inside and eat some dried meat, wanting to keep nausea at bay and knowing that I will soon need to get the food strapped up high in a tree a good distance away. When I finish eating, I bundle up the remaining meat and step outside. The sudden chill surprises me. Dark clouds overhead roll toward the shelter...*a storm is coming.*

I quickly gather the skins and bring them inside, along with the bundle of meat. I make a bed for myself of skins near Abel's bow and secure the window, not ready to lose the light. Suddenly chilled and weary from the long walk, I get in bed and wrap the skins tight around me. After I rest for a moment, I will tie up the food for the night. There is still time. The currents of sorrow rock me into a deep, dreamless sleep.

When I wake, the shelter is completely dark. Outside the wind is howling and tearing at the shelter like it might take it down. *How did I sleep through this?* I get up to close the window and secure the door, when I hear the noise I most dread. The howl of wolves is unmistakable, even over the wind's whine. First one wolf sings solo with a long, smooth *oooooo. He sings like the horned owl,* I think, as he wavers up and down from one note to a second, making the hairs on my neck stand on end. Other wolves join in. Their chorus has many strands—some eerily high pitched and others lower pitched—making their pack appear bigger than it is in reality. Adam once explained that this tactic protects their territory from other wolf packs.

Dread overcomes me. I didn't tie up the dried meat. It is neatly bound in a bundle of leaves, but Adam taught me well...*Bundling it is not enough Eve; the meat has to be high up and far from us.* Now it is too late; the wind has spread the scent and the wolves are nearby. On a whim, I hoist open the window and throw the bundle of meat as far as I can, and then immediately regret my decision. Am I drawing the wolves to me? Is it too much to ask Jehovah to protect me once again? One thing I know for sure, I will not, can not, walk outside the door. The wolves will have to come to me.

I feel my way around the perimeter to find Abel's bow and arrow. I strain to remember the little I have been taught of using them, but my jittery nerves obscure my thinking. I sit in the corner, pull skins over me, clutch the bow and arrow, and I wait. The plaintive wails of the wolves edge closer. A loud boom sounds from the sky, and light flashes from around the edges of the closed windows. The door shakes unsteadily as if it could fly open at any moment. My blood has turned cold and sluggish, chilling me to my core.

"Father, why have you brought me here?" I cry, not caring if the wolves hear. In that moment, my thoughts clear as if the dark mist hanging over me is finally disappating. The real attack isn't from wolves. It isn't the temptation of another man. It is from the evil one. And although I don't understand how, I know the same one who offered me evil Nephilim is behind this attack. He mocks my fear.

"Father, show me the way," I whisper. "Teach me your peace."

And then touching the rocks at the back of the shelter, I cry, "I call to you as my Rock, please save me."[24] As the words leave my mouth, Abel's song comes coursing back...

When wolves come near,
With threatening whines,
Do not fear,
For you are mine.

Sweet flock I embrace,
Don't forget your hiding place.

Did God give Abel these words for me? I sing the rest of the song, growing bolder with each verse...

Grazing sheep,
God has given,
Enjoy the pasture,
Where you're living.

Sweet flock I embrace,
Don't forget your watering place.

Hear my voice,
When you're alone,
Let me guide you,

[24] *"To you LORD, I call; you are my Rock, do not turn a deaf ear to me. For if you remain silent, I will be like those who go down to the pit."* PSALM 28:1

Direct you home.

Sweet flock I embrace,
Don't forget your feeding place.

Romp freely,
Within these grounds,
Then follow me,
Where grass abounds.

Sweet flock I embrace,
Don't forget your resting place.

When wolves come near,
With threatening whines,
Do not fear,
For you are mine.

Sweet flock I embrace,
Don't forget your hiding place.

Between my shoulders,[25]
Within my pen,
For you are mine,
And I am his.

Sweet flock for whom I long,
Don't forget where you belong.

Then I hear God's voice...

[25] *"About Benjamin he said: "Let the beloved of the Lord rest secure in him, for he shields him all day long, and the one the Lord loves rests between his shoulders."* DEUTERONOMY 33:12

*You are mine. You rest between my shoulders. Remember
the promise? The promise removes death's sting.*[26]

Then Jehovah surprises me by repeating Abel's words.

I long for you, Eve. Don't forget where you belong.

Is Jehovah calling me outside the protection of the hunting
shelter? As impossible as it seems, I know the answer to my
own question. I don't belong shivering in the corner of a dark
hunting shelter. Jehovah breathed himself into me. I stand
up, still trembling a little, and gently lay down the bow and
arrow. *These won't be needed.* I pause to place my hand over
my womb and speak out loud to my child, "Little one, don't
be afraid. We are his sheep and he will protect us. The evil
one fears you. One day your heel will strike a fatal blow to
his head."

Although I want to stride confidently towards the door,
I shimmy towards it in small spurts like a timid little mouse.
With each small move forward, I feel peace increase. It starts
as the tiniest whisper in my chest, almost like the first flutters
of the child I carry. Then it spreads into my stomach to
silence the butterflies circling within, flows downward to give
strength to my legs, and finally creeps up my neck, where it
shoots upwards to warm my cheeks.

By the time I open the door, I have no doubt that God
will be my shelter. Will he allow the wolves to charge me?
If he does, I know he will step in front of me. He will cover
me, just like he did with animal skins after we rebelled in
the Garden. He has told me that I will be the mother of the

[26] *"When the perishable has been clothed with the imperishable, and the mortal
with immortality, then the saying that is written will come true: 'Death has been
swallowed up in victory. "Where, O death, is your victory? Where, O death, is
your sting?'"* I CORINTHIANS 15:54-55

living, and unlike the evil one, Jehovah cannot lie.[27]

I undo the twine and loosen the door. Unexpectedly, it swings open. Although I still hear the wind, there is complete calm right beyond the door. As I step outside, I see no wolves. I still hear their moans and yelps, growing more frantic. I see only blackness.

I walk forward, arms outstretched. *I come to you Father.* Abruptly, a thorn pricks my outstretched finger. While I suck my finger, I reach out with my other hand. The light shifts enough for me to make out thick dark-green bushes closing me in…a hedge large enough to leave a small clearing in front of the shelter. A hedge that wasn't there before. *God shelters me with thorns.*

I walk around the circle, touching the hedge from time to time, not minding the thorn's pricks, even when another of them draws blood. Suddenly I see with startling clarity all that I have missed in my unbelief. It takes a few moments before I can even find a word.

"Lord, I cursed thorns…your creation. Is there a hidden blessing in pain that can redeem my darkest fears?"[28]

Beyond the hedge, the wolves continue to protest with barks of protest. One of them leaps high against the hedge and then cries out in pain. Following the bold one's lead, each tries its weight against the hedge. Moments later, the pack limps off whimpering.

I am perfectly sheltered.

Near the left side of the hedge, under the window, I notice a single skin, long and wide enough to make a bed. I kneel down and stroke the downy fur of a doe. The skin is pure white, the softest I have felt. Next to the skin, I see the

[27] *"God did this so that, by two unchangeable things in which it is impossible for God to lie, we who have fled to take hold of the hope set before us may be greatly encouraged."* HEBREWS 6:18

[28] *"And I will give you the treasures of darkness and hidden riches of secret places, that you may know that it is I, the* LORD, *the God of Israel, Who calls you by your name."* ISAIAH 45:3 (AMP)

packet of dried meat, untouched and ready to provide the nourishment I will need in the morning. Now I understand... I am not a thorn. I am the tender blossom, the bud that can only bloom protected by thorns.

Before I can rest, I have one last task. I reach up, and ignoring the nasty pricks, pull off a branch bursting with thorns. I walk back to the white skin, ease myself onto its creamy softness and lay the thorns on my chest. I don't need to protect myself with my loving Abba nearby. Rather, I entrust to my Father a long journey full of thorns.

Father, I see now that pain is part of your goodness.[29] *I thank you.*

As I drift towards sleep cocooned between skins and thorns, I watch in reverence as the violent wind tosses the treetops around me. I know this storm will pass, just as the wolves limped off in bitter defeat.[30] Beyond this tempest, there is a life to be lived. There is a child to be nurtured in my womb's soft warmth. There is one son to remember, a son buried in the dark earth but now nestled in his Abba's arms. There is another son, still living and still wandering, to be prayed over and entrusted to God. Before I leave I will take the golden eagle's feather and tuck it in the door of the shelter as a signal to Cain. *Fly home, my lost son.* And there is a husband, no doubt anxiously awaiting my return. That thought makes my heart warm with anticipation.

[29] *"Lord, by such things people live; and my spirit finds life in them too. You restored me to health and let me live. Surely it was for my benefit that I suffered such anguish. In your love you kept me from the pit of destruction; you have put all my sins behind your back."* ISAIAH 38:16-17
[30] *"When the storm has swept by, the wicked are gone, but the righteous stand firm forever."* PROVERBS 10:25

PART THREE

Rest

By the seventh day
God had finished the work he had been doing;
so…he rested from all his work.[1]

THE SPIRIT THAT HOVERS
OVER THE DARKNESS[2]

[1] GENESIS 2:2
[2] GENESIS 1:2

You will go out in joy and be led forth in peace;
Instead of the thornbush will grow the juniper,
and instead of briers the myrtle will grow.
This will be for the LORD's renown.[3]

ISAIAH, WHOSE NAME MEANS,
"THE LORD GIVES SALVATION"

[3] *from* ISAIAH 55:12–13

CHAPTER NINE
The Return

WHEN I ARRIVE HOME, IT IS LATE afternoon. From a distance, I see Adam sitting in front of our home carving a piece of wood. Deep in thought, he does not yet hear me approach. Something appetizing is cooking over a fire. My jaw aches and my mouth waters. I pause a short distance away, unsure of myself. The only communication we've had since we separated has consisted of flowers, meat, water and bread, so words are slow to come to mind. Did Jehovah take Adam on a journey similar to mine? Will Adam be ready to embrace the deep places of the heart? Surely he won't expect that we can pick up where we left off without acknowledging what has passed. This I cannot do. Although only six days have passed since we were last together, it seems like Jehovah has given new birth to creation—everything looks different, sounds different, feels different.

I squat for a moment behind some orange flowered olive bushes, not quite ready for Adam to see me. Although the small blossoms are fragrant and fragile, the olive green leaves are ragged edged. Cain once exclaimed, "Mother, they have teeth!" I pick off a cluster and lift it to my nose. Even the smallest actions can circle me back to one of the seven memories...*the way I distracted Adam when I didn't want to tell him about meeting with Serpent.*

Although these flowers have no briars, unlike the thorny myrtle branch I carry with me as a reminder of my time with Jehovah Shelter, my heart is pricked. This flowing of the past into the present, like a muddy stream joining a clear, untainted river, will no doubt happen often. I can only hope that further downstream, the two will become so one that the uncleanness won't be so noticeable. That the dirt will be flushed to the bottom, where it can fertilize plants and provide hiding places for the smaller fish.

Earlier, on the long walk home from the shelter, I counted back through the seven memories Jehovah gave. Seven memories and one miracle. Some of the memories brought joy...Jehovah rejoicing over me with singing. Adam and me delighting in our differences. Most brought pain...from the agony of losing the Garden to the curse of thorns and an adversary who wouldn't leave us alone. Before the memories, there was only darkness and a cloak that could cover me but never touch my sorrow. Now there is light creeping in, begging to flood the horizon. I stand up and start making my way to my husband.

Laying his tools aside, Adam stands up and puts his hands on his narrow hips in his man-like way. Lifting his eyes, he sees me. His face is bright and his steps are buoyant as he closes the gap between us. He smiles, seeking to reassure me with his eyes, yet he seems a little unsure, even a little shy, much like a day long ago when Jehovah first joined our hands. Yet as he nears, I see something different in his eyes, a new frontier to explore. I pray that he sees something as fresh as the morning dew in mine as well.

"Beautiful plant," he nods towards the myrtle I am carrying. "I've prepared a meal for us," he adds, holding out his hand. "I know there is much to say, but perhaps we could refresh ourselves first. You must be famished after your walk."

I nod, surprised that he knew when I would return. *Surely Jehovah prepared him.* I reach for his hand and enjoy the vitality it presses into mine. I have an urge to press my ribs against his, to reunite my rib and flesh with his, to restore the smallest bit of what we have lost. *There will be plenty of time.*

"Thank you for letting me know where you were with the arrow," he says as we walk towards our home. His voice is hoarse with emotion. "I would have never forgiven myself if anything happened to you. As soon as I saw the feathers I knew." Adam paused and smiled at his own logic. "It all made sense. After all, that is where you knew Jehovah was calling you from the beginning...before I insisted that I be the one to leave."

This is so uncharacteristic of us. Adam talks and I simply listen. He motions to the skin he has carefully laid on the ground by the flowers blooming by our home.

Adam glances at my bounty. "Would you like help planting that before we eat?" Again, I nod. Adam doesn't seem to notice that I haven't said a word.

Together we tenderly take the myrtle blossom, bursting with buds and a healthy wad of root, and plant it in the ground, in a barren place where I can encourage it up the side of our house. I know it will produce thorns, but I say a silent prayer that it will also give us the glorious blossoms I've come to treasure.[4] After we both cleanse our hands, Adam resumes his preparations while I sit down and wait. Soon we are enjoying roasted rabbit and roots. My inhibitions seem to have disappeared. I greedily suck the bones and then lick my fingers wanting every little tasty morsel. We eat in silence, both full of our own experiences.

"It's good to be home. And good of you to prepare us this meal," I say.

"Jehovah provided. A big fat rabbit wandered nearby and waited patiently while I got my bow and arrow." Adam chuckled. "I just had enough time to prepare the meat before you arrived home."

"How did you know?"

Adam raises his brows and glances at me across his shoulder.

"When I would arrive," I add.

"I didn't find the arrow until the sun was low, so I moved as quickly as I could to the hunting shelter. It was well into the night when I arrived and the wind was moving tree limbs back and forth." Adam scratches his chin. "I was greeted by the strangest sight. I'm not sure you'll believe me. I don't know if I do."

"What did you see, Adam?" I lean in, curious.

"In front of the shelter there were three shining men who each carried weapons, like the messenger at the Garden. The light was blinding. I fell on my face in fear, remembering the angel with the sword who kept us from returning to the Garden. Then Jehovah told me to return home, that you were safe in his care. As I turned to leave, I saw Zayeb standing guard with the men. He sat erect, ears up, eyes alert, light

4 "...Do not be afraid, though briers and thorns are all around you and you live among scorpions..." EZEKIEL 2:6B

beaming around him. I wanted to run to him, but didn't dare. After I hiked through the night to get home, I fell into a deep sleep. I woke up wondering if it was all a dream, then the rabbit appeared."

For a moment I am too stunned to reply. Was there even more than I experienced? Did God send his angels to protect me?[5] Is it possible that Zayeb is alive?

"Zayeb?" I murmur, dumbfounded. Zayeb disappeared the day we found Abel. "Adam, I didn't see angels or Zayeb, but Jehovah surely protected me." Suddenly overwhelmed by the thought of that day, the day we found our lifeless son, I add, "I'm not sure where to begin."

For a long moment we are both alone with our thoughts. Then it is Adam who breaks the silence. "You can tell me more, later...when you are ready."

I give his hand a squeeze, thinking...*so this is how it is not to know what to say.*

"There's something else," Adam offered. "When I came home, there was a wolf dog here, a young female. She is asleep inside." Adam speeds up as he talks, nervous. "Although she's only been here for a short while, she has warmed right up to me. Like Jehovah wants to restore part of what we have lost. I have named her Chaya."[6]

I glance at the door just in time to see the dog poke her nose out.

"Hello, woman wolf, Chaya," I say, surprised to my core. I silently remind myself that wolves are not just foes; they can also be trusted friends.

"Come Chaya," Adam says, tenderly patting his leg and leaning forward.

175

[5] *"For he will command his angels concerning you to guard you in all your ways."* PSALM 91:11
[6] *Chaya, a Hebrew girl's name, means alive, living.*

With her tail between her legs, Chaya limps slowly outside and gingerly deposits herself at Adam's feet, where he fondly pushes his fingers through her splotchy fur.

"She's hurt," I wince, seeing a large raw cut on her right flank and noticing her tired, wistful eyes.

"I put some healing balm on her wound," Adam says. "I thought she could stay with you while I am in the fields. You can nurse her back to health and then I can slowly train her for our sheep."

In Adam's plea I see Abel's brown eyes lifted towards me, begging for a baby bird's life.

"She will need time to heal," I say, speaking not only of Chaya but also of us. "And her recovery may be slow."

"Perhaps she is the start of something good," Adam adds.

Seeing Adam's quick love for the dog, I say a small prayer for Chaya, beating back jealousy that Adam so easily embraces her and tends to her wounds. Then I remember my prayer at the spring in the ravine, after I survived the cruel attack in the cave...*Lord may my eyes be full of light.*

"My heart is glad to be home with you," I say, pushing myself to be vulnerable, but surprised at how difficult it is. How clumsy I feel. How it seems like a risk to be the first to admit that the time apart has been difficult. Fear is still in me. Fear that I'll never reach the deep places inside of Adam. I kneel down and extend my hand for the dog to sniff. She takes a whiff and then gives my hand a friendly lick.

"Chaya, may you bring life to this home. May you heal and run free." Blessing the dog is my way of giving consent to Adam. After Cain left and the dog disappeared, Adam kept vigil for days on end. Losing Zayeb was like being kicked in a gaping wound. Even worse, Adam didn't talk to me about it, lest I point out that the loss of the dog was nothing compared to the loss of our boys.

After we clean up the meal, Adam leads Chaya into a cage with a vessel of water.

"Nod's cage?" I ask, again surprised.

"I made it bigger," Adam explains. "Just to protect Chaya from any wild animals that come near while she is weak."

As Adam stands over the dog, reluctant to leave her, I touch his arm. "I'm glad you saw Zayeb. Even if it was a dream. Perhaps it is a sign that he will return."

"Or perhaps it means that Zayeb is with Abel," Adam counters sadly.

We go inside to our bed. Our losses are once again crowding around me, insisting on entrance—Chaya, the bird Abel found, Nod, the willow branch cage, Zayeb, the orange olive flowers…my two sons. Adam senses my need for his physical presence and turns on his side. I move in close to him and bend my knees to rest next to his, let the top of my feet touch his soles, press my chest against his back, with my lips next to his neck. Cuddled up against my husband, I wet his back with my tears until the rising and falling of his chest lulls me into a dreamless sleep. Sometime during the night, we roll away from each other, but when I wake, just as the sky starts to shift from darkness to light, our feet are still touching.

By the time I roll back towards Adam, he is awake, his head on one elbow, watching me. "How did you rest?" he says, reaching out to touch my hair. "I've been awake for a while."

"Couldn't sleep?" I ask, yawning.

"I woke up thinking of the times I slept away from you," he says, his voice husky. "Like when I climbed up in the tree and dozed off. I blamed you for shutting me out with your grief, when I was the one who shut you out."

Then in the way I always find so endearing, Adam sits up, crosses his legs and stretches, reaching his long arms over his head. Even the tufts of dark hair under each of his arms are a welcome sight. He crosses his arms and sighs. "When you were gone, I felt divided from my own flesh, like I could no longer see around me." Then acknowledging my weeping in the night, he adds, "I know I've hurt you."

I nod and swallow. My hurt runs deeper than Adam knows. Although my throat is dry, my eyes are welling up again. I get up, get a drink of water and return to Adam's side, remembering my prayer...*thank you, Jehovah, that even after my sin, you find a way to cover.*

Just as it cost Jehovah the skin of an animal to forgive me, letting go will not come easily. Then I remember my other prayer at the ravine, as I brushed my lips with the feather of a golden eagle...*please help your words to be mine.*

"I forgive," I say, breaking loose a trickle of forgiveness. Cain for killing Abel, Abel for the ways he provoked Cain, Adam for threatening to burn the cloak, and even Zayeb for deserting us. And then I realize I need to forgive Jehovah. Silently I pray...*Father, even though one day I'll understand you've always acted for our good, I forgive you for letting Cain choose evil, for not preventing him from killing Abel.* Then I hear Jehovah's prompting as clearly as if he whispered it in my ear.

Eve, will you forgive yourself?

Adam wipes away a single tear crisscrossing its way down my cheek. "Thank you, my beautiful one," he says simply.

"We should check on Chaya," I say. "And then would you like to walk and talk in the cool of the dawn? We could bring some fruit to eat." I know I am making my way around Jehovah's question. But forgiving myself will take time. It is as if every fiber within my body—muscle, tendons, skin and bones—holds the guilt of the fall.

Adam interrupts my thoughts, "I too would like to walk."

I smile, "Perhaps you should bring your bow...just in case another animal decides to lay his life before you." Throwing back my head, I laugh at my own humor.

Adam smiles at me with the smile I yearn for, but am not quite ready to trust.

After I ready myself and gather some fruit, he returns with the bow and arrows, a cloak for me and Chaya nestled into one of his arms. "I will leave her with some meat and water. She can stay in the house while we are gone."

I motion for Adam to put Chaya into my arms. I smile with the secret knowledge I will soon share with Adam that Chaya will have more than me to protect.

"So Jehovah has provided a dog, a female," I say. The thought of a she-dog protecting us encourages me, like I will have my own ezer. "Should we walk to the overlook?"

I stroke the dog's head and then nestle her into a blanket. "While we are out, I will look for something to use in a poultice for the dog's wound. I yearn for a glimpse of the morning sky. And, when you're ready, I would like to learn to use the bow."

Soon after we venture onto the path to the overlook,

Adam takes my hand. There is just enough light in the forest to walk, but it is still full of shadows. It is my turn to plunge into the deep waters that still stand between us.[7] *Fall towards him*, I urge myself. I give his hand a squeeze, feeling the strength of his grip.

"Do you remember the last thing Cain said to us before he left?" I know no other way to share than to go straight to the heart.

"Honestly, no. I was too angry to remember."

"Cain said that Jehovah had warned him. He wanted me to know that Jehovah had tried to stop him."

Adam is silent. The memory is beyond his grasp.

"Now I see that Cain was trying to protect my faith," I add. "Although he didn't have a shard of hope for himself, he didn't want me to feel deserted by God."[8]

I take a deep breath and continue.

"Even though he was consumed by darkness, there was light." I motion around us at the barely illuminated forest. "He wanted me to know that Jehovah had been there, wanting to give him a way out. Don't blame yourself for not remembering. Perhaps Cain gave these words for me alone."

Adam gives my hand a squeeze as a thank you for the grace. Then he stops both of us in our tracks. "Shhh...look in the thicket over there. A deer and her little one."

I crouch for a better look. They don't seem frightened by us. The little one follows his mother, pulling branches with his teeth to pick off the tender young leaves. The mother seems unguarded, but the little one stops occasionally and puts his ears up, looking for danger. *Your mother has trained you well.* My breath catches in my throat. If only I had prepared

---

[7] *"The purposes of a person's heart are deep waters, but one who has insight draws them out."* PROVERBS 20:5

[8] *"We are foreigners and strangers in your sight, as were all our ancestors. Our days on earth are like a shadow, without hope."* I CHRONICLES 29:15

my boys better. *Cain and Abel*.

I stand up, sending the deer deeper into the thicket. When we start walking again, I'm grateful for silence.

"Do you remember when God gave us the skins?" I finally ask.

"How could I forget? He showed us compassion."[9]

"I hated the bloody smell. It saddened me to think that an animal had to be killed and skinned so that I could be warm. I've never told you this, Adam, but I burned those skins one day when you were out hunting. I sought to deceive you. Please forgive me."

"I noticed they were gone, but thought it best to say nothing." I don't hear even a trace of judgment in his voice.

"We've built a life on saying nothing," I remark, wanting to speak truth even if it hurts. I inhale the cool morning air, savoring its crisp, clean smell and continue. "I prayed that the terrible smell of the burnt skins would be gone by the time you returned. But now I understand. Jehovah saw me clinging to fig leaves sewed together with a few twisted vines. He sacrificed for us when we should have sacrificed."[10] Thinking of the deer and her little one, I add, "How it must have pained Jehovah to kill his creation."

"Your tender heart humbles me, Eve."

"I did the same with Abel's death. God sought to comfort me, but allowing his presence could mean more pain. And I didn't think I could ever survive anything like that again… I'm sorry I didn't let you comfort me, Adam."

I look over to see tears rimming Adam's eyes, as light pushes through an open spot in the woods. The breeze brings a woodsy aroma. Adam once told me that each tree has its

181

[9] "*[H]e redeems your life from the pit, he surrounds you with grace and compassion,*" PSALM 103:4 (CJB)
[10] "*This is love: not that we loved God, but that he loved us and sent his Son as an atoning sacrifice for our sins.*" I JOHN 4:10

own scent and that it releases this scent at sunrise.

"Adam, I won't think less of you if I see you mourn." After the words slip out, I clap my hand over my mouth, surprised at my boldness.

Dropping the bow and arrow, Adam leans against a tree by the path and puts his head into his hands. Falling to his knees, he begins to cry, first softly and then loudly. I kneel before him and he pulls me close to him so that we can weep together. As our shoulders shake in unison, I feel his ribs pushing up against mine. After a few moments, I let my head move into the crook of his neck and inhale his scent, lifting my head slightly to rub my chin against his whiskered one. He lifts my face in his hands and gently kisses me, tears still running down his cheeks. The intimacy is almost more than I can bear.

"I will gather some herbs for the dog's wound," I say, sensing Adam's need for space. "I won't be far."

I walk on a little ahead praying that Jehovah will carry both of us between his shoulders. Help me to open up. I know of a slippery elm tree, and if I can find a dry branch, I can strip some gummy bark for a poultice. When I circle back, Adam is sitting on the ground. His brow is furled, but his face looks softer. I reach down a hand, and with a little help from his strong legs, hoist him to standing. He nods at the bark in my left hand, pleased. After he picks up his bow, we walk on towards the overlook.

"I was angry with you after I left," Adam says, pushing the words together as if he doesn't trust himself to continue if he pauses. He takes a deep breath and then continues more slowly. "I was angry with Cain, angry with Jehovah and angry with myself. I thought you might follow me and take all the blame as you've always done, and then when you didn't, I thought... 'Who is this woman to think she can live without me? She was made from me. I named her. She carries my rib.'"

"I see." His vehemence causes anger to snake up my spine. It hurts me that he talks about the rib like I stole it from him. With great difficulty I prevent myself from jabbing him with my elbow in his remaining ribs.

"My pride..." Adam starts and then sighs, finding it difficult to get the words out. "I thought like one whose head touches the clouds.[11] My pride held me captive and banished me from joy and gladness. The light left my eyes." He glances over at me and I see humility in his eyes. "Do you understand?"

I nod, thanking Jehovah that I kept quiet. *Keep talking, Adam*, I will silently.

"When I was alone with Jehovah in the Garden, he taught me how to protect you. After Cain killed Abel, I thought I had failed. Your grief reminded me of my weakness. I wanted you to stop grieving for you, but even more so for me."

"Now you humble me," I chide gently.

"Jehovah will help keep us on the right path," Adam replies. "And I promise to lead in a new way. A way that is more like Jehovah."

"And I will find a way to follow, to help."[12]

As we walk towards the overlook, I see a flash of pale yellow and brown right in the path of Adam's foot. A viper lifts its ugly horned head from a hole in the ground. Fear grips my chest, reminding me of the evil one's taunts.

"A snake, Adam. Right at your foot!" I yelp.

183

11 *"Though his pride reaches to the heavens and his head touches the clouds, he will perish forever, like his own dung; those who have seen him will say, 'Where is he?'"* JOB 20:6-7 (NIV 1984)

12 *"When the princes in Israel take the lead, when the people willingly offer themselves—praise the LORD!"* JUDGES 5:2

"Hold perfectly still," Adam whispers.

Setting his bow, Adam pulls back an arrow and puts it straight through the snake's head. With a swish of his yellow tail, the viper is dead. Adam steps on the snake's neck, removes his arrow and then takes the animal by its tail. He walks up to the edge and then throws it over the overlook. We find a rock to plop down on a safe distance from the edge. Although I am still trembling, the sun is well up over the horizon and dawn's colors linger, bathing us in light.

"You saved me from being bitten," Adam says finally, shaking his head.

"But you acted so quickly. You didn't even flinch."

"But I wouldn't have brought the bow without you. You see danger when my eyes are elsewhere."[13]

"How I wish I'd seen danger in the Garden," I sigh. I don't know what I want Adam to say. I know he cannot resolve my guilt.

Adam puts an arm around me and uses both hands to rub up and down my arms.

"Eve, you are so much stronger than you know. And you might surprise yourself how well you will do with the bow with a little practice." Then he pauses, "May I call you ezer again? There was a time when…"

"Of course you may," I interject. "I can't promise I won't ever give in to fear, but I will tell you the truth of what I see."

"Speaking of truth, I have something else to tell you." Adam takes his arms from around me and wraps them around his chest.

"Is it about Serpent?" I ask, suddenly afraid.

"Were you attacked by him while we were apart?" Adam

---

[13] *"The prudent see danger and take refuge, but the simple keep going and pay the penalty."* PROVERBS 22:3

asks. I nod slowly.

Adam takes a deep, sharp breath. "I was brought a woman in a dream…a naked woman. Something in me desired her and it terrified me that my heart could be so quickly led astray. I, I reached out for her, and then caught myself and fled. It was so real. I woke up afraid that I had betrayed you."

Even the thought of a naked woman in a dream pains me. I scoot away, just far enough that we no longer touch. It takes everything within me not to ask about the other woman, what she looked like, whether she said anything. I let the sun warm my face, calm me. For just a moment I consider not telling him about Nephilim, lest I turn his focus on me instead of his own temptation. But this would leave me vulnerable to Serpent's attack, so I speak, "I also encountered Serpent. He offered me a man." I pause to catch my breath. "He called him Nephilim. And I did long for his strength."

My shame feels so great, I wonder if Adam can hear my heart pounding.

"But then Jehovah showed me that Serpent's man intended to strip me of everything good. The evil one wanted me to believe that you had forsaken me, Adam. That you only cared about fighting thorns and weaver birds. When I cried out to Jehovah, he saved me."

Now, neither of us knows what to say. For a long time, we sit quietly, both with our own thoughts, both hurt by Serpent showing up with yet another forbidden fruit. Then I remember my second prayer from my journey to the shelter…*help me to listen for your instruction*. And just as quickly, I remember something Jehovah told me in the Garden when I asked him what it meant to be an ezer:

*Adam's sight is firmly planted straight ahead. He engages
one task and then moves to the next. It keeps him pushing
forward, eager to subdue the world around him. This is his
gift. But your sight ranges all around you. It is part of your
complexity, the mystery of being a woman. You see danger
whispering in the background that Adam doesn't notice.
Eve, being an ezer is a powerful calling. I AM your ezer.[14]*

Being an ezer in the Garden seemed so simple. It
meant supplementing Adam's focused view with my wider
perspective. Pointing out glories that he might miss, like the
jasmine that blooms only in the night, sending out white
stars on the base of long dew-drenched tubes shimmering
in the moonlight. Or pointing out that the comical moves
of certain birds were courtship dances, and then laughing
as Adam surprised me with an imitation, wildly flapping
his arms while holding large ferns, strutting around me and
swooping in to claim his partner. But can I be an ezer now?
After the Garden?

Then it occurs to me how difficult it must have been for
Adam to flee the vision of a woman with his sight planted
firmly ahead. When I ate the forbidden fruit in the Garden,
Adam watched, unable to protest or stop himself from joining
me. Remembering that Adam was the first to be humble this
morning, I sigh and push myself closer, so that our legs touch.
Just as he protects us from physical danger, I can help us cross
the currents of pain, fear and faithlessness swirling between
us. He reaches over and takes my hand.

"Thank you for telling me the truth," I say. Then digging
deep, I add, "I think we were vulnerable because we were

186

[14] *"Blessed are you, O Israel! Who is like you, a people saved by the
LORD? He is your shield and helper and your glorious sword. Your
enemies will cower before you, and you will trample down their high
places."* DEUTERONOMY 33:29 (NIV 1984)

apart. We need each other and Jehovah."

Then Adam glances at me, in the way he does when he has something to tell me, but is unsure whether he will proceed. My heart jumps at the thought of another confession. "What, my strong one? Was there more?"

"While I was away from you, missing you, I asked Jehovah for strength. Then he reminded me that he is our ezer, our helper. So I wrote him a song."

Adam's mention of a song opens my ears, and suddenly I hear birds in the forest behind us, whistling, chattering, warbling, cawing and crowing, like Jehovah himself prepares to accompany Adam's tune, to remind us that there is a way for light to overcome darkness.

"Would you sing it for me?"

Adam takes a deep breath and sings to the sun, sings to me, and most of all sings to Jehovah, overflowing with the authority of the firstborn of creation...

> Blessed are you Jehovah.
> Who is like you?
> And who are we?
> A people saved by you,
> Our ezer, Jehovah God.
>
> The snake lifts his head.
> But who is he?
> His threats are lies.
> He cowers before you,
> Our ezer, Jehovah God.

Those who wage war
Will be as nothing.
For our Ezer
Says do not fear
Our ezer, Jehovah God.

So we do not fear.
With his help
We will rejoice.
The Holy One,
Our ezer...Jehovah God.[15]

When we arrive home, Chaya is in a deep sleep. She hardly stirs when I sit beside her and lightly touch her neck, feeling for her heartbeat like I did with our children.

"Looks like she ate some of the meat," Adam muses. "And drank the water."

"I'll prepare a poultice," I say. Then noticing my husband's weary eyes, I add, "Why don't you rest?"

Adam settles himself onto the bed and is soon singing a different song...a wheezing, buzzing, clucking, growling crescendo of snores. *Ah, my husband, which animals do you imitate now?* I prepare the poultice by grinding slippery elm, dandelion and thyme and mixing it with the healing balm. I place it on Chaya's wound carefully. She whimpers a little... and then starts snoring.

"The snoring seems like a good sign," Adam whispers, still half asleep yet stirred by Chaya's whimpers.

"You would know!" I laugh.

We decide to wander down to the springs to enjoy the

---

[15] *Inspired by* DEUTERONOMY 33:29 *and* ISAIAH 41:10-20.

afternoon. When we arrive, a flood of nausea reminds me that I have news. But before we commit ourselves to the new life growing within, there is something more that is needed.

"What is your favorite memory from these springs?" I ask Adam.

"Hmmm," he hesitates. "When I would play here with the boys?" I think to myself that the far off longing in his eyes might break my heart.

"How about you?" he asks, not quite ready to circle back to his grief.

"Do you remember where we first consummated our relationship?"

"Oh yes," he says with a grin. "It was by the springs in the Garden of Eden."

One thing I love about Adam is how his singularity can refocus him with a few simple words. Our loss has moved out of his line of vision, at least for the moment.

"And what do you treasure most about that memory?" I ask playfully.

"Looking deeply into your eyes and seeing such trust. I felt that I had been given a gift like no other."

"After we left the Garden, we came here often...gave ourselves to each other," I add. "It was almost like we were in the Garden again."

I hold out my hand to Adam. He raises his eyebrows in question and then takes my hand and presses his lips to it. Then I lead him to the spot, the place where we often enjoyed our bond as husband and wife.

When I kneel, he follows my lead.

"I love you, Eve," he says huskily.

"I'm ready," I say, tracing his arm with my finger.

Our time together is refreshing, like two new creations have just emerged from the mist of the dawn.[16] When I look deeply into his eyes, I see the hope of a new world, of generations to come in spite of thorns, pain, sorrows and a snake bound to continue to chase us. And when Adam looks into my eyes, I seek to give the gift of complete favor, much as Jehovah gives to me.[17]

It seems that some larger drama is being acted out in our time together. As if the continuance of life hinges on us being able to love each other in our brokenness and our grief. As if our pushing past death to claim life will be our greatest struggle, but also our best gift. And Chaya…could she be a reminder from Jehovah that healing takes time and patience?

Afterwards, as we relax in the afternoon's glow, I take his hand and place it on my stomach. I then take his finger and trace my womb. Startled, he looks up at me with a question in his eyes. I nod and smile.

"Another child? Are you sure?"

"All the signs are there."

Adam rolls over so that he can lay his head on my stomach, as if he can hear the lifeblood of the child rushing to and fro.

"A little man?" Adam questions, with a grin.

"That would be a great gift. But would you mind if I asked Jehovah for a woman-child?" Then remembering my boys, I add, "Or a brother for Cain…and for Abel."

And then Adam does exactly what I hope he will do. He lifts me in his arms, stands up, and walks straight into the springs…the springs meant to nourish us in the valleys of our life together.[18]

[16] MARK 10:6-8
[17] "For his anger lasts only a moment, but his favor lasts a lifetime; weeping may stay for the night, but rejoicing comes in the morning." PSALM 30:5
[18] "I will make rivers flow on barren heights, and springs within the valleys. I will turn the desert into pools of water, and the parched ground into springs." ISAIAH 41:18

"The water is cold!" I protest, although both of us know that this is my desire as well as his. In order to consecrate this child to Jehovah, we must consecrate ourselves.

Adam can barely get out the words. "Thank you for another precious life. We offer ourselves to guide this child in your way, as you would have us do."

And then all three of us go under the water, Adam and I, and this new little one peacefully oblivious in the safety of my womb. We come up from the water sputtering. Laughing and weeping.[19] Mourning two sons. Celebrating new life.

"Now we must warm you two up and get something to eat." Adam retrieves the skin that was lying in the sunlight and wraps it around my shoulders.

"Let me lie here in the sun for a moment. The sun will warm me." And so I rest, naked and unashamed, letting the sun kiss my skin, my heart, my womb and even the tears which still stream down my face. And then I watch as Adam raises his arms up high and dances before the Lord.

After we dress and finish our dinner, Adam suggests that invite Jehovah to walk with us. Although we don't hear him or sense his immediate presence as we did in the Garden, we know with confidence that he is there. As the four of us walk together—Jehovah, Adam, me, and the new little one awaiting his or her own story—my heart is still full of Abel and Cain. I think my heart might break with sorrow and joy.

Then I hear Jehovah's whisper…

I haven't forgotten Cain.[20]

[19] *"…Blessed are you who weep now, for you will laugh."* LUKE 6:21
[20] *"Has God forgotten to be merciful? Has he in anger withheld his compassion?"* PSALM 77:9

I wait for the LORD
more than watchmen wait for the morning,
Put your hope in the LORD,
for with the LORD is unfailing love
and with him is full redemption.[1]

DAVID, MURDERER AND ADULTERER
MAN AFTER THE HEART OF JEHOVAH

[1] *From* PSALM 130:5–7

CHAPTER TEN

Redemption

S TANDING IN FRONT OF THE MYRTLE PLANT I put into the ground when I was barely pregnant, I inhale its pungent aroma, willing myself to remember its lessons. The night I slept outside the hunting shelter between a white doeskin and thorns already seems a distant memory, covered with the mist of time. Adam saw angelic guards and our wolfdog Zayeb posted to protect me, while I saw a hedge full of thorns. On most days, we are convinced that both of our recollections are true. But on days when our faith is weak, or the memories seem distant, we wonder whether either was true. I do know that when I awoke with the sun the next morning, the hedge was gone, and in place of the thorns on my chest was a full branch of budding myrtle, roots intact, a miracle in itself. When I brought it home and planted it, the myrtle took off, growing at a dizzying pace, almost as if it had a mind of its own, climbing up the side of the house and filling the air with its sweet aroma. To make sure I would remember what Jehovah taught me that night, I took to inspecting the myrtle for thorns and for growth daily, often pricking my fingers as I pruned the bush, a reminder that pain and beauty do thrive together.

But God gave me even more evidence. After a long, difficult labor that saw me writhing in pain, Adam finally cut the cord on a lusty new little boy, with a large cry and an equally large head, thus the difficulty pushing him out. Adam remarked that he hoped that one day his body would catch up with his head! Adam gave me the honor of naming him, and I pronounced his name to be Seth, meaning *granted*. I have no clear memory of this in all the excitement, but Adam says that my first words were, "God has granted me another child in place of Abel, since Cain killed him."[2] I can hardly imagine saying such a thing, but to have a little boy when I'm missing two boys so desperately is nothing short of miraculous.

I feel so blessed by Jehovah to be entrusted with another young man to raise. *Jehovah, thank you for granting us with life once again. May you help us learn from our errors with Cain and Abel. Teach us to raise Seth well.*

From the time Seth was born, I determined to teach him of Jehovah and his goodness. And I knew from my very first memories from Eden that the starting place of God's goodness was his creation. The only good that came from the transgression in the garden was that knowledge...the knowledge of good. And I was sure that if I didn't rehearse it daily, I would be in risk of losing it, of believing the evil one's lie that evil is stronger than good. So I established a nightly routine, a little clapping rhyme. Taking Seth's baby hands and pressing them together with the beat, I chant, first quickly and then more slowly until I finally lift his hands to my lips for a kiss...

God shines the light, and the morning is good.

[2] GENESIS 4:25

Light wakes the plants, and the flowers are good.
Plants kiss the earth, and the land is good.
Fish ride the waves, and the water says "Good!"
Birds sing in tune, and their songs sound good.
Husband hugs wife, thinking, "God is good."
Father tills the ground, and the food is good.
Mother rocks her son, and he is good.
Night whispers, "Rest!"
And God replies, "Good."
Good night my son.
God is good.

After Seth made his initial adjustment to eating and
sleeping, around the time he gave us his first sweet smile,
Adam planned the sacrifice to thank Jehovah for granting this
new life. After we had devoted Seth, we prepared a special
offering for our all of our boys—both the living and the dead.
Adam knew it was important to me to honor Abel and affirm
our faith that Cain was alive and well. To believe in the mark
Jehovah put on him to protect him. For both of us, the whole
ceremony was emotional. Streams of tears ran down our
faces, dripped from our noses and salted our tongues, as we
laid our hands on our son and prayed.

SETH IS NOW FOUR MONTHS OLD AND DELIGHTING
us every day with new attempts at talking, new mannerisms.
Already he is a very physical baby, up rocking on his knees
like he might just take off crawling at any moment. While
he takes his morning nap, I go outside to tend my flowers.
Seeing a large blossom, I reach towards the myrtle, thinking

I'll put the purplish red blossom in my hair. Instead, a nasty thorn pricks me.

"Ouch," I cry, and then thinking of my sleeping baby, whisper, "Yes my Abba, I remember well. The prick comes with the glorious smell."

Sucking my throbbing finger, I see something flash across my range of vision. Do my eyes play tricks on me? Is this an illusion—like the one of Abel sitting on the hill, his cloak billowing behind him—sent to taunt a love-weary mother? I look closer and will my eyes to tell me the truth. Coming over the knoll towards our home is a more grown-up Cain and Zayeb, our wolfhound.

"Cain!" I cry out! "Cain!"

Picking up the edge of my garment, I run to him, and without the slightest indication from him that this is what he wants, I wrap my arms around him and hold him tight, taking in his smell, kissing him on his red whiskered cheek.

"Mother, Mother..." he says, partially touched, partially embarrassed. "I'm here."

I note that he doesn't use the word home. A dagger starts twisting its way into my heart.[3] He isn't planning on staying.

"Cain, it's been so long. Look at you! You've changed so much." Right away I notice that Cain has a small jagged scar on the left side of his face. I am not ready to ask, not just yet.

"Indeed I have," he says with an authority tinged with sadness.

Zayeb wags his tail and pushes up against my leg, wanting acknowledgment as well.

"And you, Zayeb! We thought you were gone for good. Look at you boy!" I scratch his neck and he rolls over, seeking

[3] *See* LUKE 2:34-35

the same for his belly.

"Where's Father?" Cain asked.

"He's out laboring in the fields. We have a new field he's harvesting. There are still thorns to reckon with, but the results have been promising." I make a quick decision to let Adam introduce Chaya, who is with him at the field. "Do you want me to point the way?"

"No, no, I'll wait."

"Please sit down, Cain," I say, pointing to the stumps that surround our firepit. Thinking we need a neutral place to start, I ask, "So tell me how Zayeb came to be with you."

"Zayeb the persistent wolfdog," he answers with a boyish grin.

I still feel like I am seeing an apparition instead of my son in the flesh. I want to memorize every bit of him—from the new way he holds his head to the way his shoulders have broadened.

"After I left, I was full of remorse and grief. Although I knew what I'd done, part of me felt like it was some terrible nightmare that I could still wake from. And the last thing I needed was Abel's dog following me. Besides, I knew Zayeb was needed here for the flocks." Cain sighs and picks up a stick to stir the firepit, so he doesn't have to deliver all this eye to eye.

"Yes, son." The word son is sweet on my tongue, even if he is my wandering son. The temptation is there to argue that Zayeb was never just Abel's dog, he belonged to all of us, but I think better of it. *Don't minimize his pain, Eve.*

"I tried everything I knew to be rid of him. I led him to the field where the sheep graze and pointed the way home, repeatedly telling him 'Go home, Zayeb!' When he insisted on following me, I tried to lose him through various obstacles, crossing a river and climbing through a thicket, and yet he remained. I climbed up a steep hill made of large boulders and he spent the night down below crying and whining. Finally, in the early morning, I climbed back down, and there he was wagging his tail and barking at me. This time when I scaled the side of the hill, Zayeb followed me. Who knew that a wolfhound could climb rocks?"[4]

Cain laughs and scratches Zayeb's head. I am grateful for Zayeb's bond with Cain. *Jehovah, thank you for giving Cain a companion for his journey.*

"So the scar on your face?"

"Actually, that was from Zayeb as well. When he followed me up the hill, I squatted down to rebuke him eye to eye... 'Zayeb, you are determined to make me carry Abel with me!' Then Zayeb growled and snapped at me, catching me on the left cheek."

I am shocked. "Zayeb has always been such a gentle dog."

"I knew I deserved it and much more. I told him, 'Zayeb, go ahead and bite me again,' and offered the other cheek. Instead, he settled down and put his head on my feet, looking up to me with sad eyes. You can say that we made peace."

Looking at the dog, Cain takes on his special tender voice that I'm realizing is reserved just for the dog, "Isn't this true, Zayeb?"

My head is spinning...fresh anger with Cain for killing Abel, anger with Zayeb for biting Cain, yet gratitude to Zayeb for leading my son one step towards peace. I bite my lip so hard, I'm afraid that it will bleed.

[4] *Thanks to Craig Childs for his description of a wild dog in* The Animal Dialogues.

"I was so thankful you sent some healing balm with me, Mother. I knew what to do...with the wound that is... because of you. I washed it with the lye soap you sent and then bandaged it with the healing balm. I thought of you and how you ministered to me when I was hurt."

This might be the best Cain can do at expressing his affection for me, so I gently turn his head towards me and examine the scar. I long to minister to so many parts of him... the callouses on his feet, the dark circles under his eyes, signs of the restlessness that Jehovah predicted.

"It looks like it is healing well, son."

"Ever since that time, Zayeb has showed me only affection. I'm watching for a female wolfdog that I can raise to breed with him. Unless, that is," Cain adds nervously, "you want Zayeb to stay here."

Could Chaya and Zayeb parent pups? I smile at my son, "I don't think we could get him to stay if we wanted to. He's your dog now, Cain."

Seth begins to whimper, and then wail, ready to be picked up and have his milk. Surprise washes across Cain's face. "A new baby?"

"You have a new little brother, already four months old. Wait here." I am afraid that Cain will disappear as suddenly as he appeared.

After I attend to Seth's soiled garments, I bring him out to see Cain.

"Cain, meet your brother, Seth." It seems the most natural thing in the world to walk over and put Seth in his brother's arms. Yet it takes all the faith within me to entrust Seth to him. "Seth, this is your big brother Cain."

Seth looks up at Cain with trusting eyes and smiles.

"Well hello, Seth," Cain says, taking him and then awkwardly bouncing him on his knee. "He looks a lot like Abel."

"I see both of you in him…your eyes, Abel's hair." I am amazed that we can talk so casually about Abel. Like what happened didn't happen. But I know from my own experience, after my sin destroyed all I had in the Garden, that Cain needs compassion rather than judgment.[5] *Help me to treat him as you treated me, Lord.*

"So this explains why you've added on to the house. It looks good," Cain says, looking into the innocent eyes of his little brother.

"Yes, your father went right to work, once he knew I was pregnant again. Where you boys slept is now our sleeping place and Seth has a new room of his own, waiting for when he is old enough. "I pause and breathe in my son, silently praying for wisdom. "So what about you? Where have you been living, Cain?"

I long to know his story, yet don't want to push too hard, too fast. I see Cain's protectiveness of Seth, even though it makes him uncomfortable to hold him. I utter a silent prayer that they will know each other one day, somehow. I pray silently that Seth will give me a few moments with Cain before his hungry tummy tells him it is time to nurse.

"After I left, I couldn't imagine being far from you," Cain says. "So I made circles farther and farther away, sometimes visiting the hunting shelter after first making sure Father wasn't there, sometimes circling close to your home at night."

Again the words "your home" clatter around in my skull.

[5] *"Speak and act as those who are going to be judged by the law that gives freedom, because judgment without mercy will be shown to anyone who has not been merciful. Mercy triumphs over judgment!"* JAMES 2:12–13

"Eventually my circles became larger and larger as I got used to tending to myself. Zayeb became an excellent hunter, helping me catch large birds and rabbits. I made my own bow and arrow, using Abel's as a model."

"Thank you for leaving Abel's bow and arrow in the shelter," I say.

"Eventually, I found a place to settle and built my own home. It needs more work, but it's only a place to come back to on my journeys. Now I'm ready to circle to the east, find out what is there, what Jehovah wants to show me. There is some beautiful land to the east of Eden. But first, my feet brought me here."

I thrill a little to hear him even mention Jehovah. Seth starts to fuss a little in his arms, and Cain awkwardly brings him over.

"He wants his milk." I put my little finger in his mouth for him to suckle.

"I'll go find Father while you attend to him."

"Cain, will you stay for a time?" I am almost afraid to hear the answer.

"I'll stay overnight, but then I must go." The restlessness, the wanderlust in his eyes is painful to witness. If anything, it has only become greater since the day he left.

"You'll find your father in that direction." I point to the other side of our home from our old fields, the ones ravaged by birds. "You can't miss him."

As I nurse Seth, I rock and weep, remembering my first time nursing little Cain and stroking his red head. I remember his eyes of total trust. *Lord, did I fail him?* And now, it seems like so little has been said of what needs to be said. What I don't want to do is to heap accusation on him, drive him further away from Jehovah and from us. *Please give me the words, Jehovah. I commit Cain to you.*[6]

When Cain and Adam finally return, with Zayab and Chaya trotting alongside, neither says a word to me about what has transpired. Yet Cain's grin as he surveys the two dogs tells me that he is pleased. I feel sure Adam and Cain had quite a talk about the dogs and the new garden. I also guess that Adam had likely asked Cain the same questions I had. It is good to see Adam loosely throw an arm around Cain's shoulders for a moment and to see Cain smile at his father. The two dogs seem smitten with each other, chasing each other around. Chaya is feisty, nipping at Zayeb's ears, but Zayeb easily puts her in her place.

After a hearty dinner of elk stew and Cain asking numerous questions about how to build a house[7]—furniture is Adam's latest pursuit starting with the beds he built, one ready for Seth when he gets older and an even larger bed for us—the men, along with the two dogs, go outside to sit by the fire, as I minister to Seth inside. I crack the door so I can hear their conversation, knowing Adam won't be able to relate it to me with the detail I hunger for. As I nurse my son, I listen with the earnestness of a mother in the pains of labor, longing for her child's birth.

"Cain, I'm so glad you came," Adam starts.

"It's been good to be with you and Mother...and Seth." He smiles and reaches down to pat Chaya's head, "And you, girl."

"We wish you could stay longer."

"You know I can't stay, Father...remember the curse?"[8]

[6] *"Let your conversation be always full of grace, seasoned with salt, so that you may know how to answer everyone."* COLOSSIANS 4:6

[7] *Cain's interest as predicted by his future... "Cain made love with his wife, and she became pregnant and gave birth to Enoch. Cain was then building a city, and he named it after his son Enoch."* GENESIS 4:17

[8] GENESIS 4:11

"I've come to see curses in a different light, Cain," Adam says with a special tone of voice reserved for our children.

"What do you think Jehovah meant…when he said that I am under a curse, driven from the ground?"

"It seems to me that Jehovah had to withdraw his blessing on the ground you tend, because he could never bless ground that had received bloodshed. Perhaps a curse is really just an absence of a blessing.[9] There was no curse put on you Cain, just on your relationship to the ground."

Adam pauses for a bit and then adds softly, his voice emotional in a way only I would recognize, "And that's why you need to keep the ground moving under you."

"Will Jehovah never bless my life again?" Cain blurts out.

I want to rush outside and tell Cain how much Jehovah can still bless, and how he must turn the thorns into good, yet it is best to let Adam have this time with him.

"Removing his blessing from the ground doesn't prevent him from blessing you in other ways," Adam muses. "What I've learned is that this depends on me."

"What do you mean, Father?"

"Cain, your mother and I sinned against Jehovah in the biggest of ways in the Garden. He trusted us to follow one simple guideline and instead we chose our own way… Serpent's way."

"You mean not to eat the fruit of the tree of the knowledge of good and evil?"

"Yes, son. You remember correctly."

"Do you really believe a snake had that much power over you?"

"Serpent deceived us. But we had the power to choose

[9] *See John H. Walton's explanation in "Hebrew Corner 9: Curse and Bless" at koinonia: biblical-theological conversations for the community of Christ, www.koinoniablog.net.*

righteousness all along. You have the same power, Cain. Just because the evil one led you astray once does not determine the rest of your life. You can hand down a different legacy to those who follow after you."[10]

"How can you believe in me when I killed your son... my, my brother?" Cain cries out, finally expressing his heart's true fear.

There is a long silence as Adam gives Cain room to grieve. Knowing my husband, he is pushing back his own tears. Finally Adam says, "We grieve Abel every day, Cain, but there is hope, because we know he is with Jehovah. It is a different kind of pain to love you, long for you, yet not know where your wanderings have taken you, what hardships you're facing. Yet we believe that just as Seth signals good things ahead, Jehovah still has good in mind for you."

"You're sorry you had me..." Cain says. The jagged edge in his voice has the power to cut my heart in two.

"No, my son. To stop loving you would be deny our very nature."

My husband pauses again. Knowing Adam, I guess that he is reaching for some way for Cain to understand.

"It's like when a seed dies to give birth to a plant. Every fiber of the plant points back to the seed, yet the plant continually recreates itself, as if the old no longer matters.[11] My hope is that you can remember the good, yet grow beyond the hurt we passed down."

"There was much...good," Cain says slowly, his words somewhere between a statement and a question. "Which hurt do you refer to, Father?"

"In the Garden of Eden, the ground thrived under God's

[10] *"Who, then, are those who fear the* LORD*? He will instruct them in the ways they should choose. They will spend their days in prosperity, and their descendants will inherit the land."* PSALM 25:12–13

[11] *"Therefore if any person is [ingrafted] in Christ (the Messiah) he is a new creation (a new creature altogether); the old [previous moral and spiritual condition] has passed away. Behold, the fresh and new has come!"* 2 CORINTHIANS 5:17 (AMP)

protection. I simply tilled it and it produced wondrous bounties. I wish you could have seen the way the Garden swelled with color, texture and flavor. The smell alone was enough to make the mouth water. After my sin, my punishment was similar to yours. Jehovah withdrew his protection from the ground."

I marvel at Adam's voice, how it rises and falls, along with the story he tells. At points, his thoughts are so heavy with emotion, I hear his effort in pushing them towards Cain.

"It hurts to lose the ground," Cain says, following his father's vulnerability.

"We battled briars and thorns, but instead of accepting this from the Lord's hand, I let thorns steal my faith. I made you share the curse, by making you share the burden of the ground." Adam sounds like he could burst into tears. "It was a burden too heavy for you, son."[12]

"There was a time when I loved the ground," Cain starts.

"Yes, my son. And I'm so sorry that love has been taken from you. I'm sorry for how I hurt you."

Cain is silent, not understanding that his father's words are a call to forgive.

"Son, do you remember the year when the birds stole the crops?"

"How could I forget?"

"I did not consider the possibility that Jehovah allowed the birds to take our crop. Remember your prayer and how you felt Jehovah didn't answer?"

"I don't want to talk anymore."

"Cain, just a few more words, please."

"If you must."

[12] *"...the Lord! A God merciful and gracious, slow to anger, and abundant in loving-kindness and truth...forgiving iniquity and transgression and sin, but Who will by no means clear the guilty, visiting the iniquity of the fathers upon the children..."* EXODUS 34:6-7 (AMP)

"Jehovah did answer your prayer. That ground was worn out from our use. We had never rested it. Jehovah allowed the ground to go to weed so that we would need to till new ground, fresh ground. And my refusal to sacrifice that year made it even more difficult for Jehovah to bless me. Should he bless a child in rebellion?"

"Why are you telling me this, Father?"

"When Jehovah needs to withdraw a blessing, he looks for a way to give another.[13] We were banished from the only home we ever knew. But yet, God killed an animal, part of his good creation, to cover us with skins."

"I remember you telling me, when I was a child, that you were naked in the Garden of Eden...before the skins. Naked as in no garments?"

I smile at Cain's directness. He may be turning into a man, but I still hear the little boy who had the most probing questions.

"We didn't know the word, naked, until after we fell," Adam replies. "There was a freedom, a total lack of self-consciousness, but it wasn't just about not having clothing. There was no shame, guilt or regret."

"Maybe it's better I wasn't raised in Eden then!" Cain laughs, unable to move past the idea of no clothing. "But it would have made things interesting."

I wait until their laughter recedes and peek out of the door. Cain is leaning back with his arms crossed. I'm happy to see light in his eyes. Adam glances my way and nods, letting me know they are finished. I step outside and come around the back of Cain, loop my arms around his neck and whisper the words I long to say, "I love you, son."

13 ...*return to the Lord, your God, for He is gracious and merciful, slow to anger, and abounding in loving-kindness; and He revokes His sentence of evil [when His conditions are met]. Who knows but what He will turn, revoke your sentence...and leave a blessing behind Him [giving you the means with which to serve Him]...*" From JOEL 2:13-14 (AMP)

"I know you were inside listening," Cain says. "I saw the door was open."

My son still sees right through me.

"Ah Cain, you've always known me well...my firstborn son."

Cain yawns. "I'm quite tired. Where would you like me to sleep?"

This is my son's signal that he has had enough talk of Jehovah and curses and blessings. My anxious mind spins. *What is most important to tell him, Jehovah?*

"Cain, you can have Seth's bed, he is already asleep in ours. But there is something I would like to share."

Cain sighs softly. He knows he cannot hear Adam out and then refuse to hear what I have to say. As much as he wants the conversation over, he loves me. This I am sure of and it warms my heart. "Of course," he says.

"After you and Abel were gone, I couldn't sleep, I couldn't eat." Moisture gathers in the corners of my eyes as I speak.

Cain touches my shoulder and lets his hand linger for just a moment, before he pulls it away.

"So your father went away for a time, while I spent time with Jehovah. I was trying to understand why I felt so lost, like I couldn't breathe. Like your father, I had much regret."

"I never wanted to cause you such pain."

"It was more about me than you, Cain. What I did in the Garden. How you boys never could live there because of my choice."

"And my silence," Adam adds. "I had the commandment first."

My tongue feels heavy, as if the words wrap themselves

around it to weigh it down."The signs I saw that you were unhappy," I say. "Unhappy and yet disregarded. The ways I unknowingly compared the two of you. You and Abel."

Cain lifts his chin. "Mother, I alone am responsible for what I did."

"While your father and I were apart, Jehovah took me back through my most beautiful and my most painful memories. He taught me a truth I hope I'll never forget." I pause, waiting for Cain to give me permission to share.

It takes a long moment, but Cain finally mumbles, "What is that, Mother?"

"I learned that in the midst of my pain, even when it seemed I'd been cut off from all I loved, God wanted me to trust him, to believe he was speaking to me through the pain. Like God wanted his way of seeing things to flow through me."[14]

"I have to make my own way now."

"You and Zayeb," I remind him, silently thanking Jehovah.

"But what hope is there for someone who's been condemned to wander the earth?" Cain blurts out, looking down. "Someone who has some invisible mark of Jehovah on him?" The hopelessness in his voice crackles and pops around me, threatening to flare up and burn down the hope that has been so difficult to build.[15]

Adam finally answers. "After we sin against Jehovah, we receive our rightful punishment. Yet he never banishes us from his heart. Like when Zayeb bit you and then you adopted him as your dog. In a small way, you redeemed each other."[16]

208

[14] *"Praise be to…the Father of compassion and the God of all comfort."* 2 CORINTHIANS 1:3

[15] *The mighty man will become tinder and his work a spark; both will burn together, with no one to quench the fire."* ISAIAH 1:31

[16] *"Like water spilled on the ground, which cannot be recovered, so we must die. But that is not what God desires; rather, he devises ways so that a banished person does not remain banished from him."* 2 SAMUEL 14:14

Zayeb hears his name and stands up. First he lays his head on Cain's knee. Then he sits, lifts a paw to claw at Cain's leg, looking up at him with pleading eyes.

"Zayeb, the redemption wolfhound," Cain muses, as he strokes his head.

We all sit quietly as the remnants of our shame swirl above us like smoke and then disappear into the dark night.[17]

Adam clears his voice. "You know, Cain, I was alone with Jehovah for what seemed like an endless time before he brought me your mother. When we were together in the Garden of Eden, it was as though time disappeared. Time alone with Jehovah is not something to be feared."

"How can time be endless when it only takes us in one direction?" Cain muses. "Perhaps there is a way it always circles us back to the very beginning."

I am momentarily stunned by my son's insight.

"I pray you are right, my son," Adam replies. "I would like that."

I glance at my husband and see his face glowing.

"There is one more thing," Adam says with a smile. "I have a feeling that Zayeb may have left Chaya with a gift."

Seeing Cain's surprise, Adam continues, "She is in heat and when they were romping in the fields, I think they found each other, if you know what I mean." He laughs. "We may have pups coming."

Cain's face lights up. "How long would it take?"

"If I am right, I'm guessing she will deliver in two months or so. If she is pregnant, I'd like for you to have the best of the litter."

"I will wait to travel to the east until we know for sure.

[17] *Do not be afraid; you will not be put to shame. Do not fear disgrace; you will not be humiliated. You will forget the shame of your youth…"* ISAIAH 54:4A

Can you leave some kind of sign at the hunting shelter, so I'll know?" Then Cain goes to his pack and pulls out the eagle feather, smiling. "I found this and knew you wanted me home. Perhaps you can leave it for me at the shelter when you know Chaya is pregnant."

"Son, you'll need to wait until the dog finishes nursing to take a pup."

"I know, Father," he says, scratching Zayeb's head. "Look at *you,* big boy," Cain says. And catching each other's eyes, we all burst into laughter, which grows louder and louder, until we are all holding our sides with the pain and joy of it.

My heart is comforted. My son will not rest until he knows whether pups are coming. *Thank you, Jehovah, for giving Cain a reason to return to us.*

As we all stand, Adam awkwardly embraces Cain and gives his blessing, "If you ever want to start a flock of sheep, I will share my herd with you."

"How would a restless wanderer take care of sheep? But thank you, Father."

I will never forget Cain's words.

WE GINGERLY MOVE SETH BETWEEN US AND ADAM is quickly asleep. It is likely that when we wake in the morning, Cain and Zayeb will be gone. And so, I quietly get out of bed and go to Cain. There is one more calling I need to fulfill. I want to pray over my son. He has always been a sound sleeper. Adam used to joke that an entire herd of elephants could tromp by and Cain wouldn't ever know it. I kneel beside his bed and touch the hem of his garment with my hand and then begin to pray softly, believing that God has taught me everything I need to know how to petition for my son...

Jehovah Creator,
Thank you for Cain and the years you've given us with him. It seems a miracle to kneel beside him in prayer right now. Yet it grieves my heart to see him so lost. Thank you for not letting Cain walk alone by leading Zayeb to follow. Lift Cain up after his fall and minister to him, just as you've done for me.[18]

Jehovah, Giver of Living Water,
Thank you for teaching us the cost of rebellion, then offering us the water of life. Even now, I know my son suffers due to his sin, and yet you haven't forgotten him—you yearn for him to walk with you. Remind Cain of his early days at the springs, and how you are the source of all good things.[19]

Jehovah Shepherd,
Thank you for remaining after I hid from you in the garden. In your mercy, you nudged my fears into the light and brought me into your pen, as a sheep needing your protection. Now I ask you to semember Cain not just in light of his sin, but in light of your goodness. Search for him, shepherd him and then carry him forever.[20]

Jehovah Provider,
Thank you for the ways you used Cain's love for the soil to help provide for our family. Now help Cain to learn the better sacrifice, of his will.[21] I pray one day, in your mercy,

---

[18] Read ISAIAH 40:28-31
[19] "...but whoever drinks the water I give them will never thirst. Indeed, the water I give them will become in them a spring of water welling up to eternal life." JOHN 4:14
[20] "Save Your people and bless Your heritage; nourish and shepherd them and carry them forever." PSALM 28:9 (AMP)
[21] See 1 SAMUEL 15:22

you'll provide Cain the good gifts of a wife and children who fear you. Preserve his spirit as he sees the way you provide.[22]

Jehovah, my Covering
I pray now that you will cover Cain. Please whisper to him in the night. Remove the pride that still reigns there. I entrust Cain's wandering to you, even as it takes him far from us, knowing that you alone can cover him.[23]

I pause as the tears begin to flow more rapidly. Sitting here beside my firstborn Cain, I know I am being called to the altar not just to pray for my son, but also to sacrifice my own selfish will...

Jehovah Shelter
My son Cain is a gift from you, even though the evil one incited him against his brother. I forgive Cain for taking away Abel as you have forgiven me. Please teach Cain that you are his only shelter. Please help him to learn that there is redemption for those who wander. Hide him in the secret place only you know. Whisper to him in the night, reminding him to cry out to you."[24]

Feeling a burden lifting off my soul, I go on to softly tell Cain the whole story of the banishment and how I burned the skins. I tell him of my night at the shelter and how Adam saw Zayeb standing guard. I hope against all hope that Cain is secretly listening, just pretending to still be asleep. But I know the story is worth the telling whether he remembers it or not.

Then weary, and sensing Jehovah's urging once again, I

[22] *Inspired by* JOB 10:12 (AMP)
[23] *"But let all those who take refuge* and *put their trust in You rejoice; let them ever sing* and *shout for joy, because You make a covering over them* and *defend them..."* PSALM 5:11 (AMP)
[24] *"For in the day of trouble He will hide me in his shelter; in the secret place of his tent will He hide me; He will set me high upon a rock."* PSALM 27:5 (AMP)

go and fetch Abel's cloak. After Adam brought it back to me, I folded it away, keeping it in a special place where it could never be lost. And so I take the very cloak that ministered to me when I needed a way to keep the pain from destroying me, the cloak that Adam took with him as a reminder of his son, and most of all the cloak that still carries my son's essence— and I lay it over Cain as a covering of blood, knowing that it was made from the skin of an animal. *Jehovah, Abba, please help Cain to accept this gift.*

As I put my hand on his back one last time, feeling his heartbeat, I could swear that his veins course into mine. I kiss my hand and place it on his cheek. I whisper, "I love you, son."

And knowing with confidence that Abel is rejoicing in the presence of Jehovah, having forgiven his brother, and even longing to see him again, I say…

"Abel would want you to have this."

Blessed is the one whom God corrects;
so do not despise the discipline of the Almighty.
For he wounds, but he also binds up...
From six calamities he will rescue you;
In seven no harm will touch you.[1]

ELIPHAZ, FRIEND OF JOB THE SUFFERER

[1] JOB 5:17-19

CHAPTER ELEVEN

Eve's Song

J ust twelve months after Seth was born, the Lord again intervened, this time bringing a woman child. We named her Taleh, or as Adam nicknamed her, "my little lamb."[2] While Taleh jostled around in my womb, Adam sang songs over her and from her very first minutes, his voice calmed her. She knew her earthly Abba. The easiest of four children to deliver, she slid out with three pushes. Did Jehovah favor me with an easier delivery to comfort me after the immense pain with Seth? Although Seth's head came out shaped like a yellow squash, longer than it was round, Taleh's head emerged perfectly round. As we cleaned her from the travails of birth, Adam and I marveled at her dark brown curls and pink cheeks. *Beauty is not enough, my child. Jehovah, help her to grow into a woman who walks securely before you.*

Seth was just beginning to toddle around on two legs when Taleh was born. From the very first day, he was protective of his little hazel-eyed sister. When she cried, and I didn't attend to her quickly, he pulled on my garment and pointed towards her, jabbering his displeasure. All I can make out is his word for Taleh, learned from Adam, "wamb."

There is no need for Seth to fetch me when Adam is

---

[2] *Taleh is Hebrew for lamb.*

around. Her urgent cries, so different from those of the boys, cause Adam to spring into action. I thank Jehovah for Adam's attentiveness because taking care of an ever-active little boy and an infant is a whirlwind of tasks. Needing to give my milk to Taleh (and not ready to juggle two at the breast), we weaned Seth onto goat's milk. He surprised us by taking to it greedily, slurping it from the vessel Adam fashioned from a piece of wood, smoothed with sand held in a small piece of skin, and then rubbed with the oil of the olive tree until it shone. After Seth spilled it all over himself (and us) again and again, Adam took some leaves and wrapped them tight around the cup, securing them with a cord, to fashion a small opening where the milk could flow. After I told Adam the cup was the most beautiful and useful thing we owned, he spent many hours fashioning a second cup that will be ready for Taleh when she weans from the breast.

After I nurse Taleh, I sing to her. The song is Seth's cue to climb up onto my lap next to her, cradling his cup. I sing for them both...

> Little lamb who made you?
> Gave you skin so fair?
> Tender eyes he gave you,
> Softest curly hair.
>
> Little lamb, I'll tell you.
> Your Abba loves so true.
> Jehovah God, he made you,
> Loves you through and though.

Little lamb who needs you?
Hears your every cry?
Wants to hold and love you?
Stop your every sigh.

Little lamb, I'll tell you,
Me and brothers three.
Papa, how he loves you,
Rocks you on his knee.

Little lamb who feeds you?
Strokes your gentle cheek?
Cares for you and holds you,
When it's milk you seek.

Little lamb, I'll tell you,
Mother loves to give.
Cares for you and loves you,
Stroking your sweet head.

Little lamb who made you?[3]
Gave you skin so fair?
Tender eyes he gave you,
Softest curly hair.

Little lamb, I'll tell you,
Your Abba loves so true.
Jehovah God, he made you,
Loves you through and through.

[3] *Inspired by William Blake's poem,* The Lamb.

As I sing, I point to Seth's skin, eyes, hair, ears, knees and cheeks. He touches Taleh's arm at *skin so fair*, and then points to his knee at *rocks you on his knee*, touches her cheek at *strokes your gentle cheek*, and to her mouth, *when it's milk you seek*, and then leans over and pats her head at *softest curly hair*, which is my signal to reach up and pat his. At the end of the song, he picks up his cup and resumes drinking. But once Taleh is tucked away for the night, and it is Seth's time, he always claps his hands and says "good" in his toddler drawl. He wants the creation rhyme...not only a reminder of God's goodness, but of his status as older brother.

Taleh was not the only new addition to our family. Sure enough, Chaya turned out to be pregnant and had a litter of two pups. The littlest one was robust at birth, but lost interest in nursing on his second day. Despite Adam doing everything he could to revive the pup, including offering goat's milk, the dog died, devastating both of us and bringing another round of grieving over Abel. We named him Zakai,[4] wrapped him carefully in white-tipped moss and buried him by Abel. I put a myrtle branch full of blossoms on his grave, picturing Zakai leaping and dancing with Abel, circled by the small bird Abel sought to revive as a boy, chirping in joy.

After we buried Zakai, Adam shook his head in sorrow and said, "Now Zayeb has lost a son as well."

The remaining pup grew strong quickly, and sure enough, four months after Adam took the eagle feather to the shelter, Cain came along with Zayeb, with Abel's cloak draped over his shoulders. My heart leapt with joy to see him with the cloak. *Does he remember that it was Abel's?* Adam had rehearsed a long speech of why Cain should take the remaining pup,

4 *Wolf in Hebrew.*

how it would be easier for us to find another mate for Chaya in the future, but he didn't need it. Cain was immediately smitten with the little she-wolf with her reddish face with dark brown muzzle, black back and light brown legs. All Cain could say was, "I'm sorry about Zakai." And then a few moments later, "Are you sure, Father?"

Adam smiled and then said, "It is better for you to have a little one. We have our hands full, and I'd rather wait for another pup for when the children are older."

"Then, my little beauty, I shall call you Yafah.[5]" Cain lifted her high in the air in exultation. When he lowered her to his face, she licked him right on the mouth.

"Ah, Cain, now you have a woman in your life," I jested, thinking...*Cain cannot begin to comprehend the sacrifice his father gives freely.*

Again Cain stayed one night, but he and Adam spent long hours discussing how to domesticate the little one, like getting the cub used to being touched all over her body including her ears, paws and inside her mouth, and how to correct her by crying out if she mouthed him too hard. So the time alone I longed for with my son never came. I had to remind myself that in helping Cain to care for the pup, Adam helped him open his heart.

As quickly as Cain came, he was off again, his heart set towards the east. I got up in the wee hours of the morning to make sure I was able to kiss my son's cheek one last time. As he strode away, Zayeb at his side and Yafah curled in a sling I fashioned, he never looked back. With tears running down my face, I prayed over my son until he was illuminated by the early morning light, bathed in gold and then lost from

[5] *Hebrew for beautiful.*

my sight once more. I reminded myself of the golden eagle feather in my possession, one that I would again put on the door of the hunting shelter when Jehovah nudged my heart. *Fly home once more, my lost son.*

TODAY, TALEH IS SEVEN MONTHS OLD. I STRAP HER on my chest with the sling I fashioned from soft cloth spun out of cotton. It is mid-morning. Time to hike to where we will offer a sacrifice to Jehovah in thanksgiving for Taleh and commit her journey to him.

"Remind me again, Eve, why you want to go to that particular spot for the sacrifice?" Adam says as he hoists Seth onto his shoulders. He is referring to the place where we found Abel with his life-breath gone. "How long has it been?"

"I haven't been there since Jehovah himself took me there." I look him in the eyes and smile, to convince him, and convince myself, that I am ready.

"Eve, remember that Abel is not there, he is with Jehovah," he chides gently. "Are you sure you want to give thanks for life at a place of death?"

I reach up and touch my heart as if to say...*trust me, Adam.* I know Adam can't understand how loss buries itself into a mother's soul. How I have two hearts instead of one—the heart that is fully present, fully in love with my two new little ones and my wandering son, and the other heart that only knows the weight of sorrow, that cannot possibly be set free until it is reunited with the child it yearns for.

He shrugs. "Do we have everything?"

I check my bag. I have pieces of clean cloth lined with soft mosses for Taleh's bottom. I've packed a lunch for the rest of us, including goat's milk for Seth. He has a lusty appetite and little patience when it comes to eating.

As we walk up the hill that looks down on the field, the morning sun caresses us. A soft breeze blows, kissing the drops of sweat on my brow from carrying a skin of water and Taleh, who is quickly acquiring chubby arms and legs. Seth holds tight to his father's hair. A young goat is on a rope and follows along innocently, intent on staying by Adam's side. This is the time of year when the ground is dry, so the going is easy.

I glance at my husband. "Thank you, Adam, for choosing a goat." Having lost two sons, I don't feel prepared to offer a lamb for Taleh, our little lamb. It rubs too close to the thought of something happening to her.

He nods and smiles.

When we reach the top of the hill, Seth points down into the valley and claps his hands in delight.

"A herd of elk," Adam says. "No doubt they are enjoying the plenteous grass at this time of year."

Seth starts trying to climb off Adam's shoulders, motioning at the elk.

"Looks like he wants down," I laugh.

Seth gets down on his arms and legs and walks like an elk. Then Seth points to Adam's beard and points to the elk, jabbering in his baby language.

"Why, he thinks the elk have beards like me," Adam laughs.

Seeing us laugh makes Seth laugh all the harder, and soon Taleh is gurgling and smiling in response. Seth starts running down the hill to catch the elk, and Adam springs after him, catching him by the back of his garment. "Hold on, little man!"

Lugging Seth back up the hill, Adam quips, more to himself than to Seth, "One day I'll explain to you why there is a division between you and them, but for now you must stay here."

Before we hike downhill to the field, we decide to spread a blanket to allow Taleh to nurse and Seth to have something to eat. Looking over the field, watching the elk slowly amble away, it strikes me that the river no longer seems to resemble a snake, even when the clouds pass overhead. After the children have been fed and Adam and I have eaten a few quick bites, we pack up all our goods and make the hike down to the field. My heart starts to beat hard. *Am I really ready for this? Was this a mistake?* Then I remember the whispers of the evil one the last time I made this journey...

Nothing but trouble! Do you really think you'll find what you're searching for? Abel isn't there. The All-Sufficient One won't be there. You should have thrown yourself over the edge of the cliff.

But I also remember Jehovah's rebuttal when I cried out to him...

Not your strength, Eve. Not your power. My strength.

As if he senses my internal battle, Adam begins to sing the song he first sang when I bounced Cain on my shoulder as we walked to the overlook for us to devote Cain to Jehovah, not thinking it might stir the deep waters of grief still left to be explored...

Come, let us bless the Lord,
Offering thanks to him.
He injures and heals,
He tears and binds up,
Lending hope of new birth.

Come, let us honor the Lord,
Offering thanks to him.
As the sun rises and sets,
He redeems and restores,[6]
Promising hope of new birth.

Come, let us praise the Lord,
Offering thanks to him.
As dawn kisses the west,
The spring rains appear,
Granting hope of new birth.

Come, let us praise the Lord,
Offering thanks to him.
Fruit of his love,
Through a firstborn lamb,
Growing hope of new birth.

Come, let us wait for the Lord,
Offering thanks to him.
Maker of heaven,
Creator of earth,
Proving hope of new birth.

[6] *"Come, let us return to the* LORD. *He has torn us to pieces but he will heal us; he has injured us but he will bind up our wounds. After two days he will revive us; on the third day he will restore us, that we may live in his presence."* HOSEA 6:1-2

But along with sorrow over my lost son Cain, the song also brings comfort. I think about how much the song predicted Jehovah's care of us within and outside the Garden. How Jehovah promised new birth in our very names, Adam for humankind, Eve for mother of the living, believing our seed could be the seed of many. But is the new birth only Taleh's? Or is it Adam and I who have been reborn, created anew?

I smile at Adam. "I love your song, but even more so, I love you." I reach over and give his elbow a squeeze.

His impish grin reminds me that this is the same man who came up behind me in the Garden, threw me over his shoulder, and then took off running, whooping at the top of his lungs. The same man, only purified by suffering.

As we trudge downhill towards Abel's grave, a silence descends on the four of us. Taleh is now asleep in the sling. Seth is draped over his father's head, snoozing until he gets jostled. He opens his sleepy eyes for a second, and then goes right back to sleep. Adam and I are out of words. When we find the marker, we lay down blankets for the children to finish their nap. Worried about the afternoon sun, Adam announces that he will put together a shelter that provides just enough shade for two small bodies.

"Do you mind if I go find a couple of branches?" he asks, concerned about whether I'm ready to be there alone.

"I'll stay here with the children," I say. "Thank you."

I look at the innocent goat staring at me with trust in his eyes. I feel deep regret that God's creation suffers due to our rebellion. I speak to him gently, as though he understands. "Thank you for giving yourself for my little Taleh. In offering yourself for her, you also redeem us in our unworthiness to receive such a gift."

The goat abruptly lowers himself to the ground and puts his head between its legs, and then dozes off, leaving me as the only one awake. A wave of grief comes, as the vision of all that Cain described, and all that I imagine, comes back.

Cain invites Abel out to the field. Abel innocently follows a short distance behind. Cain turns and hurls a rock straight at Abel's forehead, stunning him. Cain tackles Abel and they roll in the grass. Abel gains the advantage for a moment and pins Cain on his back, saying breathlessly, "You threw a rock at me on a day of sacrifice?" Then he glances at Cain's tunic and smiles, "Now you have the blood of the lamb on you." Cain roars and seizes Abel by the throat, thrusts him to the ground and shakes him until his body is limp. Cain releases his grip, backs away in horror, then turns on his heel and runs.

I cannot cry out with my babes sleeping next to me, but my chest squeezes like a fist. *If only you had apologized for throwing the rock, Cain. If only I had apologized to Adam for talking to the serpent without telling him.*

I picture the earth splitting apart beneath me, and then falling, falling, falling until I hit the ground hard. Remembering my little ones, and unwilling for them to be swallowed by the earth, I push the vision away and pull my daughter close enough to feel her breath rise and fall. Weary to the bones, I close my eyes, if only for a moment.

The next thing I know, Adam is nudging me awake, "Eve, Eve...where is Seth? I look around me confused. Taleh is snuggled into my side. The goat is lazily eating some grass, oblivious. But Seth, where is Seth?

"I couldn't have been asleep long!" I say, gently disengaging myself from my daughter. "I had a terrible vision of the boys. If only we had brought Chaya. She would have prevented him from wandering off."

"Seth, Seth!" Adam calls. Adam ties the goat, now awake and standing, to the bundle of sticks. "Eve, you take Taleh and circle to the right. I'll circle to the left."

"Adam, I'm frightened. I, I can't lose another child."

"Eve, we will find him," Adam says, although I see fear in his eyes.

With Taleh in my arms, I walk in a big circle to the right, calling for my son. The high grasses and bushes make it difficult to see. My heart beats so hard, I'd swear it isn't far from exiting my body and throwing itself on the ground. When we come back together, neither of us having found Seth, I feel faint.

Then I remember, "Adam, the elk. He wanted the elk."

"I'll get him," Adam says. "You wait here, in case he is asleep nearby, wakes up and calls for you."

Adam turns on his heels and runs. I stand up and scan all around me. Taleh begins to cry, feeling our fear, and I hold her tight, rocking back and forth to calm her and myself. Visions of the elk, or another wild animal, or even a snake finding Seth flood through my head. *How could I have fallen asleep?* Then I remember our Abba, the Shepherd who found me when I was lost and who, even now, carries me on his shoulders. The only one able to protect us from wolves, and even more, from the evil one's taunts.

I murmur to Taleh, "Regardless of what happens, we will go on, my child."

Just when I wonder if Seth is gone for good, I see Adam running towards me with a small body nestled against him. Adam is running so fast that Seth is bobbing up and down, his arms and legs flailing like the little lamb Adam brought out of the Garden.

When he reaches me, we clasp our children between us, christening them with our tears.

"He almost made it to the hill," Adam whispers.

The shadow of loss has once again passed over us, yet the very ground we stand on testifies that the bond of family is stronger than death. For just a moment I am tempted to insist on packing up everything, including the goat, and head back home. Yet, isn't finding Seth another gift to thank Jehovah for? I push away a single tear and look into Adam's eyes.

"We have a sacrifice to offer," Adam and I say in unison.

"Bone of my bones and flesh of my flesh," Adam says, as his eyes flicker with love and pride.

Seth leans over and puts a big open-mouthed kiss on my cheek and then holds his arms out to me. I hand Taleh to Adam and bring Seth to my chest in a long embrace. Adam kisses Taleh on top of her dark-brown curls.

Adam surprises me with what he says next. "I would like to do our sacrifice in a different way."

"What do you mean?"

"I think Jehovah would have us pray over Taleh and then put our hands on the goat and confess our shortcomings. When we are finished, we will drive the goat away. And no blood will be shed."[7]

227

[7] *'He is to lay both hands on the head of the live goat and confess over it all the wickedness and rebellion…and put them on the goat's head. He shall send the goat away into the wilderness…'* LEVITICUS 16:21

"Surely Jehovah has instructed your heart," I say, wiping my leaky eyes.

We kneel on our blanket. Laying a sun-weathered hand on Taleh's tender head, Adam utters a prayer for our daughter...

"Jehovah God, we bring our daughter, Taleh, before you today in thanksgiving. Although she is without sin, she unknowingly bears our losses and those of Cain and Abel. Although we desire to protect her, we know that her journey will have both beauty and thorns. Today, we commit her to you. Just as this goat represents how your goodness triumphs over our sins, we ask you to bring good out of all that is to come in her life. You alone are good."

Handing Taleh to me, Adam places his hands on the goat's head and confesses his sins...sins of being afraid and quiet, sins of selfish pride, sins of words that were needed that weren't spoken, sins of doubt, fear and rebellion against the Almighty.

When it comes my turn, Adam takes the children. I place my hands on the goat, half expecting him to kick me. Yet Jehovah himself quiets him, and he bows his head before me. I confess my disobedience and pride, hiding from Jehovah and Adam, favoring Abel, my distrust and anger toward Jehovah, burying my gift of being an ezer and hiding behind Abel's cloak. Most of all, I confess my sin in the Garden—the sin of grasping after what wasn't given as if all was owed to me.

When I lift my hands, it feels like a burden has lifted.

Adam takes the cord off the goat's neck and gives him a swift slap on the rump. Startled, the goat takes off running to who knows where. But this I know, Jehovah will not permit him near us again. Adam holds Seth by the neck of his garment. Sure enough, Seth is straining to run after the goat. We both laugh.

"One wanderer in the family is surely enough," I say.

After our sacrifice, my intention had been to ask Adam to take the children so I could have time alone at Abel's spot... the spot he exited this life and went to the next. Instead, I hand Seth to Adam, so that he has one child on each hip, and kneel in front of the marker. I lift a hand to my lips, press a kiss to it and then press it to the ground.

"I will never forget you, Abel. You know this," I say. "But as you live in the presence of Jehovah, you would want me to live with abandon, trusting Jehovah is nearby."

With the afternoon disappearing quickly, we decide to head home. When we reach the hill, the elk are back. So we lay down a blanket and sit there for a time watching the elk go down to the river for water. By the time we arrive back home, it is time to feed the children and put them down for the night. While I nurse Taleh, Adam attends to Seth. I smile as I hear Adam do his best to do the clapping rhyme.

After Taleh is sleeping soundly, I come outside. There is still a conversation that I know needs to be had.

I ask softly, "Can we talk?"

"Is something wrong?" Adam says, as he finishes preparing a fire for us to sit by. I plop down on one of the stumps and yawn. I am weary. I reach down and stroke Chaya's head. She wags her tail, pleased that we are home.

"Everything is right," I say. "The sacrifice was beautiful. I feel lighter. But still, so much has been lost."

"Is it Cain?" he asks, showing he knows me, oh so well.

"Do you remember the look on Cain's face when we found him after he killed Abel?" I finally say. "He looked so terrified.

When he came to visit, he seemed more self-assured." I burst into a cry of anguish. "Will Cain ever understand the dark place the evil one took him? That what Jehovah desired from him wasn't a matter of vegetables or meat, but a matter of the heart?[8] Why can't he say he is sorry? Is it because we never let him see our sorrow after the Garden?" I put my head in my hands and quietly weep.

When my grieving has run its course, Adam tenderly offers the sleeve of his garment to wipe my face. He reaches over and strokes my back, the way that Seth does sometimes when he notices that I am hurting, and then says, "Are you alone responsible to bring Cain back to Jehovah?"

"If I hadn't eaten the fruit, and then given it to you, Cain and Abel would have been raised in the Garden. Cain wouldn't have had to bear the brunt of the thorns." Guilt and shame course through my veins, "I should have seen the danger." I take a deep breath. "Cain wouldn't have killed Abel if it weren't for me."

Adam turns towards me and takes my hands. His eyes seek out mine and in his gaze I see love. "Does Jehovah hold himself responsible for your sin, Eve?"

I sigh. "No, of course not. He put the forbidden fruit in the Garden, but he didn't lead me to break the boundary. It was me. I desired what the evil one offered."[9]

Reaching up and brushing away a remnant of tears making a path down my face, Adam continues, "Not just you, Eve, it was both of us. And instead of forcing us to say we were sorry before we could fully understand what we had done, Jehovah gave us the skins. He covered us."

"We love Cain because Jehovah breathed love into us," I

[8] *For the kingdom of God is not a matter of eating and drinking, but of righteousness, peace and joy in the Holy Spirit.*" ROMANS 14:17
[9] *"but each person is tempted when they are dragged away by their own evil desire and enticed."* JAMES 1:14

say as peace rises up within me like a spring of fresh water, pushing its way upwards through parched ground.

"Cain will not wander alone," Adam says. "We can only pray that Cain will not despise Jehovah's discipline, but see it as evidence of love."

"Adam, giving Cain the dog," I say. "It was breathtaking."

Joy rises up in my chest and with it the urge to laugh. Why I would want to laugh when moments earlier I was full of despair, I am not sure.

Seeing mirth in my eyes, Adam asks, "Can I tell you one of my memories that came back to me while I was gone?"

"I would love that," I say.

"You awoke to Jehovah singing over you."

"My first memory from my time with Jehovah."

"The first thing I remember is laughter," Adam continued.

"Laughter?"

"I awoke and immediately sought to spring into action, jump in the air and touch the limb of a tree. But I didn't know how to use my hands or my feet quite yet. I couldn't get very high off the ground. And then I heard Jehovah laughing. He wasn't laughing at my antics. It was a laugh of pure, unfiltered joy in me. As we laughed together, I felt him in me and me in him—a glorious foolishness with no shame.

"Show me," I tease.

Adam stands up and acts like he is trying to reach a branch, all clumsy arms and legs. I begin to chuckle, first softly, putting a hand over my mouth to suppress the sound. Then Adam starts laughing, trying to muffle himself as well. Hands over our mouths, we laugh so hard that we cry. Our mirth is a joyous song, rising and falling.

Not wanting to lose the moment, I put a finger in front of my lips, "Shhhhh."

Adam whispers, "Have you ever noticed that weeping and laughing are brothers?"

"Brothers?" I whisper back.

"Weeping and laughing spring from the same place—a heart that refuses to be shut down.[10] When we laugh together, my heart feels free again."[11]

I take a deep breath and add, "I think Abel would be glad that we weep and laugh. He was such a wise soul."

Adam nods, stretches his long arm above him and then picks up a stick to stir the fire. "We can let it burn down from here. Would you like to pray together? We could lie on our backs and look at the stars."

Adam's prayer is short. I have only prayed for a short time, when I hear my husband making his own melody. *Ah Lord, you reserve this time for me alone.*

I am glad because another melody has been tugging at the edges of my consciousness begging to be sung. I sit up and grasp my knees. Although I don't know the words, I let my Abba guide my thoughts as I sing softly to him in cadence with the crackling of the dying flames.

> I will tell of your kindness,
> The deeds that praise you,
> For all you have done.
> Yes, for all the good,
> I say, Abba Father.

> I will tell of your love and mercy.

[10] *"...consider it pure joy, my brothers and sisters, whenever you face trials of many kinds, because you know that the testing of your faith produces perseverance."* JAMES 1:2-3

[11] *"The troubles of my heart have multiplied; free me from my anguish."* PSALM 25:17

In my distress, you saved me.
For the angels you sent,
Messengers of mercy,[12]
I praise, Abba Father.

I will tell of your mighty power,
Your love that never fails.
For breathing yourself,
Into my soul,
I boast, Abba Father.

I will tell of your forgiveness,
After I slipped and fell.
For redeeming me,
Through your grace,
I shout, Abba Father.

I will tell of my loving Abba,
Who knows my every care.
For walking with me,
In your goodness,
I sing, Abba Father.

Glancing at Adam, I see he has rolled over on to his side. I curl up next to Adam. But instead of waking him to roll over so I can cuddle with him from behind, as I am accustomed to, I scoot my back into the front of him. He yawns and then throws an arm around me, pulling me close. His chest is pressed to my back, his knees curled into mine, the soles of his feet against my arches, his chin snuggled into my neck. As he

[12] *"Yet if there is an angel at their side, a messenger, one out of a thousand, sent to tell them how to be upright, and he is gracious to that person and says to God, 'Spare them from going down to the pit'...let them be restored as in the days of their youth...they will see God's face and shout for joy."* JOB 33:23–26

exhales, I inhale. As he inhales, I exhale, feeling his heartbeat echo through my veins.

I pray to Jehovah that Adam's heart will run free, that he will leap like a young stag even when the hills are rugged.[13] I pray that I will be soft as the lilies, as righteous as my calling of being an ezer to my husband.[14]

And as I drift off to sleep I think of my four children, Abel, Cain, Seth and Taleh and the gifts each of them have brought to my life. I pray that Cain and Seth, and all my sons to come, will follow in their father's footsteps, knowing they will only run free in Jehovah.

Then my thoughts turn to Taleh and the daughters I feel sure will come after her. Will my daughters strive for Eden in some way they don't understand? Will they think they will only find Jehovah in their own perfection? I pray that they can learn to go to the deep waters in their own hearts, where their Abba dwells, to find peace.

Then feeling Adam draw me closer, I imagine Jehovah there with us, his mighty arms sheltering us. As sleeps washes over me, I am completely content.

When I stir in the early morning, barely awake, I roll over to find Adam gone. In his place is an arrow.

You have gone hunting, my husband.

I don't hear the children yet, so I invite sleep to return. I imagine myself floating on the river, the clouds moving over me, pointing my heart to the heavens.

As I drift, a dream comes...

I am sitting under the oak tree where Abel kept watch over his sheep, when I look up to see women coming to me,

[13] *"I run in the path of your commands, for you have set my heart free."* PSALM 119:32 (NIV1984)
[14] *"My beloved is mine and I am his; he browses among the lilies. Until the day breaks and the shadows flee, turn, my beloved, and be like a gazelle or like a young stag on the rugged hills."* SONG OF SONGS 2:16-17

women with coverings of every color and design imaginable. They are diverse—bone, skin, eyes, hair, color and size speak to their differences—yet all are magnificent. As they come closer, they sit in the grass, circling around me. We are all curious, yet there is no shame, no comparisons, no judgment...only anticipation. Their eyes speak of sorrow and joy, love and loss, longings deferred and longings fulfilled.

Instead of bringing me children to nurse, they bring me stories. Tales that beg to be told and heard. In the listening, I begin to understand...*It is neither your story, nor mine. Our stories are so one, I can no longer tell the difference.*

"Throw your hearts open wide," I urge them, as they nod their heads in agreement. "Sing your song without shame. For he wounds, but he also binds up. He allows calamity, but he alone is your rescue."

A woman with glistening brown skin and a smile as bright as the sun replies, "Surely Jehovah has instructed your heart."

The telling goes late into the night, yet darkness never comes. It seems as if our stories have the power to shed light into every crevice of our souls, turn the rough places into smooth and make way for goodness, hope and truth—not just in our own lives, but in the lives of all who will follow.[15] As I hear their stories, I laugh with them and cry with them, musing to myself....*Jehovah, the glory far exceeds the pain.*

THE FIRST PEEPS OF TALEH CALL ME OUT OF THE dream, yet the vision is so sweet I can hardly bear to let it go. It is then I notice the smell of lemongrass and thyme. Am I still dreaming? Then I hear Jehovah's song rise up from the ground, descend from the sky and surround me in its warmth.

[15] *"I will lead the blind by ways they have not known, along unfamiliar paths I will guide them; I will turn the darkness into light before them and make the rough places smooth. These are the things I will do; I will not forsake them."* ISAIAH 42:16

I lie there mesmerized, as Jehovah sings a song of rebirth, of
new creation...

> Nature prepares for the sound of my steps,
> Mighty trees stretch gnarled arms upward.
> Joyfully, they herald my presence.
> Flowers timidly open their buds
> For the season of singing.

> Blossoming vines burst with flavor,
> Flocks of birds break into chorus.
> The fig tree forms its fruit,[16]
> Ready to bestow a blessing
> On all who taste.

> Cooing of doves is heard in the mist,
> While the sheep climb to the peaks,
> Beckoning to see who will follow.
> Take your hand in mine,
> Walk with me.

> Look in my eyes and see my favor,
> Feel my heart beat in longing.
> Hear the whisper of my love.
> Do you see my face shining?
> With you alone in view?

> I betroth you to me in righteousness.
> I betroth you to me in faithfulness.
> I betroth you to me in justice and love.[17]

[16] "The fig tree forms its early fruit; the blossoming vines spread
their fragrance. Arise, come, my darling; my beautiful one, come with
me." SONG OF SONGS 2:13
[17] "I will betroth you to me forever; I will betroth you in righteousness and
justice, in love and compassion. I will betroth you in faithfulness, and you will
acknowledge the LORD." HOSEA 2:19-20

I will be your God,
And you shall know me.

After I had spoken, they spoke no more;
my words fell gently on their ears.
They waited for me as for showers
And drank in my words as the spring rain.[1]

FROM JOB'S FINAL DEFENSE

[1] JOB 29:22–23

Epilogue

S O MANY DAYS HAVE COME AND GONE. MY days have stretched longer than I could have ever imagined. Adam announced to me that we recently reached 700 years after the Garden. We are less sure of Adam's age, being that his time in the Garden of Eden before me is impossible to discern. He likes to say that he was 130 when Seth was born, to which I reply, "Ah, you are as old as the ages, my strong one." And he retorts, "And your love goes to the depths of creation, my ezer." To be sure, the desire to sing my story hasn't gone away. Rather it has only grown, matured by the perspective that comes from distance and space.

What do you need to know from a woman full of years? I can tell you that the years have passed more rapidly than you would imagine. The thorns continued. The losses were far from over. I birthed two children whose time on earth was limited to their time jostling in my womb, listening to our voices through the veil of my flesh. One was born with my cord around its neck. Another was born with a weak heart that refused to beat. One of my granddaughters lost a child to wild animals. One of my grandsons fell off a cliff and died instantly. Sickness came and took the life of some. The evil one continued to attack, seeking more deceptive methods. But none of these losses compared with the devastation of seeing the darkness grow to the point that some followed in the way of Cain and chose violence, even murder, over the knowledge of God.

Yet there was happiness. Seth never ceased to delight and worry me—he became my second wandering child. More than once did I run outside upon hearing my son's cries, to find that the only thing preventing him from getting away was Chaya holding his garment in her teeth. Five more times before the age of eight, he wandered off and was found by Chaya, who became his personal shepherd. Adam and I joked that in addition to Chaya, Seth most likely had a pack of invisible angels entrusted with keeping him alive. By the time Seth was ten, he knew the lay of the land better than I and was trying to get Adam to allow him to hunt on his own. One day Chaya took off after a deer and then Seth took off after Chaya. As Adam and I stood and laughed, we saw the deer circle back around with its wild eyes and panicked wide gait, followed by Chaya, running and barking furiously, and then Seth running with all his might, with his long arms outstretched, yelling, "Stop Chaya...you're scaring off the animals!" Seth brought a whole cadre of pets to our family, which he dutifully shared with the younger children. As Seth grew into a mighty man, a seeker of Jehovah, he lived up to his name...granted, a gift from God.

Taleh, the first of my daughters, was born feminine to the core. To her, everything was a baby, from the rabbits Seth brought home to the little doll I made for her from rags and fur, when she was just a toddler. Seeing my struggle to keep the doll clean, Adam carved another doll from soft wood that Taleh carried with her everywhere.

One day I asked Taleh if her baby had a name, and she took her thumb out of her mouth and declared solemnly, "Affra."[2]

Not sure if I heard correctly, I asked, "Affra, my love? You have named her Affra?"

And Taleh nodded, adding one more time in her toddler drawl, her eyes reprimanding me for asking a second time, "*My* Affra."

Taleh particularly liked to recreate my story of being made from the dust and Adam's rib and waking to Jehovah's song. I would find her kneeling, rubbing dirt all over the doll and singing a little tune that we couldn't decipher. Then she would lovingly wash Affra and feed her by putting her under her clothing, just like she saw me do with the little woman-child that came after her, a little red-headed beauty that favored Cain. We named our fifth child, and second daughter, Ayvah (although Adam liked to call her Eva after me).

As the firstborn daughter, Taleh grew up too quickly and was such a comfort to the children coming in rapid succession after her that they nicknamed her, "little mother." It didn't surprise us too much when Taleh and Seth announced their love. By the time she was 20 and he was 21, they had their first child, a little boy. Their union seemed right to Adam and me. After all, we were brother and sister as well as husband and wife—born of the same flesh and rib, brought to life with breath from the One who alone is goodness and redemption. Although our children looked to us for wisdom and loved to hear our stories, we could not determine their steps.

---

[2] *Hebrew for dust.*

Cain continued to wander and somehow in all his travels, he managed to become quite a builder of dwellings. His brothers and sisters begged him to build for them, but getting him to stay long enough to complete a project was a challenge. Just when I thought he might remain a single wanderer for a lifetime, he fell in love with a daughter of one of my daughters. She was a spirited child from the beginning and smitten equally by Cain and the idea of seeing new places and things. I worried for them. Yet, hope springs eternal.[3] I knew that this would just call for more prayer, more love, more sacrifice. Every so often, when Cain and his family would visit, Jehovah would pull back the curtain and I would see faith in my son. Although these moments were far between, I treasured them in my heart.

Seven hundred years after Eden, our seed has grown and spread as far as the imagination and beyond—the stories are too many to tell. One of my most sacred joys has been the growing companionship of women from my own lifeblood. My relationship with Adam is like a wellspring, less active in some seasons and overflowing in endless refreshment in others. There are times when the women can minister to me in ways Adam simply can't. My sons are like arrows in a sheath, sometimes nestled safely under my arms, but other times flung outward to conquer the harsh world around them. But my daughters are like the streams that cross the meadows to keep us all connected, their seed becoming little ones that have helped us grow to a clan with more members than I could possibly count, with a constant tide of children underfoot. The little ones never tire of hearing stories from the seven memories, clamoring onto my lap and saying...

[3] "Hope springs eternal in the human breast; Man never is, but always To be blessed; The soul, uneasy and confin'd from home; Rests and expatiates in a life to come." ALEXANDER POPE, "AN ESSAY ON MAN"

"Tell us about the thorns, Mother of All." Or, "tell us about the Shiny One. What did he say?" But then I wonder...will they see these as simply stories, embellished by the mother of all who live, or will they understand that they are life? I can only pray that my words will fall gently on their ears.

To be sure, I sense that it won't be too long before I am with Abel and with all who were released into the eternal before me. Sometimes my lost children come to me in my dreams, surrounded by pure light. Even though I am still bound by a physical body, their love bathes me, almost like I can inhale it, touch it, feed on it.

It is only through my dreams that I get a glimpse of what it was to walk with Jehovah in the Garden. The purity of his presence. The joy that emanated from him. Then I know that there is a part of me that can never give up on Eden. I wonder sometimes whether there is an angel still posted there with a flaming sword. Adam has a theory, one that he loves to expound on with the men, that Eden will be restored.[4] That all those with a fire within their hearts will taste the Garden again, only with no Serpent, no temptation, no death, and no tree of the knowledge of good and evil.

This thought warms my heart, because although the knowledge of good and evil has long departed, from time to time, something happens that floods back part of the visions. This can leave me reveling in the beauty of life or weeping rivers of tears, despairing that my rebellion in the Garden can never be undone.

In those times Adam likes to remind me, "Eve, my ezer, even if Jehovah doesn't restore the Garden, what he has for us will be absolutely perfect, because he is perfect."

[4] *[Eden Restored] Then the angel showed me the river of the water of life, as clear as crystal, flowing from the throne of God and of the Lamb."* REVELATION 22:1

And I reply, "And being with Jehovah will be more than enough."[5]

Yet I must admit, I not only long for Jehovah, and for my own flesh and blood, I also long for the women who still occasionally visit me in my dreams. The women of every color, shape and dimension who circle around me with stories as varied as the animals Adam named. When they come, I seek to memorize them—their features, the expressions on their faces, the way their arms and hands move gently in rhythm with their stories—although in truth, within a few short days of a dream, they begin to fade away. I sense that one day I will know them, sit with them and the stories will be... oh so marvelous. And although our tales will include times where we wondered if our sanity had blown away like a lone leaf in the wind, we will laugh. I like to believe that our levity will be like the laughter of Adam in his first moments on this earth, totally absent of shame.

Then, we will muse how our time on earth was like the early-morning mist that rises up and then disappears, or like the grasses that spring tender and green but are withered by the afternoon. Jehovah himself will sit with us, wiping away our tears and telling us all the ways he wove our stories together, bringing pure gold out of soul-wrenching tests and extending comfort when despair became a constant companion. He'll explain how he brought good out of each and every circumstance, showing us how good always has been and always will be stronger than evil.

When I express my sorrow over the legacy of sin I handed down to all who would follow me, Jehovah will say...

[5] *"The thief comes only in order to steal and kill and destroy. I came that they may have and enjoy life, and have it in abundance (to the full, till it overflows)."* JOHN 10::10 (AMP)

The way you came back to overcome the evil
one, Eve…it was absolutely breathtaking.

When you tell of a day when you fell hard or when loss made you wonder whether there was a reason to live, he will gently remind you of how you refused to give up, found a way to persevere. Then with all the love of the universe, he will look in your eyes and say,

You were glorious on that day.

Then the song of old will resonate as it did in the beginning, yet with the freshness of a spring rain after a long dry season…

To tell is to mourn,
To mourn is to accept.
But redemption comes
From God alone.

Born of Adam's rib
and the breath of God,
Daughter of creation,
Helpmate of man.

My song rises and falls.
As much as it gives
It takes away,
To rise once again.

But I wonder...
Is it my song or yours?
Or so one, we cannot
Tell the difference.

This I do know.
Adam proclaimed me,
Woman out of man,
Mother of life.

Yet I became to him,
And all to come...
Bearer of sin,
Firstborn of death.

Now there remains,
A song of Jehovah
Only I can sing,
Only he can witness.

Then I wonder,
Is it my song or yours?
Or so one, we cannot
Tell the difference.

Darkness is over the deep.
Chaos laughs, mocks,
Then the spirit commands
A new creation.

I cannot mistake
The love in his voice,
Echoing through my soul.
Embracing all after me.

So I must obey
As Jehovah whispers…
Sing your song, Eve.
Sing without shame!

Then I realize,
It is my song and yours.
Now so one, we cannot
Tell the difference.

Questions for Discussion

CHAPTER ONE – THE CLOAK

1. In Eve's beginning song (before Chapter One), she says, "Then I realize it is my song and yours." What part of her song do you relate to? Why does she need to tell her story and why do we need to listen?
2. Eve insulates herself from pain with a cloak. How do you insulate yourself from hurt, loss or pain?
3. Eve says that her regrets wash back like waves of the sea. Think of an unwanted heartache in your life. What regrets do you have?
4. Why do Adam and Eve argue over the cloak? What does Adam really want? What does Eve really want? Why can't they come together?
5. Adam calls Eve, "my ezer" (pronounced ē-zer), Hebrew for helper. In the earliest forms of the language, there is a word picture for ezer—a large eye and a person with a weapon, i.e. *the eye that sees the danger.*[6] Why might this nickname be significant?
6. Do you sense that God brought you to this book for a journey of your own? What question of yours might he want to answer?

[6] Ancient Hebrew Word Pictures, *Dr. Frank Seekin*

CHAPTER TWO – THE SONG

1. How do Adam and Eve grieve differently? Why is it difficult for Adam to understand Eve's grief? What does Adam need from Eve? Eve from Adam?
2. After Adam leaves, Eve says, "It seems with one hand I push Adam away, and with the other I seek to pull him back." Do you ever find yourself doing the same in your relationships? What form does it take?
3. Eve remembers how, right after Cain's death, she took off one day for the shelter, Adam following behind. Why does she throw rocks at the shelter? How do you relate to what transpires there?
4. Eve wonders whether giving Abel's clothing to Cain clothed him in shame. Is there anything in your past or present that brings you shame? Has it ever made you question God's love for you?
5. In Chapter Two, we have the first appearance of Satan in answer to Eve's question, "Who would know or care if I fell?" How do unanswered questions of the heart leave us vulnerable to Satan's attack?
6. What moved you most about the first memory? How does it symbolize what Eve is searching for? How does it resonate with you?

CHAPTER THREE – THE SPRINGS

1. Eve says that she buried some of her memories away in a "storehouse of dark earth." Yet the memories from the streams are all good memories. How do good memories prepare us for our more painful ones?
2. In Chapter Three, we see the beginning clues of the rivalry between Cain and Abel. How did Adam and Eve unknowingly fuel this? How do you see them handling it with grace?
3. Read Job 39 and then read back through Eve's song over her boys at the springs. What does her song say about the nature of being a boy? A man?
4. Re-read Jehovah's song before he brings Adam and Eve together. What evidence do you see that God created intimacy not just for good times, but for bad? Not just for in the Garden of Eden, but for after the Garden?
5. What do you see about God's gift of relationship from reading the second memory? About the differences between man and woman? How does our relational nature mirror the nature of God?
6. Think of a time when you were disappointed with God. How did you handle it? How are anger and mourning related? How can they point us to our real desires?

CHAPTER FOUR – THE SHEPHERD

1. It seems to Eve that the wolves' song is personal, a narration of her fall. How do unmourned losses make us vulnerable to Satan's attack?
2. What do you learn from Abel's song about having a relationship with God? Which of these verses would Jehovah sing to you today?
3. Do you think Adam and Eve made a mistake to give Cain and Abel separate duties? How do we unknowingly take on our parents' losses? Hand down our own losses to our children?
4. Go through the third memory and write down every way Satan attacks. How might these parallel ways he has attacked (or still attacks) you?
5. Why is it so significant that Eve decided not to tell Adam about the encounter with the serpent? Think of a time where you kept quiet when you needed to talk. Why does Satan want us to be silent?
6. At the end of the chapter, Eve asks God, "Why would you give me the desire to protect without the ability to carry it out?" Do you ever feel this way? How are we tempted to overcompensate for our helplessness?

CHAPTER FIVE – THE SACRIFICE

1. At the beginning of the chapter Eve wishes there was a simple way to release her accused heart. What does it mean to have an accused heart? How do you see it in Eve? In yourself?

2. Read Genesis 3:17-19. How does Eve's view of thorns evolve from the beginning to the end of the chapter? What thorns do you currently have in your life?

3. In the fourth memory, birds attack the family's garden. How does this impact Adam? Cain? Abel? Eve? How might this help explain the rivalry between Cain and Abel? In what ways do we unintentionally set up our own children to be rivals?

4. Within the crisis, we see Eve ministering to her family, but don't see her grieving her own loss. Do you routinely put others' need for comfort above your own? How might this come back to haunt you?

5. Eve chose to sacrifice. Adam chose not to sacrifice. And Eve chose for the boys. Do you agree with Eve's choice to sacrifice without Adam? How can a good thing like seeking to please God cause tension in a family?

6. When Eve asks Jehovah what sacrifice he would like, he says simply, "Come." Why is such a simple request from God so difficult? What can Eve teach us about trusting God?

CHAPTER SIX – THE SKINS

1. As Eve runs to the place Jehovah has called her, the evil one attacks. Eve says, "Shiny One's familiar though inaudible voice lures me toward self-pity and doubt as if there is comfort and resolution to be found in these feelings." What is the allure of self-pity and doubt?

2. Why does Eve need to go to "the very bit of earth where Abel left?" What does Eve realize that offers hope to you?

3. Read Hebrews 11:4. Why was Abel's sacrifice more pleasing to Jehovah? What did he understand that still evaded Cain?

4. Eve remembers the day when she found Abel dead, learned Cain was being banished, and felt a rift opening up between her and Adam—three losses in one. How is Eve's experience of tragedy similar to yours? Different from yours?

5. Eve senses that Jehovah's breath, the infusion of his nature, is chipping away at her "carefully built wall of denial." What areas of denial have been/are most difficult for you to overcome?

6. Eve has a dream in the night of being cast out of the Garden, remembering it as if she is hovering over top. What does she learn about God through her dream? What do the skins signify to us?

CHAPTER SEVEN – THE SHELTER

1. Although Cain killed Abel, Eve realizes that she can never stop loving him. How does the heart of a mother mirror the heart of God?
2. As Eve travels to the shelter she reminisces about how Adam helped Cain and Abel to build a hunting shelter and finds herself again in pain over her boys. When Jehovah tells her, "I have always covered you," her first response is anger. How does pain push us towards bitterness?
3. At the riverbed Eve discovers a mossy bed and asks, "Did you prepare this for me, Jehovah? For one that accuses you?" How does God's kindness lead us towards repentance? (See Romans 2:4.)
4. The sixth memory is Eve's most dreaded one—of falling in the Garden. What nuances did you see in Satan's attack? How does he discredit God? Create doubt? Prey on Eve's fears?
5. After the memory of evil, Eve says, "The thought of giving myself to Adam, as I did before the fruit, filled me with dread. I feared that with no coverings, Adam would look straight through me and see me for who I was..." How does sin compound our insecurity?
6. Re-read the knowledge of good and the knowledge of evil. What keys do you see in each to understanding God? Understanding grace? Understanding spiritual warfare?

CHAPTER EIGHT – THE STORM

1. Eve is reeling from her memory of the fall. Jehovah's words haunt her, "Where are you?" What do these words show about God's nature? When does God ask you the same question?

2. Satan wants Eve to believe that her vulnerability is a curse. She is tempted to believe that only Adam can save her. Do you ever wrestle with the illusion that another person can save you? What do you want to be saved from?

3. Eve relates a third encounter with the shiny one in the cave where he offered her a man named Nephilim. What about the memory shocked you?

4. The last attack in the cave is on Eve's beauty. What does Satan want Eve to believe? How can we overcome the self-doubt that can come from society's obsession with beauty? What do we need to surrender to find deliverance?

5. When the wolves come, Jehovah tells Eve, "Don't forget where you belong." She comments, "I don't belong shivering in the corner of a dark hunting shelter. Jehovah breathed himself into me." How can this same knowledge help you?

6. Sheltered between a white doeskin and a branch full of thorns as the storm roared about her, Eve muses, "Father, I see now that pain is part of your goodness." What did you learn from Eve's experience at the shelter?

CHAPTER NINE – THE RETURN

1. Coming together after a separation or conflict can be tricky. How did Adam and Eve show grace? Give the benefit of the doubt? Look to God for help?
2. When Adam and Eve walk in the forest, Eve comments, "We've built a life on saying nothing." What new growth do you see in their relationship since they've come back together? What can we learn?
3. Adam and Eve make confessions to each other, bringing up hurt and anger. Why is confession so messy? How does confession clear the way for healing in relationships?
4. Before Adam left, Eve asked him not to call her an ezer any more. Why was it so important for Eve to reclaim that calling? How does Adam make it easier for her? In what ways do you need to reclaim your calling?
5. After Adam and Eve come back together intimately, Eve says, "It seems as if the continuance of life hinges on us being able to love each other in our brokenness." What does this mean to you? How can you apply this to your life?
6. After they've restored their relationship, Eve tells Adam about the new child. Why was her timing important? What is significant about the way they celebrate?

CHAPTER TEN – THE REDEMPTION

1. Eve does a little clapping rhyme every night with Seth. Why is the knowledge of good so precious to Eve? What does the rhyme communicate?
2. When Cain returns, it is obvious he no longer considers their home his home. Eve says, "A dagger starts twisting its way into my heart." Why is this so difficult for Eve, even with all the pain Cain has brought?
3. Where does Eve find compassion for Cain? What does she keep in mind? What from the seven memories helps her?
4. After Cain goes to find Adam, Eve says, "As I nurse Seth I rock and weep, remembering my first time nursing little Cain and stroking his red head...Lord, did I fail him?" How difficult is it for you to give up regret? What are you learning?
5. How does Adam explain to Cain his changed relationship to the ground? How do you see Adam's redemption in the wisdom he offers his son? How can this apply to times you've felt rejected by God or others?
6. After the family goes to sleep, Eve fulfills a calling from Jehovah to pray over Cain. How does Eve live out her prayer in giving Cain Abel's cloak?

CHAPTER ELEVEN – EVE'S SONG

1. After Seth, Eve quickly has a little girl, Taleh (pronounced Tah-la). What has Eve learned about loving her children individually? How is she fostering a relationship between the two?

2. How does Adam flesh out God's heart when he gives Cain the remaining pup? How does he nudge Cain towards redemption?

3. After Seth wanders off, Eve says, "The shadow of loss has once again passed over us, yet the very ground we stand on testifies that the bond of family is stronger than death." How can you testify to this from your own life?

4. Adam suggests they lay their hands on a goat, confess their sins and send it into the wilderness. What does this symbolize? How do you see yourself in their confessions?

5. At the fire, Eve agonizes over Cain's inability to apologize for killing Abel and her fear that she caused all this pain. What conclusions do Adam and Eve reach? How can you apply this to your battles?

6. At the end of the chapter, Eve sings a song to Jehovah and then Jehovah sings a song to Eve. Do you sense a renewal of vows taking place? A celebration of covenant? What new meaning does Jehovah's song have now?

EPILOGUE

1. Taleh likes to take her doll, Affra, and rub her with dust. Read Psalm 103. Why is it so important for us to remember that we were created from dust?

2. Eve mentions that Seth and Taleh married, saying, "Their union seemed right to Adam and me. After all, we were brother and sister as well as husband and wife." Does this make sense to you? Do you have a different theory?

3. Eve tells about the dream of women surrounding her, women of "every shape, color and dimension," with "stories as varied as the animals Adam named." Why is it so important for us to tell each other our stories?

4. Eve ends her story with the song she sang at the beginning of the book. How does the song read differently now? What new meaning do you find here?

5. Go back through the three title pages for each of the three sections of the book, *Darkness Over the Deep, Re-Creation* and *Rest,* and the scriptures on each. What do these have to say about how God is working in your life?

6. Some Hebrew scholars believe that the Genesis account was written as a reminder to the Jews that the God of creation could still bring light from darkness (despite their failings). How has reading *Eve's Song* influenced your view of Adam and Eve? Of God?

Afterword

A WORD FROM THE AUTHOR, ROBIN WEIDNER

THERE IS AN OLD JEWISH LEGEND THAT GOD threw truth down from the heavens to the earth when he created man and woman—those who wouldn't always hold to the truth. When the angels questioned his judgment, God told them that he was planting truth as a seed. Now planted in the ground, truth would be able to grow and blossom on the earth. This story tugs at my heart because as much as I love truth, there is part of me, a part that I don't always like (in fact, sometimes that I outright hate), that participates in the fall that occurred in the first pages of the Bible. A part that struggles to hold on to truth and can be enticed by lies—lies that the evil one began assaulting me with from the time I was a young girl: *You'll never be enough. You need to be perfect. Who could ever accept you? No one will ever love you wholeheartedly.* I can't help but believe that God knew we would need truth embedded deep within our nature to help us to overcome these lies.

Yet I've also come to see that this first story, this planting of truth on the earth, holds enormous hope. After all, planting any kind of seed is an incredibly hopeful act. Seeds in their very nature demand hope. Hope that death will bring life. Hope for a small green shoot, then a stem, then leaves and a bud, until fruit appears...a beautiful flower, shade to rest under, something delicious to eat. Like seeds, stories have incredible redemptive power. Hope that letting go of oneself holds immense potential for good. Hope that the suffering we endure (the time we spend buried in the hard, dark earth) ultimately points toward the greater good God can and will bring as we surrender our stories to him. These are the truths I've sought to communicate through this biblical allegory.

As my dear friend Linda hinted at in the foreword, in many ways Eve's story is my story. And that explains why Eve often finds herself in tears. Over the last four years, I've found myself weeping in coffee shops, weeping late at night and in the early morning, as the story flowed through me (as God himself led me to deep places of my own losses) onto the screen of my computer. To this day, reading just one of these vignettes in these pages can bring me to tears and, at the same time, fill me with awe at the enduring nature of hope.

As I told one of my book groups as I choked back tears, "God's grace is breathtaking!" And one of my friends replied, with the rest of the women around the table nodding their heads vigorously in agreement, "Robin, be sure to put that in the book!" But yet, it is also a tale of joy. Like Eve, I've learned to laugh more, take myself less seriously and lean more heavily on God's grace.

In writing this allegory, my heart's desire has been to be true to the Bible. Because of this, I have spent uncountable hours looking up scriptures, doing searches on Bible Gateway and reading numerous books. In order to help you gain the full value of this allegory, I've reflected some of my use of scripture in the footnotes. They are at the bottom of the pages to make them accessible to you as you seek to take this study deeper. I believe with all my heart this is God's story. Inspiration came largely from the scriptures and prayer. For instance, when I set to write the temptation scene, I asked myself, "Where does Satan show the way he works most vividly in the scriptures?" My thoughts immediately went to Proverbs 5 to 7. If you study these chapters and then compare them to Eve's memory of the fall, you'll see many parallels.

Let me be clear that this is *not* an attempt to explain theologically all that happened, (matters the Bible is largely silent on like where Adam and Eve's children found mates, what led up to Cain killing Abel, or how long it took Adam to name all the animals), but rather to demonstrate truths about God, relationship, longing, mercy, grace, loss, sin, healing and much more. I had this sense that if God doesn't change his fundamental nature, which the Bible assures us of, that the way he loved his first son and daughter would be consistent with the way he's interacted with human beings throughout time. And, in fact, because Jesus perfectly reflected his Father (John 1:18), God's relationship with Adam and Eve would also reflect the way Jesus interacted with sinful, broken people. My hope was that if I could help dispel the shame of Adam and Eve's story, then others could better despise and ignore the shame of their own humanity, their own brokenness (see Hebrews 12:2 Amplified). That together, we could walk more securely.

So if I could, I'd like to take these final moments to urge you, "Sing your story without shame!" Form book groups, call a friend, plan special events, give the book to family members, do whatever you can to help others tell their stories. Because as we do, we show that God's planting of truth was far from being in vain.

Acknowledgements

It took over four years to wrote *Eve's Song*, counting the starts
and stops and the long process of letting other women read
and comment, which eventually turned into book groups
that read with me. With that I owe a huge debt of gratitude
to many who have helped form and shape this allegory. I
owe a special thank you to Mitch Temple, author of *The
Marriage Turnaround*, who helped me in the very early stages
of *Eve's Song* to make connections with a few publishers that
gave me critical feedback, that in turn led to some radical
shifts in direction. I also want to thank Mary Owens (coauthor of *Witness*), who immediately fell in love with the
story and encouraged me to keep believing, keep writing.
I also appreciate the savvy editing of my daughter, Rebekah
Weidner (also a writer), Linda Brumley—whose long years of
ministry to women made her a trusted advisor on the spiritual
journey reflected in these pages—and Maxine Heath, whose
long-time experience as an editor in the publishing industry
not only helped me to see my blind spots, but also validated
that God was doing something unique and powerful through
this project. At the last minute, Cindi Royce stepped in and
volunteered numerous hours of editing and companionship.
Before *Eve's Song* went to press three eagle-eyes (or
proofreaders as we like to call them) went through the book
line by line...thanks to Josh Weidner, Gina Poirier and Steve
Haberkorn.

The beauty of this book is due to some very special people
as well. Jeffrey Little donated the original painting that
makes the cover come alive. Jeff, from the very first words
I penned, I knew I would want your artwork on the cover.

Thank you. A big thank you to Shari Poirier (my niece, who is also an accomplished graphic designer) for spending many long hours perfecting the typography for the cover and the inside pages. Lastly, I want to thank Tara Lynn Price who took Shari's typography and made it into a functional book. Tara, I couldn't have done this without you.

Most of all, I'd like to thank my early readers. These women sat with me in book groups week after week and thrilled with me at all God was doing in each of their lives: Loy-Dee Ballejos, Melissa Breech, Darla Frank, Judy Gill, Stephanie Hailey, Monica Hollingsworth, Diane Parsons, Laurie O'Kelley, Caroline Sofarelli, Michelle Sutton, Carrie Uriguen, Tami Jo Van Ackern, Corrina Washington and Tina Williams. A special thank you to the women in my earliest *Eve's Song* book group in DeKalb, Illinois, who, due to Dave and I moving, never got past the middle of the book. You encouraged me to believe that I could write an allegory and opened wide your hearts week after week. Thank you, my dear friends.

Lastly, to you my reader (yes, you!) currently holding this book in your hands...know that you now are a part of a sisterhood (and brotherhood) of readers. I welcome your thoughts, your feedback and your own story. You can reach me directly at rwcopywriting@comcast.net.

Book List

H ERE IS A PARTIAL LIST OF SPIRITUAL BOOKS
(that I read during the writing of this book) whose
truths are somehow reflected in *Eve's Song*:

Addiction and Grace, Gerald May
Animal Dialogues, Craig Childs
*Broken Open: How Difficult Times Help
Us Grow*, Elizabeth Lesser
Desiring God, John Piper
Evil and the Justice of God, N.T. Wright
Free of Charge, Mirsoslav Volf
Hinds Feet on High Places, Hannah Hurnard
Knowing God, J.I. Packer
No Man is an Island, Thomas Merton
Searching for God Knows What, Donald Miller
Secrets in the Dark, Frederick Buechner
Springs in the Valley, Mrs. Charles E. Cowman
Suffering and the Sovereignty of God,
John Piper and Justin Taylor
The Awakened Heart, Gerald May
The Dark Night of the Soul, Gerald May
The Life Story of Adam and Havah, Shira Halevi
*The Lost Books of the Bible and The Forgotten
Books of Eden*, Meredian Books
Undefiled, Harry Schaumburg
Wounds that Heal, David Seamands

Book Group

EVE'S SONG IS A BOOK THAT BEGS TO BE READ and discussed with others. By getting together weekly, and following a few basic guidelines, you'll live out Eve's vision of women gathering together to tell their stories.

Before Eve's Song was released, it went through three different book groups, one early in the writing process, and two groups that finished up right before the book's release.

Here is what we found makes for a deep, meaningful and relationship-building group:

1. **Read out loud** — Go around the table, having each person read 3 to 4 pages. If someone doesn't want to read, they can simple say, "Pass." Reading the whole book out loud will help book group participants...

    * Go deeper — Most of us skip words when we read silently. In *Eve's Song*, there are many layers of meaning. Hearing every single word helps group members process the book.

    * Hear and see — By engaging two different senses, your retention will increase. Read along and mark the places in the book that leap out at you.

    * Take time to process — As another person reads, you'll hear her interact with the book. When you hear someone becoming emotional, ask yourself, "How do I relate?" Take risks to open up and others will follow.

2. **Let the discussion breathe** — Pause at the natural breaks in the book for discussion. The leader can ask simply, "What stood out to you? Did anything touch your heart?

3. **Use the study guide** — At the end of the group, ask each person to pick a question or two from the study guide to journal on during the week. At the start of the next group, allow people to share what they learned.

4. **Take advantage of the footnotes** — Likewise, encourage group members to go back through the scriptures at the bottom of the pages in between meetings. These scriptures help form the scriptural basis of the story, and help with application.

5. **Set some guidelines** — An *Eve's Song* group, by its very nature, is an intimate exploration into each other's hearts. Some simple guidelines will help people open up and look forward to the group.

    - Safe Haven — This is a confidential group. What is shared in the group stays within the group.
    - Sharing — When someone in the group shares, we will all simply say, "Thank you for sharing." This is not a time to try to fix anyone else, but for us all to safely process our losses, spiritual struggles and ongoing situations in our lives.
    - Support — We are all committed to open our hearts to God and to each other. We will look for ways to support each other outside of this group.
    - Spirit — We come together in expectation of the Holy Spirit working. As we read the book, we will pray specifically for each of our hearts to be receptive to

the Spirit's prompting and to what God would have us learn from each other.

I love to hear from book groups! Send your stories, responses and questions to questions@secureinheart.com.

Robin Weidner
Author, *Eve's Song*

About the Author

ROBIN WEIDNER IS ALSO THE AUTHOR OF *Secure in Heart*, another vulnerable look into the heart of a woman (www.secureinheart.com). Alongside her husband of 32 years, Dave, Robin speaks in the United States and abroad about insecurity, marriage, and sexual integrity. Their *Purity Restored* Ministry touches individuals around the world. Dave and Robin currently lead a church in Boise, Idaho. They have three adult children and a black lab Mojo, affectionately known as their *recovery dog*.

As the principal of Robin Weidner Copywriting & Consulting, Robin writes for health organizations and other businesses. Robin earned her BS from Western Illinois University's Board of Governors program (concentrating in English) and has four years of study in Social Work.

Robin is a popular speaker at women's days and retreats. You can reach Robin at rwcopywriting@comcast.net.

Secure *in* Heart

Overcoming Insecurity in a Woman's Life

Robin Weidner

New Edition Includes Bonus Chapter and Scripture Index

S E C U R E   I N   H E A R T

Overcoming Insecurity
in a Woman's Life

Available from the publisher, Discipleship Publications
International (dpibooks.org) and on amazon.com

SECURE IN HEART CHARTS A PATH TO SECURITY
that women across the world are finding life changing. By
taking us into her own struggles, and deep into the hearts
of other women, Robin demonstrates how to translate the
knowledge of God into a battle-tested security. It addresses
an issue that continues to be a huge need in our culture today.
You'll want to read this book and recommend it to others."
—Mitch Temple, Marriage Expert
and author of *The Marriage Turnaround*

"*SECURE IN HEART* STRIKES A CHORD THAT IS IN
every woman's heart, 'Do I really matter?' Thank you for the
truth that God says, 'Yes, you are worth it all!'"
— Mary Owen, Recovery Group Leader,
Coauthor of *Witness*

"I HIGHLY, HIGHLY RECOMMEND THIS BOOK TO Christian women's groups and to ladies who are caught up in their insecurities."

— Reader's Views.com

"WRITER AND SPEAKER ROBIN WEIDNER SHARES biblically-based insights she has learned through her own trials in life as she encourages women to discover and confront their own sources of insecurity."

— *Journey Magazine/Lifeway Publications*